LITERATURE
Uses of the Imagination

The suggestions of reviewers have aided us in our final preparation of materials for this book. We gratefully acknowledge the critical assistance of:

Richard Calisch
Elk Grove High School
Elk Grove, Illinois

Jack D. Cundari
Wayne Hills High School
Wayne, New Jersey

Sister Margaret McBrien
Merion Mercy Academy
Merion Station, Pennsylvania

Conrad Stawski
David H. Hickman High School
Columbia, Missouri

W.T. JEWKES

Professor of English
The Pennsylvania State University

Supervisory Editor
NORTHROP FRYE

University Professor
University of Toronto

The Perilous Journey

HARCOURT BRACE JOVANOVICH, INC.

New York   Chicago   San Francisco   Atlanta   Dallas

ISBN 0-15-333520-3

ACKNOWLEDGMENTS: *For permission to reprint copyrighted material, grateful acknowledgment
is made to the following sources:*

Christ's College, Cambridge: From "Asclepius" from *Gods, Heroes and Men of Ancient Greece* by W.H.D.
Rouse © 1957 by arrangement with Christ's College, Cambridge and the New American Library, Inc.,
New York.

Commonweal Publishing Co., Inc.: "Heroes" by Witter Bynner from *Commonweal,* February 20, 1929.

Crown Publishers, Inc.: Excerpt from *Superman;* Edited by E. Nelson Bridwell, © 1939 Detective Comics,
Inc.; renewed © 1966 by National Periodical Publications, Inc.; © 1971 National Periodical Publications, Inc.

Doran William Cannon: Three adapted excerpts from the original screenplay "Brewster McCloud" by
Doran William Cannon.

Doubleday & Company, Inc.: "Sonnet XXVI" by Feng Chih, "The Ricksha Puller" by Cheng Min, and
"The Song of Youth" by Ai Ch'ing from the book *Twentieth Century Chinese Poetry* by Kai-yu Hsu,
copyright © 1963 by Kai-yu Hsu.

E.P. Dutton & Co., Inc.: "A Bao A Qu" from the book *The Book of Imaginary Beings* by Jorge Luis Borges
with Margarita Guerro, trans. by Norman Thomas di Giovanni in collaboration with the author,
copyright, ©, 1969 by Jorge Luis Borges and Norman Thomas di Giovanni. Published by E.P. Dutton
& Co., Inc.

E.P. Dutton & Co., Inc. and *The Bodley Head Ltd.:* "The Return of Oisin" from the book *The High Deeds
of Finn MacCool* by Rosemary Sutcliff, text copyright © 1967 by Rosemary Sutcliff. Published by E.P.
Dutton & Co., Inc.

Farrar, Straus & Giroux, Inc.: "Losses" by Randall Jarrell from *The Complete Poems* by Randall Jarrell,
copyright © 1948, 1969 by Mrs. Randall Jarrell.

Follett Publishing Company, division of Follett Corporation and *Frederick Muller Ltd.:* "The Man Whose
Luck Was Asleep" from *Persian Fairy Tales* retold by Eleanor Brockett, copyright © 1962 by Eleanor
Brockett. First published in 1962 by Frederick Muller Ltd., London, England. Published in 1968 in
the U.S.A. by Follett Publishing Company, division of Follett Corporation.

Joan and Robert Franklin, the Estate of Sir Arthur Conan Doyle, John Murray (Publishers) Ltd. and *Basker-
villes Investments Ltd.:* "The Final Problem" from *The Memoirs of Sherlock Holmes* by Sir Arthur Conan
Doyle.

Emmet M. Greene, Executor of the Estate of Padraic Colum: "Heracles," and an adaptation of "Lemminkainen" from *Myths of the World* by Padraic Colum, published by Grosset & Dunlap.

The illustrations on pages xvi-1, 48-49, 92-93, 170-71, 210-11, and 274-75 are by Alan E. Cober.

Contents

1   The Rightful Kingdom

2   More Than Man

3 To Do What Must Be Done

4 The Golden Cup

5   Might for Right

6   To Find Out Who I Am

INTRODUCTION

Without a sense of pattern in life, man would always feel like a lonely child, lost in a vast forest with night coming on. But man's powers of observation do enable him to perceive patterns in the world around him: day and night; spring, summer, autumn, winter; birth, maturity, death, and rebirth.

In addition to these outer, physical patterns, man is conscious of patterns in his inner world. His emotional life also works in patterns. He fears the harshness of winter, disease, and death. He remembers with longing the warmth of summer, health, and life. With his imagination he relates his inner world to the outer world. He constructs a pattern for his life that will help him to live in harmony with the world around him, to turn his wishes into reality.

How the imagination transforms the materials of outer reality into an image of desire can be seen in the way our dreams work. But dreams are too fragmentary and fleeting. Man longs for some more permanent and extensive vision of human life made over into the image of desire. It is this longing that has produced literature. It is this vision that has formed the backbone of every mythology.

Just as patterns recur in the physical world and in our own inner worlds, they also recur in our imaginative expressions, that is, in our literature. In fact, the recurring imaginative patterns of the whole human race are reflected in literature. As we read more and more, we find that there is a "larger" pattern into which all our reading experiences can fit. This larger story pattern takes the shape of a quest. This quest story tells of how man once possessed the secret of life; somehow he lost that secret, and he tries to regain it by his own efforts.

The story of man's quest for his lost inheritance can be seen as the story of human civilization. The human race itself has embarked from the dawn of time on a quest for a truly civilized society. This vision, expressed in literature, has carried civilization forward against the dehumanizing powers that have always tried to hold it back. Today, just as throughout history, these powers are still trying to capture our imagination and force it to serve their ends. Whenever such powers try to imprison the creative imagination, they are trying to steal man's inheritance from him. But poets and storytellers have no ulterior motives. Their only aim is to free our imagination, as we share with them the creative experience of building a truly human society.

W. T. J.

I Think Continually of Those Who Were Truly Great

I think continually of those who were truly great.
Who, from the womb, remembered the soul's history
Through corridors of light where the hours are suns,
Endless and singing. Whose lovely ambition
Was that their lips, still touched with fire,
Should tell of the Spirit, clothed from head to foot in song.
And who hoarded from the Spring branches
The desires falling across their bodies like blossoms.

What is precious, is never to forget
The essential delight of the blood drawn from ageless springs
Breaking through rocks in worlds before our earth.
Never to deny its pleasure in the morning simple light
Nor its grave evening demand for love.
Never to allow gradually the traffic to smother
With noise and fog, the flowering of the Spirit.

Near the snow, near the sun, in the highest fields,
See how these names are feted by the waving grass
And by the streamers of white cloud
And whispers of wind in the listening sky.
The names of those who in their lives fought for life,
Who wore at their hearts the fire's center.
Born of the sun, they travelled a short while toward the sun,
And left the vivid air signed with their honor.

STEPHEN SPENDER

1

THE RIGHTFUL KINGDOM

The Golden Age

A Greek myth
Retold by MARY M. INNES

In the beginning was the Golden Age, when men of their own accord, without threat of punishment, without laws, maintained good faith and did what was right. There were no penalties to be afraid of, no bronze tablets were erected, carrying threats of legal action, no crowd of wrong-doers, anxious for mercy, trembled before the face of their judge: indeed, there were no judges, men lived securely without them. Never yet had any pine tree, cut down from its home on the mountains, been launched on ocean's waves, to visit foreign lands: men knew only their own shores. Their cities were not yet surrounded by sheer moats, they had no straight brass trumpets, no coiling brass horns, no helmets and no swords. The peoples of the world, untroubled by any fears, enjoyed a leisurely and peaceful existence, and had no use for soldiers. The earth itself, without compulsion, untouched by the hoe, unfurrowed by any share, produced all things spontaneously, and men were content with foods that grew without cultivation. They gathered arbute berries and mountain strawberries, wild cherries and blackberries that cling to thorny bramble bushes: or acorns, fallen from Jupiter's spreading oak. It was a season of everlasting spring, when peaceful zephyrs, with their warm breath, caressed the flowers that sprang up without having been planted. In time the earth, though untilled, produced corn too, and fields that never lay fallow whitened with heavy ears of grain. Then there flowed rivers of milk and rivers of nectar, and golden honey dripped from the green holm oak.

When Saturn was consigned to the darkness of Tartarus, and the world passed under the rule of Jove, the age of silver replaced that of gold, inferior to it, but superior to the age of tawny bronze. Jupiter shortened the springtime which had prevailed of old, and instituted a cycle of four seasons in the year, winter, summer, changeable autumn, and a brief spring. Then, for the first time, the air became parched and arid, and glowed with white heat, then hanging icicles formed under the chilling blasts of the wind. It was in those days that men first sought covered dwelling places: they made their homes in caves and thick shrubberies, or bound branches together with bark. Then corn, the gift of Ceres, first began to be sown in long furrows, and straining bullocks groaned beneath the yoke.

After that came the third age, the age of bronze, when men were of a fiercer character, more ready to turn to cruel warfare, but still free from any taint of wickedness.

Last of all arose the age of hard iron: immediately, in this period which took its name from a baser ore, all manner of crime broke out; modesty, truth, and loyalty fled. Treachery and trickery took their place, deceit and violence and criminal greed. Now sailors spread their canvas to the winds, though they had as yet but little knowledge of these, and trees which had once clothed the high mountains were fashioned into ships, and tossed upon the ocean waves, far removed from their own element. The land, which had previously been common to all, like the sunlight and the breezes, was now divided up far and wide by boundaries, set by cautious surveyors. Nor was it only corn and their due nourishment that men demanded of the rich earth: they explored its very bowels, and dug out the wealth which it had hidden away, close to the Stygian shades; and this wealth was further incitement to wickedness. By this time iron had been discovered, to the hurt of mankind, and gold, more hurtful still than iron. War made its appearance, using both those metals in its conflict, and shaking clashing weapons in bloodstained hands. Men lived on what they could plunder: friend was not safe from friend, nor father-in-law from son-in-law, and even between brothers affection was rare. Husbands waited eagerly for the death of their wives, and wives for that of their husbands. Ruthless stepmothers mixed brews of deadly aconite, and sons pried into their fathers' horoscopes, impatient for them to die. All proper affection lay vanquished and, last of the immortals, the maiden Justice left the blood-soaked earth.

The heights of heaven were no safer than the earth; for the giants, so runs the story, assailed the kingdom of the gods and, piling mountains together, built them up to the stars above. Then the almighty father hurled his thunderbolt, smashed through Olympus, and flung down Pelion from where it had peen piled on top of Ossa. The terrible bodies of the giants lay crushed beneath their own massive structures, and the earth was drenched and soaked with torrents of blood from her sons. Then, they say, she breathed life into this warm blood and, so that her offspring might not be completely forgotten, changed it into the shape of men. But the men thus born, no less than the giants, were contemptuous of the gods, violent and cruel, with a lust to kill: it was obvious that they were the children of blood.

What season of the year is identified with the Golden Age? Do you think it is appropriate? Why?

How do you think the myth of a lost Golden Age made people feel about themselves? What does it show they wanted to believe in?

Do you think people still believe in a past Golden Age? Why? What "age" do you think most people are living in now? Why? What substance (such as gold, iron) would you identify with our age? Why?

Do you think "Golden Age" or "Iron Age" might also represent different stages of a person's life? How? Have you ever lived in a Golden Age? When? What was it like? In what ways was it like the image of the Golden Age in this selection?

Aquarius

From the musical HAIR

When the moon is in the seventh house,
And Jupiter aligns with Mars,
Then peace will guide the planets,
And love will steer the stars;
This is the dawning of the age of Aquarius,
The age of Aquarius.
Aquarius, Aquarius.

Harmony and understanding,
Sympathy and trust abounding.
No more falsehoods or derisions,
Golden living dreams of visions,
Mystic crystal revelation,
And the mind's true liberation.
Aquarius, Aquarius.

When the moon is in the seventh house,
And Jupiter aligns with Mars,
Then peace will guide the planets,
And love will steer the stars;
This is the dawning of the age of Aquarius,
The age of Aquarius.
Aquarius, Aquarius.

JAMES RADO

GEROME RAGNI

What specific images in this song correspond to images of the Golden Age in the previous selection? Why do you suppose people so widely separated in space and time would use the same images?

Midnight Cowboy

From the novel by
JAMES LEO HERLIHY

This day in late September marked the beginning of Joe Buck's alliance with Ratso Rizzo. The pair of them became a familiar sight on certain New York streets that fall, the little blond runt, laboring like a broken grasshopper to keep pace with the six-foot tarnished cowboy, the two of them frowning their way through time like children with salt shakers stalking a bird, urgently intent on their task of finding something of worth in the streets of Manhattan.

Ratso chewed his fingernails, consumed all the coffee and tobacco he could get hold of, and lay awake nights frowning and gnawing at his lips. For he was the natural leader of the two, and upon his head rested the responsibility for thinking up new schemes for their survival.

Joe Buck, in the fashion of a follower, simply expressed his across-the-board pessimism about whatever was suggested, and then went along with it. Once, for instance, Ratso heard about a town in Jersey where the parking meters were said to be vulnerable to the common screwdriver. Joe Buck was skeptical and said so, often, but still he submitted to hocking his radio in order to raise bus fare for the trip across the river. When they got there it became clear at once that Ratso's information was out of date: the town had all new meters of a make no screwdriver could ever disturb. In the face of such a disappointment, Joe Buck was capable of behaving with magnanimity, at least to the extent of keeping his mouth shut while Ratso made excuses for the failure.

But on the whole this person with the sunburst on his boots remained cranky and disagreeable in his behavior toward the little blond runt. He realized it, too. Joe knew good and well he had become a pain in the neck, and what's more he was none too concerned about it. But there was a reason for his unconcern: He was happy.

For the first time in his life he felt himself released from the necessity of grinning and posturing and yearning for the attention of others. Nowadays he had, in the person of Ratso Rizzo, someone who needed his presence in an urgent, almost frantic way that was a balm to something in him that had long been exposed and enflamed and itching to be soothed. God alone knew how or why, but he had somehow actually stumbled upon a creature who seemed to worship him. Joe Buck had never before known such power and was therefore ill equipped to administer it. All he could do was taste it over and over again like a sugar-starved child on a sudden mountain of candy: cuss and frown and complain and bitch, and watch Ratso take it. For that's the way in which power is usually tasted, in the abuse of it. It was delicious and sickening and he couldn't stop himself. The only thing the runt seemed to demand was the privilege of occupying whatever space he could find in the tall cowboy's shadow. And casting such a shadow had become Joe Buck's special pleasure.

He enjoyed listening to Ratso, too. As they walked through the city, or shared a cup of coffee in a lunch stand or cafeteria, or shivered together in the progressively colder doorways of the waning year, he heard Ratso's views on many subjects. Bit by bit, he was able to piece together a picture of Ratso's early years in the Bronx.

Ratso was the thirteenth child of tired immigrant parents. He remembered his father as a hard-working bricklayer who in his off hours went to sleep whenever he found something even vaguely horizontal to lie upon. His mother, a burnt-out child bearer, usually sick, managed the family like a kindly, befuddled queen, issuing contradictory mandates from her bedroom. Occasionally she would pull a housecoat about her body and move through the flat trying to sort out the confusion she had wrought. On one such tour she found the seven-year-old Ratso under the kitchen stove in an advanced stage of pneumonia. Surviving this, he contracted infantile paralysis a few weeks later, and by the time he was discharged from the hospital the following year his mother was dead and gone. His three sisters and two of his nine brothers had left home, either for marriage or for other purposes. Of the eight remaining boys, none took any interest in cooking or housework; nor had Papa Rizzo ever given any special attention to the running of a family. When he thought of the job at all, it was in terms of supplying food. Therefore once a week he stocked the shelves with saltines and cans of pork and beans, the refrigerator with cheese and cold cuts and milk. For six days the boys would grab what they could, and on the seventh Papa Rizzo gave them a real Sunday dinner at a neighborhood spaghetti place. Occasionally in an earlier time—usually at Easter or on Mother's Day—he had hosted such dinners in this same restaurant, and the owner had always made him feel proud of his enormous brood by calling attention to the fact that he required the biggest table in the place. *"Ecco, che arriva Rizzo!"* he would say. *"Prende la tavola piu grande del locale!"* Even now, with only eight sons left, it was necessary to shove two regular tables together. But after the first month or so, these Sunday dinners were ill-attended, for the old bricklayer had developed a foul temper and took to using them as occasions for scolding and shouting. The boys, one by one, having learned to forage in ways they found easier than listening to the ravings of a disagreeable old man, wandered away from home altogether. Finally one Sunday afternoon at the family dinner there was only Ratso. When the owner led them to a table for two, the old man was shocked, and then embarrassed, and then chastened. He ate in silence, behaving with an almost ceremonial kindness toward the skinny, crippled, thirteen-year-old runt of his progeny. He also drank a good deal of wine, and then there came a moment in which he broke the silence and ended the meal by landing one tremendous wallop of his bare fist on the little formica-covered table, shouting his own name and reminding the world at large, and God, too, that he was accustomed to larger tables than this: *"Sono Rizzo! Io prendo la tavola piu grande del locale!"* The owner came over and the two old men wept together and embraced each other. Then Ratso led his father home. Entering the flat, the old man drew back and let out a dreadful howl. It was as if he had suddenly awakened from the longest of all of his naps and found his family wiped out by bandits and the walls of the flat all splattered with blood. Looking past Ratso as if the boy didn't exist, the bricklayer started to sob, asking over and over again the whereabouts of his sons. *"Dove sono i miei ragazzi terribili?"* Gradually, and perhaps only by default, Ratso became the favorite, and for a while life was better for him than for the others. He was given an allowance and was never scolded. The Sunday dinners continued. There was not much talk at the small table, but a silent intimacy had grown between them and the atmosphere was affectionate and peaceful. Papa Rizzo, by now a fat, benign, baldheaded old bear in his late sixties, drank a quart of Chianti all by himself, and on the way home from the restaurant he would find a number of opportunities to place his hand upon the head of his last remaining son, or, waiting for a traffic light, to wrap a heavy arm around his shoulder. On one such afternoon of a summer Sunday, Ratso was undermined by the great burden of weight his father placed upon him, and they both fell to the sidewalk. When Ratso was able to disengage himself, he found that the old man had died on him, right there in the crowded sunlight of the Bronx River Parkway.

From then on, Ratso was on his own. He was sixteen, with no special training for life. But he did have a quick natural intelligence, and, like most persons raised in large families, he was a good, fast liar. With these assets, he took to the streets.

Ratso could talk about the Bronx, and he could talk about Manhattan, and he could talk about nearly anything under the sun. But his best subject was Florida, and though he had never been there, he spoke more positively and with greater authority on this topic than on any other. He often studied folders in color put out by transportation companies or perused a stack of travel clippings collected from newspapers; he also owned a book called *Florida and the Caribbean*. In this splendid place (he claimed), the two basic items necessary for the sustenance of life—sunshine and coconut milk—were in such abundance that the only problem was in coping with their excess. For all that sunshine you needed wide-brimmed hats, special glasses and creams. As for coconuts, there were so many of these lying about in the streets that each Florida town had to commission great fleets of giant trucks to gather them up just so traffic could get through. And of course coconuts were the one complete food: This was common knowledge. Anytime you got hungry, all you had to do was pick one up and stab it with a pocketknife, and then hold it up to your mouth. Ratso was unable to tell about this without demonstrating with an invisible coconut. "Here your only problem is," he would say to Joe, sucking at the air between phrases, "—you want to know what your only problem is here, diet-wise? It's the warm milk running down your face and neck. Yeah, sometimes you got to exert yourself, you got to reach up and wipe off your chin. Tough, huh? You think you could stand that? I could. I could stand it." As for fishing, he made this sound so simple Joe actually got the impression you didn't need a rod and reel or even a pole. Without examining the picture too carefully for probability, he had formed a king of cartoon image of the two of them standing near the water saying *here fishy-fishy*, at which point a pair of enormous finned creatures would jump into their arms precooked. A silly, happy thought, and he could smell the fish plain as day. Sometimes to keep this pleasant discussion going, Joe might feed a question: "But . . . man, where in hell would you sleep? They got no X-flats down there, you can bet your smart ass on that." But Ratso had an answer for everything. At this cue he would begin to tell of the endless miles of public beaches on which had been built hundreds of pagodas and pergolas and gazebos; under these, on sun-warmed sand or softly padded benches, protected from rain and wind, one slept the sleep of Eden.

Ratso's actual "home" is a world of sickness, insecurity, and death. What is his imaginative "home" like? Would you say it is a Golden Age? Why?

Explain how the Garden of Eden referred to in the last sentence is also an image of the lost Golden Age.

Inaugural Address

JOHN F. KENNEDY

Mr. Chief Justice, President Eisenhower, Vice-President Nixon, President Truman, reverend clergy, fellow citizens, we observe today not a victory of party, but a celebration of freedom — symbolizing an end, as well as a beginning — signifying renewal, as well as change. For I have sworn before you and Almighty God the same solemn oath our forebears prescribed nearly a century and three-quarters ago.

The world is very different now. For man holds in his mortal hands the power to abolish all forms of human poverty and all forms of human life. And yet the same revolutionary beliefs for which our forebears fought are still at issue around the globe — the belief that the rights of man come not from the generosity of the state, but from the hand of God.

We dare not forget today that we are the heirs of that first Revolution. Let the word go forth from this time and place, to friend and foe alike, that the torch has been passed to a new generation of Americans — born in this century, tempered by war, disciplined by a hard and bitter peace, proud of our ancient heritage — and unwilling to witness or permit the slow undoing of those human rights to which this nation has always been committed, and to which we are committed today at home and around the world.

Let every nation know, whether it wishes us well or ill, that we shall pay any price, bear any burden, meet any hardship, support any friend, oppose any foe, in order to assure the survival and the success of liberty.

This much we pledge — and more.

To those old allies whose cultural and spiritual origins we share, we pledge the loyalty of faithful friends. United, there is little we cannot do in a host of cooperative ventures. Divided, there is little we can do — for we dare not meet a powerful challenge at odds and split asunder.

To those new states whom we welcome to the ranks of the free, we pledge our word that one form of colonial control shall not have passed away merely to be replaced by a far greater iron tyranny. We shall not always expect to find them supporting our view. But we shall always hope to find them strongly supporting their own freedom—and to remember that, in the past, those who foolishly sought power by riding the back of the tiger ended up inside.

To those people in the huts and villages across the globe struggling to break the bonds of mass misery, we pledge our best efforts to help them help themselves, for whatever period is required—not because the Communists may be doing it, not because we seek their votes, but because it is right. If a free society cannot help the many who are poor, it cannot save the few who are rich.

To our sister republics south of our border, we offer a special pledge —to convert our good words into good deeds, in a new alliance for progress, to assist free men and free governments in casting off the chains of poverty. But this peaceful revolution of hope cannot become the prey of hostile powers. Let all our neighbors know that we shall join with them to oppose aggression or subversion anywhere in the Americas. And let every other power know that this hemisphere intends to remain the master of its own house.

To that world assembly of sovereign states, the United Nations, our last best hope in an age where the instruments of war have far outpaced the instruments of peace, we renew our pledge of support—to prevent it from becoming merely a forum for invective—to strengthen its shield of the new and the weak—and to enlarge the area in which its writ may run.

Finally, to those nations who would make themselves our adversary, we offer not a pledge but a request: that both sides begin anew the quest for peace, before the dark powers of destruction unleashed by science engulf all humanity in planned or accidental self-destruction.

We dare not tempt them with weakness. For only when our arms are sufficient beyond doubt can we be certain beyond doubt that they will never be employed.

But neither can two great and powerful groups of nations take comfort from our present course—both sides overburdened by the cost of modern weapons, both rightly alarmed by the steady spread of the deadly atom, yet both racing to alter that uncertain balance of terror that stays the hand of mankind's final war.

So let us begin anew—remembering on both sides that civility is not a sign of weakness, and sincerity is always subject to proof. Let us never negotiate out of fear. But let us never fear to negotiate.

Let both sides explore what problems unite us instead of laboring those problems which divide us.

Let both sides, for the first time, formulate serious and precise proposals for the inspection and control of arms — and bring the absolute power to destroy other nations under the absolute control of all nations.

Let both sides seek to invoke the wonders of science instead of its terrors. Together let us explore the stars, conquer the deserts, eradicate disease, tap the ocean depths, and encourage the arts and commerce.

Let both sides unite to heed in all corners of the earth the command of Isaiah — to "undo the heavy burdens and to let the oppressed go free."

And if a beachhead of cooperation may push back the jungle of suspicion, let both sides join in creating a new endeavor, not a new balance of power, but a new world of law, where the strong are just and the weak secure and the peace preserved.

All this will not be finished in the first hundred days. Nor will it be finished in the first thousand days, nor in the life of this Administration, nor even perhaps in our lifetime on this planet. But let us begin.

In your hands, my fellow citizens, more than in mine, will rest the final success or failure of our course. Since this country was founded, each generation of Americans has been summoned to give testimony to its national loyalty. The graves of young Americans who answered the call to service are found around the globe.

Now the trumpet summons us again — not a call to bear arms, though arms we need; not as a call to battle, though embattled we are; but a call to bear the burden of a long twilight struggle, year in, and year out, "rejoicing in hope, patient in tribulation" — a struggle against the common enemies of man: tyranny, poverty, disease, and war itself.

Can we forge against these enemies a grand and global alliance, north and south, east and west, that can assure a more fruitful life for all mankind? Will you join in that historic effort?

In the long history of the world, only a few generations have been granted the role of defending freedom in its hour of maximum danger. I do not shrink from this responsibility — I welcome it. I do not believe that any of us would exchange places with any other people or any other generation. The energy, the faith, the devotion which we bring to this endeavor will light our country and all who serve it — and the glow from that fire can truly light the world.

And so, my fellow Americans, ask not what your country can do for you: Ask what you can do for your country.

My fellow citizens of the world: Ask not what America will do for you, but what together we can do for the freedom of man.

Finally, whether you are citizens of America or citizens of the world, ask of us the same high standards of strength and sacrifice which we ask of you. With a good conscience our only sure reward, with history the final judge of our deeds, let us go forth to lead the land we love, asking His blessing and His help, but knowing that here on earth God's work must truly be our own.

What images of the Golden Age are used in this speech?

Does this speaker think men have a right to live in a Golden Age? Do you think so? Why? Does this speaker think men bear a responsibility to struggle to rebuild the Golden Age? Do you think so? Why?

The golden world that existed in Ratso's imagination could be reached, he thought, but only by a long and difficult journey. What is the perilous journey that can bring people to the golden world described in this selection? What "monsters" must be slain? What weapons must be used against them?

Perseus

A Greek myth
Retold by JAY MACPHERSON

"You will have no sons of your own, and your daughter's son will be your death." So ran the answer of the oracle to King Acrisius of Argos, who had come to ask about his future. Acrisius went home in a fury, and promptly shut up his beautiful daughter Danae in a tower of bronze where no man could see her, but all to no purpose; for Zeus poured himself in at an opening in the roof as a shower of gold, and gave her a son, whom she called Perseus. Resisting the will of the gods, but still reluctant to kill his own flesh and blood, Acrisius set Danae and her child afloat in a wooden chest, expecting that the raging sea would soon finish them off. But their ark at length was carried to the island of Seriphos, where a fisherman named Dictys cast his net around it and drew it ashore.

Welcomed by the fisherman and his wife, Danae and Perseus lived with them for several years. Dictys' brother Polydectes, as harsh as Dictys was kind, was king of the island, and he in time demanded the stranger woman in marriage. He was greatly astonished when Danae and her son, now fully grown, resisted him, and he resolved that Perseus should be got rid of forthwith. To this end, he gave out that he had decided instead to marry a neighboring princess and invited the young men of the island, Perseus among them, to a celebration. Each of the guests brought a present: only Perseus in his poverty had none. Taunted for it by Polydectes, he flung back proudly that he was prepared to go out and win by his own efforts a rarer gift than any — "even the head of the Gorgon Medusa herself." That was just what Polydectes had hoped to hear. "Very well," he said, "we will see no more of you till you have it."

The original Gorgons were two monstrous sisters, bird-winged, snake-haired, and plain-faced enough to scare off anything, living on a solitary rock at the edge of the western sea. These two were divinely born and immortal, but a mortal woman had been sent to join them as punishment for a crime against the gods. She, Medusa, was the most terrible of the three, with a face so appalling in its ugliness and hatred that whoever looked at it was turned into stone.

Perseus' task would have been impossible had he not been helped by Pallas Athene and by Hermes, the messenger of the gods. Giving him a brightly-polished shield of bronze, Athene warned him never to look directly at the face of the Gorgon but only at its reflection in the mirror-like surface. Hermes lent him his own winged sandals to shorten the long journey and a sickle of adamant with which to cut off the Gorgon's head. They both gave him advice about the beings he must seek out for the remaining information and equipment he needed.

The first place to which Perseus' winged sandals carried him was the home of the Gorgons' three sisters, the white-haired Graeae, dwelling in the farthest west. These had only one eye and one tooth among them, and Perseus easily got control over them by snatching the eye as they were passing it from hand to hand, and threatening to throw it into the sea. They were quickly persuaded to direct him to the Gorgons' rock and to give him the things he asked for: a helmet of invisibility to wear when he was about to strike, and a leather wallet in which the head could safely be carried.

Arriving at the Gorgons' rock, he found the three horrors asleep. This gave him time to decide which was Medusa, the only one who could be killed: to attack either of the others would have been fatal. Hovering over her in his winged sandals, he struck off her head with one blow and dropped it into the leather wallet. The sister Gorgons woke at the noise and howled in fury at the murder, but Perseus sprang into the air, concealed by the helmet of darkness. As he flew back towards the east, drops of the Gorgon's blood fell from the wallet onto the Libyan sands, where they became all manner of snakes: that is why to this day the Sahara desert swarms with deadly serpents.

On his way back to the court of Polydectes, Perseus met with another adventure. He was flying over the land of Ethiopia when he saw a maiden on the seashore, chained to a rock, her arms outstretched against it. Hastening down, he learned her story from her. She was the unfortunate Andromeda, whose mother Queen Cassiopeia, glorying in her beauty, had boasted that she excelled all the daughters of the sea-god Nereus. To avenge the insult, Nereus had sent a sea-monster,

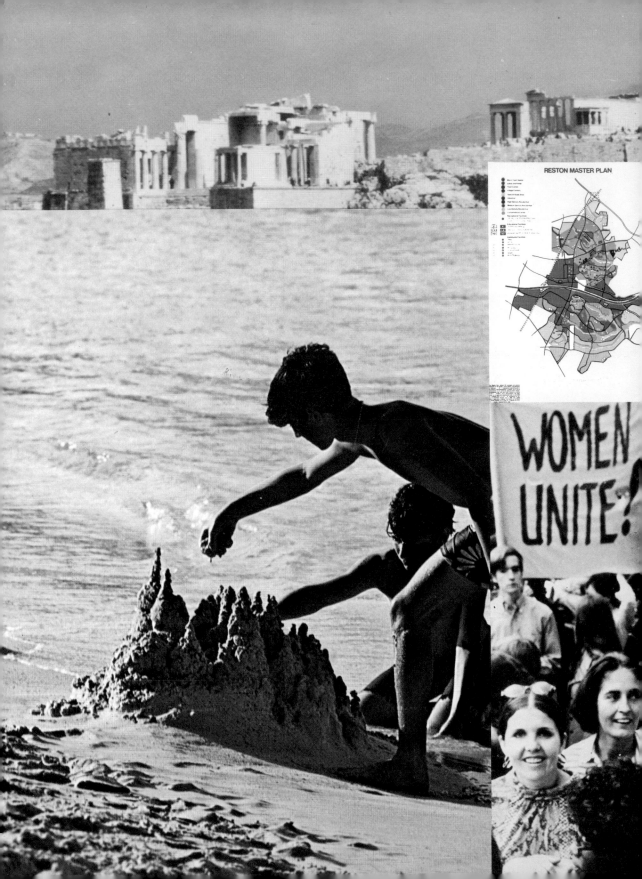

RESTON MASTER PLAN

WOMEN UNITE!

whose ravages of crops and men could be checked only by the sacrifice of the princess. While they were still speaking, the monster appeared out to sea, swimming toward the shore. Perseus, standing in front of Andromeda, snatched the head from its pouch and held it aloft, making his first trial of its powers. Instantly the great serpent stopped; its coils congealed; it was no longer a living creature, but an immense black rock, stretching far out into the waves. Before putting the head away again, Perseus laid it for a moment on some seaweed, which stiffened and became the first coral.

Andromeda's grateful parents gave her to Perseus in marriage, and she accompanied him on his return to Seriphos. They found on arrival that far from marrying a princess from the mainland, as he had said he meant to do, Polydectes was still pursuing Danae with his attentions, and that she and her protector Dictys had taken refuge in a nearby temple. Perseus went straight to the palace, where the king and his nobles were banqueting just as they were when he saw them last. "Here is the promised gift, O King"; and with that he showed them all the head. Visitors to the island are still shown the circle of stones he left behind him. Then, having no more use for the Gorgon's head, Perseus gave it to his protectress Athene, who attached it to the shield that she carries in battle.

Leaving the kingdom to Dictys, Perseus with his wife and his mother crossed the sea to Argos, hoping that Acrisius would by now have forgotten his fears and be prepared to receive them. Far from it: Acrisius fled to a neighboring kingdom. Perseus, unaware of this, happened to come there shortly afterwards to compete in the funeral games held for the king's old father. When Perseus threw the discus, the wind carried it aside so that it struck Acrisius as he stood in the crowd and killed him. Perseus buried his grandfather with due honor, recognizing in the accident the will of the gods, and returned to inherit the kingdom of Argos. There he and his family lived long and happily, and to him was born a son whose child in turn was Alcmene, the mother of Heracles, the greatest of the heroes of Greece.

Perseus wins not only his mother's freedom, but also the return of his own kingdom. How is his triumph like the victory hoped for in the previous three selections?

Many heroes are born into the world in a marvelous or mysterious way. How does Perseus fit this pattern? Why do you think people would want to believe that a great hero was not born in the usual human way?

In many hero stories, the hero grows up in exile or hiding, and then suddenly appears to the world fully grown and ready to conquer. How does Perseus fit this pattern?

List some of the characteristics of Perseus' perilous journey: his goal, his enemy, his helpers, his weapons, his final glorification.

Just as there are characteristics that always mark the hero, there are certain kinds of female figures that appear frequently in hero stories: goddesses, mothers, lovers, and witches. Describe the characteristics of each in this story.

The Street

From Black Boy
RICHARD WRIGHT

Hunger stole upon me so slowly that at first I was not aware of what hunger really meant. Hunger had always been more or less at my elbow when I played, but now I began to wake up at night to find hunger standing at my bedside, staring at me gauntly. The hunger I had known before this had been no grim, hostile stranger; it had been a normal hunger that had made me beg constantly for bread, and when I ate a crust or two I was satisfied. But this new hunger baffled me, scared me, made me angry and insistent. Whenever I begged for food now my mother would pour me a cup of tea which would still the clamor in my stomach for a moment or two; but a little later I would feel hunger nudging my ribs, twisting my empty guts until they ached. I would grow dizzy and my vision would dim. I became less active in my play, and for the first time in my life I had to pause and think of what was happening to me.

"Mama, I'm hungry," I complained one afternoon.

"Jump up and catch a kungry," she said, trying to make me laugh and forget.

"What's a *kungry?*"

"It's what little boys eat when they get hungry," she said.

"What does it taste like?"

"I don't know."

"Then why do you tell me to catch one?"

"Because you said that you were hungry," she said, smiling.

I sensed that she was teasing me and it made me angry.

"But I'm hungry. I want to eat."

"You'll have to wait."

"But I want to eat now."

"But there's nothing to eat," she told me.

"Why?"

"Just because there's none," she explained.

"But I want to eat," I said, beginning to cry.

"You'll just have to wait," she said again.

"But why?"

"For God to send some food."

"When is He going to send it?"

"I don't know."

"But I'm hungry!"

She was ironing and she paused and looked at me with tears in her eyes.

"Where's your father?" she asked me.

I stared in bewilderment. Yes, it was true that my father had not come home to sleep for many days now and I could make as much noise as I wanted. Though I had not known why he was absent, I had been glad that he was not there to shout his restrictions at me. But it had never occurred to me that his absence would mean that there would be no food.

"I don't know," I said.

"Who brings food into the house?" my mother asked me.

"Papa," I said. "He always brought food."

"Well, your father isn't here now," she said.

"Where is he?"

"I don't know," she said.

"But I'm hungry," I whimpered, stomping my feet.

"You'll have to wait until I get a job and buy food," she said.

As the days slid past the image of my father became associated with my pangs of hunger, and whenever I felt hunger I thought of him with a deep biological bitterness.

My mother finally went to work as a cook and left me and my brother alone in the flat each day with a loaf of bread and a pot of tea. When she returned at evening she would be tired and dispirited and would cry a lot. Sometimes, when she was in despair, she would call us to her and talk to us for hours, telling us that we now had no father, that our lives would be different from those of other children, that we must learn as soon as possible to take care of ourselves, to dress ourselves, to prepare our own food; that we must take upon ourselves the responsibility of the flat while she worked. Half frightened, we would promise solemnly. We did not understand what had happened between our father and our mother and the most that these long talks did to us was to make us feel a vague dread. Whenever we asked why father had left, she would tell us that we were too young to know.

One evening my mother told me that thereafter I would have to do the shopping for food. She took me to the corner store to show me the way. I was proud; I felt like a grownup. The next afternoon I looped the basket over my arm and went down the pavement toward the store. When I reached the corner, a gang of boys grabbed me, knocked me down, snatched the basket, took the money, and sent me running home in panic. That evening I told my mother what had happened, but she made no comment; she sat down at once, wrote another note, gave me more money, and sent me out to the grocery again. I crept down the steps and saw the same gang of boys playing down the street. I ran back into the house.

"What's the matter?" my mother asked.

"It's those same boys," I said. "They'll beat me."

"You've got to get over that," she said. "Now, go on."

"I'm scared," I said.

"Go on and don't pay any attention to them," she said.

I went out of the door and walked briskly down the sidewalk, praying that the gang would not molest me. But when I came abreast of them someone shouted.

"There he is!"

They came toward me and I broke into a wild run toward home. They overtook me and flung me to the pavement. I yelled, pleaded, kicked, but they wrenched the money out of my hand. They yanked me to my feet, gave me a few slaps, and sent me home sobbing. My mother met me at the door.

"They b-beat m-me," I gasped. "They t-t-took the m-money."

I started up the steps, seeking the shelter of the house.

"Don't you come in here," my mother warned me.

I froze in my tracks and stared at her.

"But they're coming after me," I said.

"You just stay right where you are," she said in a deadly tone. "I'm going to teach you this night to stand up and fight for yourself."

She went into the house and I waited, terrified, wondering what she was about. Presently she returned with more money and another note; she also had a long heavy stick.

"Take this money, this note, and this stick," she said. "Go to the store and buy those groceries. If those boys bother you, then fight."

I was baffled. My mother was telling me to fight, a thing that she had never done before.

"But I'm scared," I said.

"Don't you come into this house until you've gotten those groceries," she said.

"They'll beat me; they'll beat me," I said.

"Then stay in the streets; don't come back here!"

I ran up the steps and tried to force my way past her into the house. A stinging slap came on my jaw. I stood on the sidewalk, crying.

"Please, let me wait until tomorrow," I begged.

"No," she said. "Go now! If you come back into this house without those groceries, I'll whip you!"

She slammed the door and I heard the key turn in the lock. I shook with fright. I was alone upon the dark, hostile streets and gangs were after me. I had the choice of being beaten at home or away from home. I clutched the stick, crying, trying to reason. If I were beaten at home, there was absolutely nothing that I could do about it; but if I were beaten in the streets, I had a chance to fight and defend myself. I walked slowly down the sidewalk, coming closer to the gang of boys, holding the stick tightly. I was so full of fear that I could scarcely breathe. I was almost upon them now.

"There he is again!" the cry went up.

They surrounded me quickly and began to grab for my hand.

"I'll kill you!" I threatened.

They closed in. In blind fear I let the stick fly, feeling it crack against a boy's skull. I swung again, lamming another skull, then another. Realizing that they would retaliate if I let up for but a second, I fought to lay them low, to knock them cold, to kill them so that they could not strike back at me. I flayed with tears in my eyes, teeth clenched, stark fear making me throw every ounce of my strength behind each blow. I hit again and again, dropping the money and the grocery list. The boys scattered, yelling, nursing their heads, staring at me in utter disbelief. They had never seen such frenzy. I stood panting, egging them on, taunting them to come on and fight. When they refused, I ran after them and they tore out for their homes, screaming. The parents of the boys rushed into the streets and threatened me, and for the first time in my life I shouted at grownups, telling them that I would give them the same if they bothered me. I finally found my grocery list and the money and went to the store. On my way back I kept my stick poised for instant use, but there was not a single boy in sight. That night I won the right to the streets of Memphis.

In what ways is Richard's mother like Perseus' mother?

List some of the characteristics of Richard's perilous journey and tell how they are like Perseus': his goal, his enemy, his weapons, his helper, his triumph.

What rightful kingdom did Richard win?

Many young heroes must pass through an initiation before going off into the world, a test or calling to leave childhood and enter maturity. How is this incident Richard's initiation? What was Perseus' moment of initiation?

A DECLARATION

BY THE REPRESENTATIVES OF THE UNITED STATES OF AMERICA, IN GENERAL CONGRESS ASSEMBLED

When in the course of human events it becomes necessary for one people to dissolve the political bands which have connected them with another, and to assume among the powers of the earth the separate and equal station to which the laws of nature and of nature's God entitle them, a decent respect to the opinions of mankind requires that they should declare the causes which impel them to the separation.

We hold these truths to be self-evident: that all men are created equal; that they are endowed by their creator with certain inalienable rights; that among these are life, liberty, and the pursuit of happiness: that to secure these rights, governments are instituted among men, deriving their just powers from the consent of the governed; that whenever any form of government becomes destructive of these ends, it is the right of the people to alter or abolish it, and to institute a new government, laying its foundation on such principles, and organizing its powers in such form, as to them shall seem most likely to effect their safety and happiness. Prudence indeed will dictate that governments long established should not be changed for light and transient causes; and accordingly all experience hath shown that mankind are more disposed to suffer while evils are sufferable, than to right themselves by abolishing the forms to which they are accustomed. But when a long train of abuses and usurpations pursuing invariably the same object evinces a design to reduce them under absolute despotism, it is their right, it is their duty to throw off such government, and to provide new guards for their future security. Such has been the patient sufferance of these colonies; and such is now the necessity which constrains them to alter their former systems of government. The history of the present king of Great Britain is a history of repeated injuries and usurpations, all having in direct object the establishment of an absolute tyranny over these states. To prove this let facts be submitted to a candid world.

What is the goal of the quest described in this document? In what ways is it like the other quests in this unit?

Who is the "hero" in this document? What "monster" must the hero slay?

How is this declaration the "hero's" initiation from childhood into maturity? Would you say this "hero" underwent a mysterious birth?

Cadmus

A Greek myth
(*Original title:* The Serpent's Teeth)
Retold by PENELOPE FARMER

The great white bull reared upward from the sea, first his horns that smoothly curved, then his kind, strong head. He stood on the shore at last, his hooves among the little tippling waves. His eyes beamed mildly as the summer sea.

The king's daughter Europa played ball there with her hand-maidens. The king's son Cadmus and his followers were running, wrestling, practicing swordplay, and throwing javelins. All stopped to watch the bull, but Europa broke away and alone ran down the beach. The bull remaining quiet, she dared at last approach him, holding out her hand. She stroked his soft nose, reached up to touch his polished horns, hung garlands of flowers about his neck. She was so delighted by his beauty, so unafraid of him, that when the bull lowered his back to her, she climbed onto it immediately.

At first they stayed at the water's edge. But then the bull wheeled out from the shore and started swimming, smoothly, powerfully, farther out to sea. Europa stopped laughing and began to scream in fear, but still the bull swam on, till between the glitter of water and of sun they could be seen no more.

Everyone stood staring, thunderstruck, amazed. All suddenly moved at once, ran shouting, crying to the water's edge. Cadmus outstripped his men and plunged into the sea ahead of them. As far as his strength would take him he swam on, till he could see no land, yet saw no Europa, saw no bull. There was only the tilting of the waves all round, the gold sun burning in the huge sky.

His followers waited, anxious, on the shore. Cadmus did not greet or look at them. He strode towards the palace of the king. He heard women weeping about his path, but the king sat waiting in his court alone, gazing through olive groves to the empty sea.

"You saw her, Cadmus? Let Europa ride this bull and did not try to stop a woman's foolishness?"

"I admired the courage my sister showed, and mean to prove my courage is no less. I vow to Zeus that I will seek her to the edges of the earth, that I will not return to you without Europa at my side."

"Go, seek her then. That, Cadmus, is the most, also the least, that you can do. But we have heard your oath, the vow you have made to Zeus, father of the gods. So shall it be. Losing your sister has lost you your father and your home. Until she is found again, consider yourself for ever homeless, fatherless."

A wooden ship waited by the shore. It had a sail and a lifting prow and ranks of powerful oars to drive it through the waves. With a band of followers manning them, Cadmus sailed away across the sea — the same sea that took Europa on the white bull's back.

All round the Aegean he searched for her, along the jutting shores of Greece, asking fisherman, sailor, king, and prince alike. But no one had seen her or heard her name. He began to think himself doomed to seek for ever, to journey perpetually without a home. He would wander, lonely, while his men made camp; and one day, on the shore, he heard a voice.

"Cadmus, hear me." The voice was like the meeting of stone on steel, yet he saw only gray rocks, molded by the sea.

"Cadmus, hear me. . ." Now he saw a gray form, shifting from the rock. He saw the steely glintings of spear and shield, the plume of a helmet nodding in the breeze. Gray-eyed Athene stood before Cadmus on the shore at last.

"Have you come to mock my misfortune, goddess, to laugh at me?"

"I come to tell you, Cadmus, that you search in vain. The great god Zeus has taken Europa for his own, and those the gods love are not found by men."

"Then the gods hate Cadmus. They punish me. Must I wander till death with my warriors?"

"The gods do not hate you, Cadmus. You will found a great city to their glory. That is your fate, your destiny."

The goddess Athene faded before Cadmus's eyes, but clearly still he heard her voice. "Leave your ship, Cadmus. Seek a white heifer lowing on the mountainside. Follow her, and when at last she bends her head to graze, there found your city. There lies your fate."

The heifer might have been sired by Europa's bull, so pure, so white her back, so jewel-like her horns. There were no marks of harness upon her hide, no welts upon her neck where the yoke of a plow had rubbed. She raised her head when Cadmus came and bellowed loudly to the burning sky.

Then he drove her ahead of him, over stony passes, along waterless ravines, through red barren valleys where the only sound was the dry creakings of cicadas. The cow's coat dulled, her flesh diminished till the bones stood out, but Cadmus drove her on, relentlessly, until at last she led them down onto a wide and grassy plain.

Birds sang there among groves of trees — bright feathery trees, ripe-scented pines. From one grove the sound of water came, and here the heifer bent her head and began to graze her fill. Cadmus did not try to stop her now.

He wrenched out a handful of the grass, a clod of the damp black earth. He shouted exultantly.

"All this rich land is ours to rule and cultivate, to build on it a mighty city. We must thank Athene, gray-eyed goddess. The heifer that led us here will make our sacrifice."

None had seen stern Cadmus weep since Europa had been taken by the bull. But now he threw himself upon the earth, and wept.

His men laid aside their weapons and took bronze jugs and pitchers to fill with water for the sacrifice. They went to the grove from which the sound of water came and found a little pool, the branches bowed across. A spring slipped out of a cleft in the rocks above and fell down into it. Beyond there was a cave, its black mouth masked by foliage.

No one saw the gleam in the darkness of the cave; no one heard the small hissing and slithering within. The men were clattering their pitchers against the edges of the rock. The gold gleam stirred, reflected, like the firelight on a rounded ornament. Still the men laughed and joked too much to see.

The cave spat out a head, a sinister, thin serpent's head. There was a tongue like black lightning flickering across a golden sky. There were pointed teeth like spearheads in a row.

A second head emerged and then a third. A single body followed, thick as a pillar, supple as a rope. The heads reared, struck with teeth and darting tongues. At the touch of their poison a man fell dead.

The snake writhed, rippled, struck again. It caught men and crushed them in its body coils. Its heads shot out like lightning, so that some were felled while thinking themselves still safe.

Cadmus slept from relief and joy. When he awoke the silence puzzled him. There was only the white cow's cropping at the grass, the water falling in the spring. He picked up his weapons and went toward the grove, treading quietly, looking around him carefully. The bodies of his men lay everywhere, between the trees, along the edges of the pool. Suddenly he saw the serpent coiled, its skin like sunlight spread among the trees.

Enraged, horrified, he bent and seized a stone. The serpent as suddenly caught sight of him and reared angrily. Cadmus threw the stone with all his shoulder's force and struck its lower head. When it paused, he cast his bronze-tipped javelin. Gold met gold, the javelin pierced the serpent's throat, and its blood gushed out. Still angry tongues continued flickering, eyes glittering like jewels. As the serpent reared to crush its adversary, its poison dripped like rain upon the trees. Their leaves blackened and shriveled immediately.

Cadmus waited with his spear. Branches deflected the striking head, and at once he struck. The serpent writhed and tried to drag itself away, its blood pouring down on him. Its eyes dulled at last, its tongues lolled and slowed. Cadmus stood alone in a bloody scene. His men were flung in attitudes of death all round; the snake lay dead in its golden coils. There lived only the heifer he had meant to sacrifice.

He raged, wept for his followers, for his city that had no one to build and people it. If he had to make it with his own bare hands, a city would rise here on this lavish plain. But now, he vowed, it should be their monument.

He lay exhausted in the evening calm. From the sky, suddenly, the voice of Athene came.

"Sleep now, Cadmus. But on the morrow pluck the serpent's teeth. Plow the earth and sow them there like corn among the furrows. Armed men shall spring like poplar trees, and these shall be your citizens, your eager men of war."

The little cow had the mark of man set on her sides at last. Cadmus yoked her to a plow the next day and drove her long hours across the plain, scoring deep furrows in the rich black earth. Afterwards he cast the teeth out along the furrows. He looked back only when all of them were sown.

Already men had begun to grow like trees. The spearheads pricked first, the points of plants. Then the plumes of their helmets burst like foliage. Broad shoulders followed, armored breasts and slender waists, strong legs with bronze protecting them. Like a forest a whole army had sprung up, the plumes of their helmets swaying on their heads like leaves, the earth prickling and bristling with the weapons they had brought, with javelins and swords. The sun caught rounded shield and pointed spear alike, glittered as fiercely off steel and bronze. There were ringings and whisperings of steel as if the sun struck hard enough to make metal sound aloud.

Cadmus watching, dazzled and amazed, heard the voice of Athene speak once more. He bent and took a stone to her ordering, and again he threw with all his strength. But now he flung his stone amid the array of men.

A murmuring broke out, as if a forest spoke; each warrior accused his neighbor of attack. Each rank swayed and broke as fights began. Like a forest the tall men had grown, so now like a forest they began to fall, though cut by their own swords, not by a woodman's axe, until only the five mightiest warriors remained.

Once more Cadmus held up his hand, this time to check their fight. They turned immediately, raising their flashing spears, lifting their voices to him as if one voice.

"Hail, Cadmus, mighty king. We are come to serve you loyally. Only command, and we will at once obey."

Cadmus arrogantly raised his spear, acknowledged their obedience. His voice rang out like a trumpet across the plain. "Build my city. Defend it against its enemies. Father its populace."

The city so built was Thebes, great Thebes of the seven gates; Cadmus, fittingly, the first of its mighty kings.

Cadmus thought his quest was to rescue his sister. What greater quest did the gods have in mind for him? How is it like others in this unit?

Find these aspects of the perilous journey in the story of Cadmus: a helpful goddess, a dangerous underworld, a contest and a triumph.

The Song of Youth

A canoe, still smelling of new wood,
Leaves a tiny barren island;
A melancholy but warm-hearted youth
Thus left his little village.

I disliked that village—
As ordinary as a banyan tree,
As slow-witted as a water buffalo—
Where I spent my childhood.

Those who knew less than I made fun of me,
I said nothing, but kept a wish to myself.
I wanted to go away to see more and learn more,
I wanted to go far away—to places never dreamed of:

There everything would be much, much better than here.
There people would live like gods.
There no heart-rending sound of the ceaseless pestles would be heard,
And the annoying faces of the monks and nuns would remain unseen.

Father counted the silver dollars, five by five,
And wrapped them up in red paper, handing them to me with a lecture,
While I was thinking about things a world apart,
About the harbors reflecting the glitter of the sun.

You, chattering sparrows, what are you talking about—
Don't you know that I am about to depart?
And you, simple and honest hired hands on our farm,
Why do you always wear a look of sorrow on your faces?

The morning sun shone on the stone-paved road,
My heart went out for my poor village.
It stood beneath the mountain of twin peaks,
Like an old man, wrinkled and failing.

Good-by, my village of poverty,
And my old dog, please hurry home.
The Twin Peaks will protect you from misfortunes.
I shall return, when I grow old, to be with you.

AI CH'ING
Translated by KAI-YU HSU

Where is the new kingdom the youth must find?

In what ways is the youth like Ratso? Like Richard?

The Return

JAMES NGUGI

The road was long. Whenever he took a step forward, little clouds of dust rose, whirled angrily behind him, and then slowly settled again. Meanwhile a thin train of dust was left in the air, moving like smoke. He walked on, however, unmindful of the dust and ground under his feet. Yet with every step he seemed more and more conscious of the hardness and apparent animosity of the road. Not that he looked down; on the contrary, he looked straight ahead as if he would, any time now, see a familiar object that would hail him as a friend and tell him that he was near home. But the road stretched on.

He made quick, springing steps, his left hand dangling freely by the side of his once white coat, now torn and worn out. His right hand, bent at the elbow, held on to a string which supported a small bundle on his slightly drooping back. The bundle, well wrapped with a cotton cloth that had once been printed with red flowers now faded out, swung from side to side in harmony with the rhythm of his steps. The bundle held the bitterness and hardships of the years spent in detention camps. Now and then he looked at the sun on its homeward journey. Sometimes he darted quick side-glances at the small hedged strips of land which, with their sickly-looking crops, maize, beans, and so forth, appeared much as everything else did—unfriendly. The whole country was dull and seemed weary. To Kamau, this was nothing new. He remembered that, even before the Mau Mau emergency, the over-tilled Kikuyu holdings wore haggard looks in contrast to the sprawling green fields in the settled area.

A path branched to the left. He hesitated for a moment and then seemed to make up his mind. For the first time, his eyes brightened a little as he went along the path that would take him down the valley and then to the village. At last home was near and, with that realization, the

faraway look of a weary traveller seemed to desert him for a while. The valley and the vegetation along it were in deep contrast with the surrounding country. For here green bush and trees thrived. This could only mean one thing: Honia river still flowed. He quickened his steps as if he could scarcely believe this to be true till he had actually set his eyes on the river. It was there; it still flowed. Honia, where so often he had taken a bath, plunging stark naked into its cool living water, warmed his heart as he watched its serpentine movement round the rocks and heard its slight murmurs. A painful exhilaration passed through him and for a moment he longed for those days. He sighed. Perhaps the river would not remember in his hardened features that same boy to whom the river-side world had meant everything. Yet as he approached Honia, he felt more akin to it than he had felt to anything else since his release.

A group of women were drawing water. He felt excited, for he could recognize one or two from his ridge. There was the middle-aged Wanjiku, whose deaf son had been killed by the Security Forces just before he himself was arrested. She had always been a darling of the village, having a smile for everyone and food for all. Would they receive him? Would they give him a "hero's welcome"? He thought so. Had he not always been a favorite all along the Ridge? And had he not fought for the land? He wanted to run and shout: "Here I am. I have come back to you." But he desisted. He was a man.

"Is it well with you?" A few voices responded. The other women, with tired and worn features, looked at him mutely as if his greeting was of no consequence. Why! Had he been so long in the camp? His spirits were damped as he feebly asked: "Do you not remember me?" Again they looked at him. They stared at him with cold, hard looks; like everything else, they seemed to be deliberately refusing to know or own him. At last Wanjiku recognized him. But there was neither warmth nor enthusiasm in her voice as she said, "O, is it you, Kamau? We thought you—" She did not continue. Only now he noticed something else— surprise? fear? He could not tell. He saw their quick glances dart at him and he knew for certain that a secret from which he was excluded bound them together.

"Perhaps I am no longer one of them!" he bitterly reflected. But they told him of the new Village. The old Village of scattered huts spread thinly over the Ridge was no more.

He left them, feeling embittered and cheated. The old Village had not even waited for him. And suddenly he felt a strong nostalgia for his old home, friends and surroundings. He thought of his father, mother and — and — He dared not think about her. But for all that, Muthoni, just as she had been in the old days, came back to his mind. His heart beat faster. A pang of desire passed through him. He quickened his step. He forgot the village women as he remembered his wife. For he had stayed with her for a mere two weeks; then he had been swept away by the Forces. Like many others he had been hurriedly screened and then taken to detention — without trial. And all that time he had thought of nothing but the village and his beautiful woman.

The others had been like him. They had talked of nothing but their homes. One day he was working next to another detainee from Muranga. Suddenly the detainee, Njoroge, stopped breaking stones. He sighed heavily. His worn-out eyes had a faraway look.

"What's wrong, man? What's the matter with you?" Kamau asked.

"It is my wife. I left her expecting a baby. I have no idea what has happened to her."

Another detainee put in: "For me, I left my woman with a baby. She had just delivered. We were all happy. But on the same day, I was arrested . . ."

And so they went on. All of them longed for one day — the day of their return home. Then life would begin anew.

Kamau himself had left his wife without a child. He had not even finished paying the bride-price. But now he would go, seek work in Nairobi, and pay off the remainder to Muthoni's parents. Life would indeed begin anew. They would have a son and bring him up in their own home. With these prospects before his eyes, he quickened his steps. He wanted to run — no, fly to hasten his return. He was now nearing the top of the hill. He wished he could suddenly meet his brothers and sisters. Would they ask him questions? He would, at any rate, not tell them all — all about his sufferings, all his work on the roads and in the quarries with an askari always nearby ready to kick him if he relaxed. Yes. He had suffered many humiliations, and he had not resisted. Was there any need? But his soul and all the vigor of his manhood had rebelled and bled with rage and bitterness.

One day these wazungu would go!

One day his people would be free! Then, then — he did not know what he would do. However, he bitterly assured himself no one would ever flout his manhood again.

He mounted the hill and then stopped. The whole plain lay below. The new Village was before him — rows and rows of compact mud huts, crouching on the plain under the fast-vanishing sun. Dark blue smoke curled upwards from various huts, and formed a kind of dark mist that hovered over the village. Altogether it was very impressive and for a time he forgot his old home. Beyond, the deep, blood-red sinking sun sent out finger-like streaks of light that thinned outwards and mingled with the gray mist shrouding the distant hills.

In the village, he moved from street to street, meeting new faces. He inquired. He found his home. He stopped at the entrance to the yard and breathed hard and full. This was the moment of his return home. His father sat huddled up on a three-legged stool. He was now very aged and Kamau pitied the old man. But he had been spared — yes, spared to see his son's return —

"Father!"

The old man did not answer. He just looked at Kamau with strange vacant eyes. Kamau was impatient. He felt annoyed and irritated. Did he not see him? Would he behave like the women Kamau had met at the river?

In the street, naked and half-naked children were playing, throwing dust at one another. The sun had already set and it looked as if there would be moonlight.

"Father, don't you remember me?" Hope was sinking in him. He felt tired. Then all of a sudden he saw his father tremble like a leaf. He saw him stare with unbelieving eyes. Fear was discernible in those eyes. His mother came, and his brothers too. They crowded around him. His aged mother clung to him and sobbed hard.

"I knew my son would come. I knew he was not dead."

"Why, who told you I was dead?"

"That Karanja, son of Njogu."

And then Kamau understood. He understood his trembling father. He understood the women at the river. But one thing puzzled him: he had never been in the same detention camp with Karanja. Anyway he had come back. He wanted now to see Muthoni. Why had she not come out? He wanted to shout, "I have come, Muthoni; I am here." He looked around. His mother understood him. She quickly darted a glance at her man and then simply said:

"Muthoni is gone."

Kamau felt something cold settle in his stomach. He looked at the village and the dullness of the land he had passed through seemed to blind his vision. He wanted to ask many questions but he dared not. He could not yet believe that Muthoni had gone. But he knew by the look of the women at the river, by the look of his parents, that she was gone.

"She was a good daughter to us," his mother was explaining. "She waited for you and patiently bore all the ills of the land. Then Karanja came and said that you were dead. Your father believed him. She believed him too and keened for a month. Karanja constantly paid us visits. He was of your rika, you know. Then she got a child. We would have kept her. But where is the land? Where is the food? Ever since land consolidation, our last security was taken away. We let Karanja go with her. Other women have done worse—gone to town. Here only the infirm and the old have been left."

He was not listening; the coldness in his stomach slowly changed to bitterness. It would choke him. He felt bitter against all, all the people including his father and mother. They had betrayed him. They had leagued against him, and Karanja had always been his rival. Five years was admittedly not a short time. But why did she go? Why did they allow her to go? He wanted to speak. Yes, speak and denounce everything—the women at the river, the village and the people who dwelt there. But he would not. This thing was choking him.

"You—you gave my own away?" he whispered.

"Listen, child, child—"

The big yellow moon dominated the eastern horizon. It was like a great eye, watching two grief-stricken parents as they helplessly watched their son slip away in bitterness.

He stood on the bank of Honia River. He gazed fixedly at the river without actually seeing it. He was seeing his hopes being dashed on the ground instead. The river moved swiftly, making the same ceaseless murmurs. In the forest the crickets and other insects kept up an incessant buzz. And above, the moon shone in all her brightness. His heart began to thaw. He tried to remove his coat, and the small bundle he had held on to so firmly fell. It rolled down the bank and before Kamau knew what was happening, it was floating swiftly down the river. For a time he was shocked and wanted to retrieve it. What would he show his —Oh, then he remembered. Had he forgotten so soon? His wife had gone. And all the little things that had so strangely reminded him of her and that he had guarded all those years, had gone! He did not know why, but somehow he felt relieved. Warmth began to rise in his heart. He felt as if he would dance the magic of the night, the ritual of the moon and the river. All thoughts of drowning himself dispersed. Life was still sweet. He began to put on his coat, all the time murmuring to himself, "Why should she have waited for me? Why should all the changes have waited for my return?"

"My son!"

He quickly turned round. There, standing and looking resplendent under the bright moon, was his aged mother. For the first time he saw sorrow and untold hardships written on her wrinkled face. He felt like weeping, yes, weeping like a woman. She had all the time followed him. He looked at her and forgot all about himself.

"Mother!" It was a softened voice full of emotion. He went towards her and took her by the arm. "Let's go home!" he murmured again. This was truly his "return", and as he peered into the future, as he became aware of the beauty of life in spite of its hardships, he could see no possibility of his going away again.

How is Kamau like the youth in the previous poem?

What did his village represent to Kamau? What was his quest?

At the end of his perilous journey, Kamau had to face one final "monster." What was it? Do you think Kamau triumphed? If so, how?

The City

You said, "I will go to another land, I will go to another sea.
Another city will be found, a better one than this.
Every effort of mine is a condemnation of fate;
and my heart is—like a corpse—buried.
How long will my mind remain in this wasteland.
Wherever I turn my eyes, wherever I may look
I see black ruins of my life here,
where I spent so many years destroying and wasting."

You will find no new lands, you will find no other seas.
The city will follow you. You will roam the same
streets. And you will age in the same neighborhoods;
and you will grow gray in these same houses.
Always you will arrive in this city. Do not hope for any other—
There is no ship for you, there is no road.
As you have destroyed your life here
in this little corner, you have ruined it in the entire world.

CONSTANTINE CAVAFY
Translated by RAE DALVEN

There are two voices in this poem. Which would the heroes in this unit agree with? Why?

According to the first voice, where is the Golden Age? According to the second voice, where is the Golden Age? Which do you agree with? Why?

pity this busy monster,
manunkind

pity this busy monster, manunkind,

not. Progress is a comfortable disease:
your victim (death and life safely beyond)

plays with the bigness of his littleness
— electrons deify one razorblade
into a mountainrange; lenses extend

unwish through curving wherewhen till unwish
returns on its unself.
                             A world of made
is not a world of born — pity poor flesh

and trees, poor stars and stones, but never this
fine specimen of hypermagical

ultraomnipotence. We doctors know

a hopeless case if — listen: there's a hell
of a good universe next door; let's go.

E. E. CUMMINGS

Who is the hero in this poem? What is the monster? What has happened to
the Golden Age? Why is it appropriate to call the Golden Age "the world of
born"?

How is the quest of all the heroes in this unit to turn "the world of made"
into "the world of born"?

The poems and stories in this book come from all parts of the world, from widely separated times in history, and represent many kinds of imaginative literature. In this unit alone, there are classical myths and poems, political speeches and manifestoes, stories from America and Africa, a Chinese poem and a song from a rock musical. Yet despite their varied backgrounds and styles, they all spring from the same imaginative source—the notion of the hero's quest for his rightful kingdom.

The story of the quest is perhaps best exemplified by the Greek myth of Perseus. The princely hero begins life at a great disadvantage—the kingdom which is his birthright has been stolen from him, and if he is to recover it, he must go on a long and perilous journey. During his wanderings, he encounters dangers and tests of his courage and skill. Ultimately, however, he overcomes all the obstacles, fights one great battle with a monster, brings home a bride, rescues his oppressed family, and takes over his place of leadership in his kingdom.

Other selections in this unit retrace the pattern of similar quests. Cadmus must wander far and wide in pursuit of the mysterious heifer, finally slay a dragon, plow the hard earth, and found a new kingdom. The young boy in "The Street" must earn his right to return to his home by taking his father's place and battling a gang to bring back provisions to his destitute mother. The boy in the Chinese poem "The Song of Youth" must likewise set off in his canoe alone, in search of "places never dreamed of," where "people live like gods," an exciting kingdom he feels he has a right to discover.

What is represented by this lost inheritance that each hero must set out to regain? In Western literature it is often represented by the myth of the Golden Age, which tells of a time when all men lived in peace with one another and in harmony with nature; when, in fact, they possessed the secret of happy life. The great durability of this vision is shown by its constant occurrence in literature and in life. Its features reappear again and again: in the song "Aquarius," in speeches like President Kennedy's Inaugural Address or documents like the Declaration of Independence, in the "hell of a good universe next door" to which a poet invites us, and even in Ratso Rizzo's dreams of Florida, where a man can "sleep the sleep of Eden."

Yet the myth goes on to relate that somehow man lost this happy life, and in successive ages poverty, strife, pain, and suffering came into the world. The recovery of this lost Eden, this vanished or stolen Golden Age, is not an easy task. It takes patience, endurance, and courage—the kind of courage the speaker in "The City" does not believe in, but that most of the other heroes in this unit do seem to have. It also takes imagination, for the Golden Age may only be recovered, perhaps, at the very moment when it seems to have been finally lost. So it is that Kamau in "The Return" seems to have endured all his hardships for nothing, when the reality of his return fails to live up to the dream he has kept alive in his mind and heart for five years. It is at this moment of crisis that he achieves the vision of life still sweet and beautiful, "in spite of its hardships." Without those hardships, without the perilous journey itself, he would never have been able to discover his true home. He would never have become worthy to enter into it.

The quest for the rightful kingdom is a quest of confidence and optimism, a struggle based on the belief that the green golden world can be reachieved —and that it may be just over the next hill. All of literature is the story of this search, the search not only for what is ours by *right*, but also for what we have a *responsibility* to achieve.

2
MORE THAN MAN

Leonardo da Vinci

Alan E. Cober '73

Orpheus and Eurydice

A Greek myth
Retold by EDITH HAMILTON

The very earliest musicians were the gods. Athene was not distinguished in that line, but she invented the flute although she never played upon it. Hermes made the lyre and gave it to Apollo who drew from it sounds so melodious that when he played in Olympus the gods forgot all else. Hermes also made the shepherd-pipe for himself and drew enchanting music from it. Pan made the pipe of reeds which can sing as sweetly as the nightingale in spring. The Muses had no instrument peculiar to them, but their voices were lovely beyond compare.

Next in order came a few mortals so excellent in their art that they almost equaled the divine performers. Of these by far the greatest was Orpheus. On his mother's side he was more than mortal. He was the son of one of the Muses and a Thracian prince. His mother gave him the gift of music and Thrace where he grew up fostered it. The Thracians were the most musical of the peoples of Greece. But Orpheus had no rival there or anywhere except the gods alone. There was no limit to his power when he played and sang. No one and nothing could resist him.

> In the deep still woods upon the Thracian mountains
> Orpheus with his singing lyre led the trees,
> Led the wild beasts of the wilderness.

Everything animate and inanimate followed him. He moved the rocks on the hillside and turned the courses of the rivers.

Little is told about his life before his ill-fated marriage, for which he is even better known than for his music, but he went on one famous expedition and proved himself a most useful member of it. He sailed with Jason on the *Argo,* and when the heroes were weary or the rowing was especially difficult he would strike his lyre and they would be aroused to fresh zeal and their oars would smite the sea together in time to the melody. Or if a quarrel threatened he would play so tenderly and soothingly that the fiercest spirits would grow calm and forget their anger. He saved the heroes, too, from the Sirens. When they heard far over the sea singing so enchantingly sweet that it drove out all other thoughts except a desperate longing to hear more, and they turned the ship to the shore where the Sirens sat, Orpheus snatched up his lyre and played a tune so clear and ringing that it drowned the sound of those lovely fatal voices. The ship was put back on her course and the winds sped her away from the dangerous place. If Orpheus had not been there the Argonauts, too, would have left their bones on the Sirens' island.

Where he first met and how he wooed the maiden he loved, Eurydice, we are not told, but it is clear that no maiden he wanted could have resisted the power of his song. They were married, but their joy was brief. Directly after the wedding, as the bride walked in a meadow with her bridesmaids, a viper stung her and she died. Orpheus' grief was overwhelming. He could not endure it. He determined to go down to the world of death and try to bring Eurydice back. He said to himself,

> With my song
> I will charm Demeter's daughter,
> I will charm the Lord of the Dead,
> Moving their hearts with my melody.
> I will bear her away from Hades.

He dared more than any other man ever dared for his love. He took the fearsome journey to the underworld. There he struck his lyre, and at the sound all that vast multitude were charmed to stillness. The dog Cerberus relaxed his guard; the wheel of Ixion stood motionless; Sisyphus sat at rest upon his stone; Tantalus forgot his thirst; for the first time the faces of the dread goddesses, the Furies, were wet with tears. The ruler of Hades drew near to listen with his queen. Orpheus sang,

> O Gods who rule the dark and silent world,
> To you all born of a woman needs must come.
> All lovely things at last go down to you.

You are the debtor who is always paid.
A little while we tarry up on earth.
Then we are yours forever and forever.
But I seek one who came to you too soon.
The bud was plucked before the flower bloomed:
I tried to bear my loss. I could not bear it.
Love was too strong a god. O King, you know
If that old tale men tell is true, how once
The flowers saw the rape of Proserpine.
Then weave again for sweet Eurydice
Life's pattern that was taken from the loom
Too quickly. See, I ask a little thing,
Only that you will lend, not give, her to me.
She shall be yours when her years' span is full.

No one under the spell of his voice could refuse him anything. He

Drew iron tears down Pluto's cheek,
And made Hell grant what Love did seek.

They summoned Eurydice and gave her to him, but upon one condition: that he would not look back at her as she followed him, until they had reached the upper world. So the two passed through the great doors of Hades to the path which would take them out of the darkness, climbing up and up. He knew that she must be just behind him, but he longed unutterably to give one glance to make sure. But now they were almost there, the blackness was turning gray; now he had stepped out joyfully into the daylight. Then he turned to her. It was too soon; she was still in the cavern. He saw her in the dim light, and he held out his arms to clasp her; but on the instant she was gone. She had slipped back into the darkness. All he heard was one faint word, "Farewell."

Desperately he tried to rush after her and follow her down, but he was not allowed. The gods would not consent to his entering the world of the dead a second time, while he was still alive. He was forced to return to the earth alone, in utter desolation. Then he forsook the company of men. He wandered through the wild solitudes of Thrace, comfortless except for his lyre, playing, always playing, and the rocks and the rivers and the trees heard him gladly, his only companions. But at last a band of Maenads came upon him. They were as frenzied as those who killed Pentheus so horribly. They slew the gentle musician, tearing him limb from limb, and flung the severed head into the swift river Hebrus. It was borne along past the river's mouth on to the Lesbian shore, nor had it suffered any change from the sea when the Muses found it and buried it in the sanctuary of the island. His limbs they gathered and placed in a tomb at the foot of Mount Olympus, and there to this day the nightingales sing more sweetly than anywhere else.

What "more than human" power did Orpheus have that aided him in his quest for his bride?

What "merely human" quality did Orpheus have that turned his quest into catastrophe?

Why do you suppose people think of the world of death as "down"? Make a list of phrases, or collect a group of pictures, that express the belief that what is "up" is desirable and what is "down" is undesirable.

Annabel Lee

It was many and many a year ago,
    In a kingdom by the sea,
That a maiden there lived whom you may know
    By the name of Annabel Lee;
And this maiden she lived with no other thought
    Than to love and be loved by me.

I was a child and *she* was a child,
    In this kingdom by the sea,
But we loved with a love that was more than love—
    I and my Annabel Lee—
With a love that the wingèd seraphs of Heaven
    Coveted her and me.

And this was the reason that, long ago,
    In this kingdom by the sea,
A wind blew out of a cloud, chilling
    My beautiful Annabel Lee;
So that her highborn kinsmen came
    And bore her away from me,
To shut her up in a sepulcher
    In this kingdom by the sea.

The angels, not half so happy in Heaven,
    Went envying her and me:—
Yes!—that was the reason (as all men know,
    In this kingdom by the sea)
That the wind came out of the cloud by night,
    Chilling and killing my Annabel Lee.

But our love it was stronger by far than the love
    Of those who were older than we—
    Of many far wiser than we—
And neither the angels in Heaven above,
    Nor the demons down under the sea,
Can ever dissever my soul from the soul
    Of the beautiful Annabel Lee:—

For the moon never beams, without bringing me
       dreams
    Of the beautiful Annabel Lee;
And the stars never rise, but I feel the bright eyes
    Of the beautiful Annabel Lee:
And so, all the night-tide, I lie down by the side
Of my darling—my darling—my life and my bride,
    In the sepulcher there by the sea—
    In her tomb by the sounding sea.

EDGAR ALLAN POE

Orpheus made the perilous journey to the Underworld to rescue his bride. Is Annabel Lee also in a kind of "Underworld"? What quest does this poet undertake to try to rejoin his bride? What enemy must he conquer?

Why do you think the poet pictures himself and Annabel Lee as children? What powers and qualities of the hero and his bride are emphasized by their childlikeness? Would you say they lived in a Golden Age? Why? What happened to it? Why?

Lemminkainen

A Finnish myth
Retold by PADRAIC COLUM

Into the forest went Lemminkainen. As he went he chanted his Magic Song, "O Tapio, Lord of the Forest, aid me: lead me where I may take my quarry! Nyyrikki, O thou son of the Forest's Lord, red-capped one, mighty hero, make a path for me through your father's domain; clear the ground for me and keep me on the proper roadway!" Lemminkainen, the handsome, the light-stepping one, chanted Magic Songs to win the forest divinities as he went seeking the Elk of Hiisi. . . .

So he went through the forest; but the quarry he sought was not turned toward him. Through the trackless forest he went, across the marshes, over the heaths. At last he went up a mountain; he climbed a knoll; he turned his eyes to the north-west; he turned his eyes to the north; there, across the marshes, he saw Tapio's mansions with their doors and windows all golden.

Then once more the quick-moving, light-stepping Lemminkainen went onward. He dashed through all that lay across his path. Under the very windows of the mansions of the Lord of the Forest he came. Through the windows he saw those whose business it was to dispense the game to the hunters. They were resting; they were lolling; their worst wear they had on them. Under the windows Lemminkainen chanted his Magic Songs:

". . . Graybeard with the pine-leaf hat," he chanted, "with the cloak of moss! Re-array the woods; give the aspens their grayness, give the alders a robe of beauty, clothe the pine trees in silver, adorn the fir trees with gold, and the birch trees with golden blossoms. Make it as in the former years when days were better, when the waste places flowed with honey. O daughter of Tapio, Tuulikki, gracious virgin, drive the game this way! Take a switch; strike the game on their haunches; drive the game toward the one who seeks for it and waits for it! Master of Tapio's mansions, mistress of Tapio's mansions, make wide the doors, send forth the game that has been shut in!''

So Lemminkainen chanted; for a week he ranged through the forest. His Magic Songs appeased the Lord of the Forest, delighted the Mistress of the Forest, and made glad the hearts of all the Forest Maidens. To where the Elk of Hiisi had his lair they went; they drove forth the Elk; they turned it in the direction of the one who waited for it.

Over the Elk Lemminkainen threw his lasso. And when he held the Elk he chanted his Magic Song once more, "Lord of the Forest, Tapio; Mistress of the Forest, Mielikki, come now and take your reward for the good you have done me! Come now and take the gold and silver I scatter on the ground of the forest!'' So he chanted; then to the north, to Pohjola, he journeyed with the Elk he had captured. "I have caught the Elk of Hiisi! Come forth now, ancient one of Pohjola; give me your daughter; give me the bride I have come for!''

Louhi, the Mistress of Pohjola, came out of her dwelling, and she looked upon Lemminkainen and the Elk he had captured. "I will give you my daughter, I will give you the bride you have come for, when you capture the Steed of Hiisi, and bring it to me here.''

Then Lemminkainen took a golden bridle and a halter of silver; he went through the green and open meadows; he went out upon the plains. No sign he saw of the Steed of Hiisi. He called upon Ukko, the God of the Sky, and he chanted a Magic Song:

"Open the clefts of the Heavens; cast the hail upon the back of Hiisi's Steed; fling ice blocks upon him that he may race from where he is, that he may come to where I am!'' Ukko rent the air; he scattered ice blocks; they were smaller than a horse's head, but they were bigger than a man's head. They struck the back of Hiisi's Steed. It raced forward. Then Lemminkainen chanted, "Steed of Hiisi, stretch forth thy silver head; push it into this golden bridle! I will never drive thee harshly; with a rope's end I will never smite thee. No, with silver cords I will lead thee, and with a piece of cloth I will drive thee!'' So he chanted, and the Steed of Hiisi put forward his head; the golden bridle with the bit of silver went across his head and into his mouth.

Then to the north went Lemminkainen bringing the chestnut steed with the foam-flecked mane. He called to the Mistress of Pohjola, "I have captured the Steed of Hiisi and the Elk of Hiisi. Now give thy daughter to me, give me the bride that I have come for.''

But Louhi, the Mistress of Pohjola, answered him, "I will give thee

my daughter, I will give thee the bride thou hast come for when thou hast shot with an arrow, and using one arrow only, the white Swan on Tuonela's dark water." Then Lemminkainen took his bow. He went down into Manala's abysses. He went to where Tuoni's murky river flowed. He went to where the waters made a dread whirlpool.

There the cowherd Markahattu lurked; there the blind man waited for Lemminkainen. When Lemminkainen had come first to Pohjola he had chanted his Magic Songs; he had chanted them against the swordsmen and the young heroes who were there, and he had driven them all away, banning them with his Magic Songs. One old man he had not banned—Markahattu the cowherd who sat there, his eyes closed in blindness. Lemminkainen had scorned him. "I have not banned thee," he cried, "because thou art so wretched a creature. The worst of cowherds, thou hast destroyed thy mother's children, thou hast disgraced thy sister, thou hast crippled all the horses, thou hast wearied to death the foals." Markahattu, greatly angered, left the place where Lemminkainen had scorned him; ever since he had waited by the whirlpool for the coming of Lemminkainen.

The white Swan was on the dark river of Tuonela. Lemminkainen drew his bow. As he did, Markahattu grasped a water-snake; he hurled it; he pierced Lemminkainen with the serpent. Lemminkainen knew no Magic Songs to relieve himself from the wounds made by water-snakes. He sank into the murky river; he was tossed about in the worst of whirlpools; he was dashed down the cataract; the stream brought him into Tuonela.

There Tuoni's bloodstained son, drawing his sword, hewed him into pieces. He hewed him into eight pieces and he flung the pieces into the dark river. "Be tossed about for ever with thy bow and thy arrows, thou who camest to shoot the sacred Swan upon our sacred River!"

Only through his mother could help come to Lemminkainen. She had bided at home, troubled by his long delay in returning. One day she looked upon the comb and the hairbrush he had left behind: she saw blood trickling from the comb, blood dripping from the hairbrush. She knew that blood was coming from the body of her son. She gathered up her skirt and she went off to find him.

Valleys were lifted up as Lemminkainen's mother went on; hills were levelled; the high ground sank before her and the low ground was lifted up. She hastened to Pohjola. She came to the door and she questioned the Mistress of Pohjola.

"Whither hast thou sent my son, Lemminkainen?" "I know no tidings of your son. I yoked a steed for him; I fixed a sledge for him, and he started off from my dwelling; perhaps in driving over a frozen lake he sank into it." "Shameless are the lies thou tellst me. Tell me whither thou hast sent him or I will break down the doors of Pohjola." "I fed him; I gave him meat and drink, and I placed him in his boat; he went to shoot the rapids, but what has befallen him I do not know." "Shameless are the lies thou tellst. Tell me whither thou hast sent him or this instant death will come to thee." "Now I will tell thee, now I will tell thee truly. Lemminkainen went to shoot the sacred bird, the Swan on Tuonela's River."

Then his mother went in quest of him; she questioned the trees, she questioned the pathway, she questioned the golden moon in the sky. But the trees, the pathway, the golden moon in the sky, all had their own troubles, and they would take no trouble for any woman's son. She questioned the sun in the heavens, and the sun told her that her son was in Tuonela's River.

Then to the smith Ilmarinen went Lemminkainen's mother. For her Ilmarinen fashioned a rake, a rake with a copper handle and with teeth of steel—a hundred fathoms was the length of the teeth, five hundred fathoms was the length of the handle. To Tuonela's River she went: there she chanted a Magic Song.

She prayed the sun to shine with such strength that the watchers in Manala would sleep and that the powers of Tuonela would be worn out. And the sun stooped upon a crooked birch tree and shone in his strength so that the watchers of Manala were worn out—the young men slept upon their sword-hilts; the old men slept resting upon their staffs; the middle-aged men, the spearmen, slept resting upon the hafts of their spears. Then Lemminkainen's mother took her rake; she raked the river against the current; once she raked it, and she raked it again. The third time she raked the river she brought up the hat and stockings of her son Lemminkainen. She went into the river, and she waded in its deepest water. She drew up the body with her rake of iron.

Many fragments were wanting to make up the body of Lemminkainen—half of his head, a hand, many little fragments. Life was wanting in the body. But still his mother would not cast it back into the river. Once again she raked Tuonela's deep river, first along it and then across it; his hand she found, half of his head she found, fragments of his backbone she found, and pieces of his ribs.

She pieced all together; the bones fitted, the joints went together.

She chanted a Magic Song, praying that Suonetar would weave the veins together, and stitch with her finest needle and her most silken thread the flesh and the sinews that were broken. She sang a Magic Song, praying that Jumala would fix together the bones. Then the veins were knit together, the bones were fastened together, but still the man remained lifeless and speechless.

Then Lemminkainen's mother sang a Magic Song. She bade the bee go forth and find the honey-salve that would give final healing. The bee flew across the moon in the heavens; he flew past the borders of Orion; he flew across the Great Bear's shoulders, and into the dwelling of Jumala the Creator. In pots of silver, in golden kettles was the salve that would give final healing. The bee gathered it and brought it back to Lemminkainen's mother.

With the salve she rubbed him. She called upon her son to rise out of his slumbers, to awaken out of his dreams of evil. Up he rose; out of his dreams he wakened, and speech came back to him. Even then he would have slain the Swan so that he might win a bride in Pohjola. But his mother persuaded him, and his mother drew him back with her to his home. There the bride awaited him whom he had won in another place and on another day, Kyllikki, the Flower of Saari.

Lemminkainen, too, braves an Underworld for his bride. What is it? Can you name any other stories of heroes who try to rescue their lovers? Why do you suppose it is such a common story?

What magic power do Lemminkainen and Orpheus use? What does this suggest to you about man's belief in the power of "the word"?

In what ways is Lemminkainen's mother like the mothers of Richard and Kamau in unit one? What do they do for their hero-sons? Why do you think the role played by these women could never be played by the heroes' fathers?

How are the heroes of each of these three stories trying to do something that no mortal is allowed to do?

Daedalus, the famous craftsman and engineer, once angered King Minos and was imprisoned on the island of Crete. A man of courage and imagination, he vowed to escape.

Daedalus and Icarus

A Greek myth

Homesick for homeland, Daedalus hated Crete
And his long exile there, but the sea held him.
"Though Minos blocks escape by land or water,"
Daedalus said, "surely the sky is open,
And that's the way we'll go. Minos' dominion
Does not include the air." He turned his thinking
Toward unknown arts, changing the laws of nature.
He laid out feathers in order, first the smallest,
A little larger next it, and so continued,
The way that pan-pipes rise in gradual sequence.
He fastened them with twine and wax, at middle,
At bottom, so, and bent them, gently curving,
So that they looked like wings of birds, most surely.
And Icarus, his son, stood by and watched him,
Not knowing he was dealing with his downfall,
Stood by and watched, and raised his shiny face
To let a feather, light as down, fall on it,
Or stuck his thumb into the yellow wax
Fooling around, the way a boy will, always,
Whenever a father tries to get some work done.
Still, it was done at last, and the father hovered,
Poised, in the moving air, and taught his son:
"I warn you, Icarus, fly a middle course:
Don't go too low, or water will weigh the wings down,

Don't go too high, or the sun's fire will burn them.
Keep to the middle way. And one more thing,
No fancy steering by star or constellation,
Follow my lead!'' That was the flying lesson,
And now to fit the wings to the boy's shoulders.
Between the work and warning the father found
His cheeks were wet with tears, and his hands trembled.
He kissed his son (*Good-by,* if he had known it),
Rose on his wings, flew on ahead, as fearful
As any bird launching the little nestlings
Out of high nest into thin air. *Keep on,*
Keep on, he signals, *follow me!* He guides him
In flight—O fatal art!—and the wings move
And the father looks back to see the son's wings moving.
Far off, far down, some fisherman is watching
As the rod dips and trembles over the water,
Some shepherd rests his weight upon his crook,
Some plowman on the handles of the plowshare,
And all look up, in absolute amazement,
At those air-borne above. They must be gods!
They were over Samos, Juno's sacred island,
Delos and Paros toward the left, Lebinthus
Visible to the right, and another island,
Calymne, rich in honey. And the boy
Thought *This is wonderful!* and left his father,
Soared higher, higher, drawn to the vast heaven,
Nearer the sun, and the wax that held the wings
Melted in that fierce heat, and the bare arms
Beat up and down in air, and lacking oarage
Took hold of nothing. *Father!* he cried, and *Father!*
Until the blue sea hushed him, the dark water
Men call the Icarian now. And Daedalus,
Father no more, called "Icarus, where are you!
Where are you, Icarus? Tell me where to find you!"
And saw the wings on the waves, and cursed his talents,
Buried the body in a tomb, and the land
Was named for Icarus.

OVID
Translated by ROLFE HUMPHRIES

More Than Man **63**

What "more than human" power did Daedalus have that aided him in his quest to fly?

What "merely human" quality did Icarus have that turned his quest into catastrophe?

Why do you suppose a person's tragedy or catastrophe is called his *downfall?*

All God's Chillen Had Wings

A Georgia Sea Islands legend
Retold by JOHN BENNETT

Once all Africans could fly like birds; but owing to their many trans-
gressions, their wings were taken away. There remained, here and
there, in the sea islands and out-of-the-way places in the low country,
some who had been overlooked, and had retained the power of flight,
though they looked like other men.

There was a cruel master on one of the sea islands who worked his
people till they died. When they died he bought others to take their
places. These also he killed with overwork in the burning summer sun,
through the middle hours of the day, although this was against the law.

One day, when all the worn-out Negroes were dead of overwork, he
bought, of a broker in the town, a company of native Africans just
brought into the country, and put them at once to work in the cotton-
field.

He drove them hard. They went to work at sunrise and did not stop
until dark. They were driven with unsparing harshness all day long,
men, women and children. There was no pause for rest during the un-
endurable heat of the midsummer noon, though trees were plenty and
near. But through the hardest hours, when fair plantations gave their
Negroes rest, this man's driver pushed the work along without a
moment's stop for breath, until all grew weak with heat and thirst.

There was among them one young woman who had lately borne a
child. It was her first; she had not fully recovered from bearing, and
should not have been sent to the field until her strength had come back.

She had her child with her, as the other women had, astraddle on her hip, or piggyback.

The baby cried. She spoke to quiet it. The driver could not understand her words. She took her breast with her hand and threw it over her shoulder that the child might suck and be content. Then she went back to chopping knot-grass; but being very weak, and sick with the great heat, she stumbled, slipped and fell.

The driver struck her with his lash until she rose and staggered on.

She spoke to an old man near her, the oldest man of them all, tall and strong, with a forked beard. He replied; but the driver could not understand what they said; their talk was strange to him.

She returned to work; but in a little while she fell again. Again the driver lashed her until she got to her feet. Again she spoke to the old man. But he said: "Not yet, daughter; not yet." So she went on working, though she was very ill.

Soon she stumbled and fell again. But when the driver came running with his lash to drive her on with her work, she turned to the old man and asked: "Is it time yet, daddy?" He answered: "Yes, daughter; the time has come. Go; and peace be with you!" . . . and stretched out his arms toward her . . . so.

With that she leaped straight up into the air and was gone like a bird, flying over field and wood.

The driver and overseer ran after her as far as the edge of the field; but she was gone, high over their heads, over the fence, and over the top of the woods, gone, with her baby astraddle of her hip, sucking at her breast.

Then the driver hurried the rest to make up for her loss; and the sun was very hot indeed. So hot that soon a man fell down. The overseer himself lashed him to his feet. As he got up from where he had fallen the old man called to him in an unknown tongue. My grandfather told me the words that he said; but it was a long time ago, and I have forgotten them. But when he had spoken, the man turned and laughed at the overseer, and leaped up into the air, and was gone, like a gull, flying over field and wood.

Soon another man fell. The driver lashed him. He turned to the old man. The old man cried out to him, and stretched out his arms as he had done for the other two; and he, like them, leaped up, and was gone through the air, flying like a bird over field and wood.

Then the overseer cried to the driver, and the master cried to them both: "Beat the old devil! He is the doer!"

The overseer and the driver ran at the old man with lashes ready; and the master ran too, with a picket pulled from the fence, to beat the life out of the old man who had made those Negroes fly.

But the old man laughed in their faces, and said something loudly to all the Negroes in the field, the new Negroes and the old Negroes.

And as he spoke to them they all remembered what they had forgotten, and recalled the power which once had been theirs. Then all the Negroes, old and new, stood up together; the old man raised his hands; and they all leaped up into the air with a great shout; and in a moment were gone, flying, like a flock of crows, over the field, over the fence, and over the top of the wood; and behind them flew the old man.

The men went clapping their hands; and the women went singing; and those who had children gave them their breasts; and the children laughed and sucked as their mothers flew, and were not afraid.

The master, the overseer, and the driver looked after them as they flew, beyond the wood, beyond the river, miles on miles, until they passed beyond the last rim of the world and disappeared in the sky like a handful of leaves. They were never seen again.

Where they went I do not know; I never was told. Nor what it was that the old man said . . . that I have forgotten. But as he went over the last fence he made a sign in the master's face, and cried "Kuli-ba! Kuli-ba!" I don't know what that means.

But if I could only find the old wood sawyer, he could tell you more; for he was there at the time, and saw the Africans fly away with their women and children. He is an old, old man, over ninety years of age, and remembers a great many strange things.

In what specific ways is the story of these flying slaves like the story of Daedalus and Icarus? In what ways is it different?

Why do you think people tell stories about wanting to fly? Do you think such stories are symbols of some other human desire? What is it?

This is a brief excerpt from the script of a recent American movie about an unusual boy whose dream was, perhaps, not as unusual as it seems. The movie takes place in Houston, Texas.

Brewster McCloud

DORAN WILLIAM CANNON

NARRATOR. Flight of birds. Flight of Man. Man's similarity to birds. Birds' similarity to Man is the subject at hand. We will deal with them for the next hour or so and hope that we draw no conclusions. Elsewise the subject shall cease to fascinate us and, alas, another dream would be lost. There are far too few. In these words, the German poet, Goethe, expressed Man's desire to fly: "How I yearn to throw myself into endless space and float above the awful abyss." Man, incontestably the most advanced creature, has only to observe the flight of birds to realize the weight of the Earth's imprisonment. And so, the desire to fly has been ever-present in the mind of Man. But the reality has been long in coming. Has Man truly realized his dream? To answer that, we must isolate the dream. Was the dream to attain the ability to fly, or was the dream the freedom that true flight seemed to offer Man? . . .

SUZANNE. When will I get to see you again?

BREWSTER. Always . . . forever. I guess—you'll just have to . . . fly away with me.

SUZANNE. I'm scared of airplanes. The last time I flew it—well, I got so scared, I sweated right through my new dress.

BREWSTER. Not that kind of flying . . . Real flying . . . on wings . . . like a bird.

SUZANNE. Wings? You're kidding!

BREWSTER. Un uh. Un uh. I been workin' on them for a long time. They're almost finished.

SUZANNE. You mean . . . you've got real wings? That work? And that you can really fly with?

BREWSTER. Um hm.

SUZANNE. You're kidding!

BREWSTER. No.

SUZANNE. Where are they?

BREWSTER. Where I live . . . in the Dome.

SUZANNE. You live in the Astrodome? You're kidding! Where?

BREWSTER. In the fallout shelter.

SUZANNE. And you've got wings that really work?

BREWSTER. Um hm.

SUZANNE. You're kidding!

BREWSTER. You keep saying that. Do you think I just make that up?

SUZANNE. When can we try them out?

BREWSTER. Tomorrow. Like to fly tomorrow?

SUZANNE. Brewster, do you realize what that means if they work?

BREWSTER. I know. We can fly away together.

High angle close-up — upside-down shot on SUZANNE, *turning to look up to foreground, eyes wide.*

SUZANNE. Fly away?! Brewster, you could be a millionaire! . . .

High angle close-up — down to BREWSTER *looking off left, reacting.*

SUZANNE. . . . I've gotta get you a good lawyer, to protect you. And you'll need a patent. . . .

High-angle upside-down shot — SUZANNE *looking up, nodding her head.*

SUZANNE. . . . Tonight I'll know. Remember — he's my old boyfriend. The one that I told you about that works as a politician. . . .

High angle — down to BREWSTER *looking left.*

SUZANNE. . . . You could get a limousine — and a chauffeur . . . everything!

BREWSTER. Suzanne, you're talkin' crazy!

High angle — down to SUZANNE *and* BREWSTER *beside each other,* BREWSTER *watching her as she turns and puts her hand to his neck.*

SUZANNE. You could get a house on the River Oaks Boulevard!

BREWSTER. But we have to fly away.

SUZANNE. Why? Why can't we stay here? This is my home. I love it here.

Camera pans up and right to BREWSTER's *face as he turns his head to foreground.*

BREWSTER. They'll put me in a cage.

.   .   .

Interior Astrodome — day — high-angle zoom long shot.

SINGERS (*off stage*). All of the stars look down on your earth,
Everyone can see everything that you do
And all of the heavens have watched you since birth
And you had your chance to watch them too.
All of the trees, all of the flowers
And the goods that fly high in your way
Beg the heavenly powers to intervene
Before you reach the end.
All of the rain falls on the earth
Cannot cleanse away what's been done
And all of the winds can't blow away the curse
Nature has provided that will come.
These are the unnatural facts.
This is the last of the unnatural acts.

Exterior Astrodome concourse — day — zoom high-angle travel long shot — travel right and zoom back with squad cars' sirens wailing, racing toward corner and starting to turn toward foreground.

Interior Astrodome — day — high angle — down to BREWSTER *with his wings on his back, moving toward background through doorway.*

Exterior Astrodome — day — zoom high-angle long shot — camera zooms in past the squad cars racing toward the Dome, up toward the top of the Dome.

Interior Astrodome — Camera tracks left with BREWSTER *moving toward background ramp near top of Dome.*

Camera travels in with several POLICEMEN *racing toward background, riot guns in hand, around the outer edges of the arena.*

High-angle long shot—down to BREWSTER *looking off right then to* COP *left, who finally sees him and races up background left stairs while* BREWSTER *starts to climb the railing in foreground.*

High-angle long shot—down to POLICEMEN *racing in and up background ramp toward foreground.*

High angle—down to BREWSTER *climbing onto rail.*

High angle—down to the arena and stationed POLICEMEN *and* PEOPLE *in background below.*

Close shot— BREWSTER *looking foreground right to left and right again.*

Low-angle travel long shot—up to BREWSTER *taking off from the rail as* POLICEMAN *runs in left, too late, camera traveling right with the flying* BREWSTER, *panning down and right slightly with him.*

Close shot— BREWSTER *blowing hard and flapping his hands, snugly in the halter, flying toward foreground.*

High-angle long shot—down to many POLICEMEN *moving down the aisles toward foreground, one starting to jump the rail.*

Close shot— BREWSTER *flying toward foreground, looking down.*

POLICE *chasing* BREWSTER, *who is flying low, camera panning up and right off them as he takes off higher into the air toward background right.*

SINGERS. When . . .

Medium shot— BREWSTER, *with wing controls in both hands, flapping them as he flies toward foreground.*

High-angle travel—travel in holding the oval below and the POLICE *running.*

SINGERS. . . . you are sliding . . .

Low-angle long pan shot—Camera pans right with the flying BREWSTER.

SINGERS. . . . how . . .

Close shot— BREWSTER *flying toward foreground.*

SINGERS. . . . the bird . . .

High-angle long pan shot—Camera pans right with BREWSTER *flying,* POLICEMEN *down below left in the aisles, group seated in background center.*

SINGERS. . . . sings when she . . .

Low-angle long shot—up to BREWSTER *gracefully flying up toward background top of Dome.*

SINGERS. . . . is flying . . .

Close shot— BREWSTER *flying.*

SECOND CHORUS (*off stage*). . . . how the bird sings.

Low-angle travel long pan shot—up to the Dome. Camera travels and pans up and left to pick up the background lights.

SINGERS. . . . and how that bee stings . . .

Low-angle long pan shot—up to BREWSTER *flying toward foreground left, camera panning left.*

SINGERS. . . . he . . .

Camera pans up and left along the Dome as BREWSTER *flies.*

SINGERS. . . . knows he is dying . . .

Low-angle circular—Camera pans left in circle with BREWSTER *flying up near top of Dome.*

SINGERS. . . . White feather wings . . .
SECOND CHORUS. White feather wings.

Close shot— BREWSTER *flying right and looking down.*

SINGERS. . . . gracefully glid- . . .

Low-angle travel circular—Camera travels left and pans up and left with BREWSTER *flying near the Dome, panning right and left again as he circles and flies toward background.*

SECOND CHORUS. White feather wings.
SINGERS. . . . -ing don't turn and spin when you are . . .

Close-shot— BREWSTER *flying right.*

SECOND CHORUS. When you are sliding.
SINGERS. . . . sliding.
How the bird sings . . .

Low-angle travel up to BREWSTER *flying, camera travels fast circularly and pans left with his flight.*

SECOND CHORUS. Sliding—sliding.
SINGERS. . . . when she is flying . . .
SECOND CHORUS. Flying—flying.
SINGERS. . . . and how the bee stings
When he knows he is dying.
SECOND CHORUS. Dying—dying.

*Close shot—*BREWSTER *flying right.*

Camera travels left with the flying BREWSTER *around the Dome. Zoom back slightly.*

*Close shot—*BREWSTER *sweating and panting as he works the wings, flying right.*

Low-angle travel long shot—up to BREWSTER *straining and grunting as camera travels left with him up near top of Dome.*

*Close shot—*BREWSTER *grunting as he flies right, looks up.*

Low-angle long pan shot—up to BREWSTER *flying up toward top of Dome, camera panning right as he strains.*

*Close shot—*BREWSTER *flying, screaming grunts of straining energy escape his lungs.*

Low-angle zoom travel long shot—up to BREWSTER *flying higher toward top of Dome, camera zooms up and in and traveling right with him making bird squawks.*

Travel and zoom in and left along top of Dome.

Low-angle long shot—up to BREWSTER *flying, squawking.*

*Close shot—*BREWSTER *flying right, squawking.*

Low-angle travel long shot—Camera travels left with the flying BREWSTER *squawking.*

*Close shot—*BREWSTER *flying right, seeming tired, squawking as he looks down.*

High-angle long shot—past a foreground left flapping wing to the stadium below.

Low-angle long shot—up to BREWSTER *stopped in midair and squawking.*

Close shot— BREWSTER *trying to stay aloft.*

BREWSTER. Yeowww!

Camera pans left along Dome as wing flaps in foreground.

High-angle long pan shot—Camera pans down fast as BREWSTER *plummets down and hits the dirt with a thud, spraying dust up into the air. Camera holds on the crushed bird-figure.*

The chorus sings that nature is on Brewster's side, and yet it also says that nature is against him, calling his quest an "unnatural act." How is nature itself the "monster" to be conquered on this quest?

How much power did Orpheus have over nature? How much did Daedalus have? How much did Icarus have? Which of these is Brewster most like? Why?

Daedalus and Icarus, the flying slaves, and Brewster are all participating in the same quest, though they lived in different societies thousands of years apart. What reason did each have for wanting to succeed?

Three worlds are imagined in these myths: the upper world, the middle earth, and the lower world. According to the stories, which world is man decreed to live in? Who made that decree? What are the characteristics of the other two worlds? Why would man want to conquer them? Are the human impulses to "know" these non-human worlds still revealed by men today? How?

Asclepius

A Greek myth
Retold by W. H. D. ROUSE

This god was named Asclepius, and he was the god of healing, one who did only kind things, and never pushed out anyone else; but all men loved him and worshipped him for his deeds of kindness.

He was the son of Apollo; but when he was born, he was left out among the mountains, to live or die. There a nanny goat found him, and gave him milk, and a dog watched over him, until a shepherd came and found him. He was put in the charge of a wonderful creature named Cheiron, a Centaur; that is to say, he was half man and half horse.

Cheiron was himself the son of old Cronus the Titan, and he lived in a cave on Mount Pelion. He was the wisest and most just of all creatures on earth. He knew all the healing herbs that grow, to cure the diseases which men have. He could heal wounds, and sing magical ditties which soothed the sick and made them well. He could chase and catch the wild animals. In his cave among the hills he lived a happy life at home with his wife and mother; and all the young heroes used to be brought to him, and left to be taught, like schoolboys in a boarding school. He taught them how to ride on his own back and how to hunt and how to fight and how to use healing herbs; and he taught them the rules of good conduct. His most famous rule was: Honor Zeus first among gods, and among men honor first thy father.

Asclepius learned all this from him, but he paid most attention to the healing herbs and the salves for curing wounds and the magical ditties, for he cared nothing about hunting or war. When he grew up, he became famous for his cures; but he went too far in this. He happened one day to kill a snake; and as the dead snake lay on the ground, by and by another snake crept up, and laid an herb on the dead snake's mouth. Then the dead snake came to life again, and they both went away together. Asclepius noticed what the herb was—for he had not learned about this one from Cheiron; and he used it to bring a dead man back to life.

This made Hades angry, and he complained to Zeus. "Look here, sir," he said, "if this man goes on, my kingdom will be empty. It is not fair to me." Then Zeus struck Asclepius with a thunderbolt, and killed him. But Apollo his father begged Zeus to relent, and Zeus revived Asclepius, and placed him among the stars. I do not think he used to visit Olympus and to join the company of the gods there. He seems to have been much more interested in mankind, and did not care for grandeur. He soon had temples all over Greece, and men were glad to worship him.

What powers were ranged against Asclepius when he discovered something that no other man knew? How was his quest like that of Orpheus and the poet in "Annabel Lee"?

Did the ancient myth-makers believe that this quest could be achieved? Did they believe it should be achieved? Do you believe it can or should be achieved?

A serpent in this myth has special knowledge that humans do not have. What is it? How does a serpent in the Bible also have special knowledge that humans are innocent of? How are "snakes" used in the myths of Lemminkainen and Cadmus? Which of the three worlds do snakes inhabit? What is the imagination saying in stories of heroes who slay such monsters?

Death, Be Not Proud

Death, be not proud, though some have called thee
Mighty and dreadful, for thou art not so;
For those whom thou think'st thou dost overthrow
Die not, poor Death; nor yet canst thou kill me.
From rest and sleep, which but thy pictures be,
Much pleasure; then from thee much more must flow;
And soonest our best men with thee do go,
Rest of their bones and souls' delivery!
Thou art slave to fate, chance, kings, and desperate men,
And dost with poison, war, and sickness dwell;
And poppy or charms can make us sleep as well
And better than thy stroke. Why swell'st thou then?
One short sleep past, we wake eternally,
And Death shall be no more: Death, thou shalt die.

JOHN DONNE

Do you think Asclepius could be imagined as the speaker of this poem? Why?

This is a Christian view of death. What "perilous journey" does it describe? Who is the hero? What are his weapons? How does the outcome of this quest compare with the outcomes of the ancient myths? How are this poet's feelings and beliefs like or unlike those of Orpheus, in the song he sings to Hades, King of the Dead?

*Gilgamesh, a powerful king, discovers
a grief his power cannot subdue: his
closest friend Enkidu has died.*

Gilgamesh

From the Babylonian epic

Gilgamesh wept bitterly for his friend.
He felt himself now singled out for loss
Apart from everyone else. The word *Enkidu*
Roamed through every thought
Like a hungry animal through empty lairs
In search of food. The only nourishment
He knew was grief, endless in its hidden source
Yet never ending hunger.

All that is left to one who grieves
Is convalescence. No change of heart or spiritual
Conversion, for the heart has changed
And the soul has been converted
To a thing that sees
How much it costs to lose a friend it loved.
It has grown past conversion to a world
Few enter without tasting loss
In which one spends a long time waiting
For something to move one to proceed.
It is that inner atmosphere that has
An unfamiliar gravity or none at all
Where words are flung out in the air but stay
Motionless without an answer,
Hovering about one's lips
Or arguing back to haunt
The memory with what one failed to say,
Until one learns acceptance of the silence

Amidst the new debris
Or turns again to grief
As the only source of privacy,
Alone with someone loved.
It could go on for years and years,
And has, for centuries,
For being human holds a special grief
Of privacy within the universe
That yearns and waits to be retouched
By someone who can take away
The memory of death.

Gilgamesh wandered through the desert
Alone as he had never been alone
When he had craved but not known what he craved;
The dryness now was worse than the decay.
The bored know nothing of this agony
Waiting for diversion they have never lost.
Death had taken the direction he had gained.
He was no more a king
But just a man who now had lost his way
Yet had a greater passion to withdraw
Into a deeper isolation. Mad,
Perhaps insane, he tried
To bring Enkidu back to life
To end his bitterness,
His fear of death.
His life became a quest
To find the secret of eternal life
Which he might carry back to give his friend.

He had put on the skins of animals
And thrown himself in the dust, and now
He longed to hear the voice of one
Who still used words as revelations;
He yearned to talk to Utnapishtim,
The one who had survived the flood
And death itself, the one who knew the secret.

Retold by HERBERT MASON

How is Gilgamesh's quest like Orpheus'?

Does the poet in "Death, Be Not Proud" believe he has found what Gilgamesh is searching for? What is it?

Would you have considered Gilgamesh a hero if he had decided to accept the silence and emptiness caused by Enkidu's death? Why or why not?

Gilgamesh yearns to talk with an ancient man who "knew the secret." How is a similar character type used in the stories of Asclepius and of the flying slaves?

The Return
of Oisin

An Irish legend
Retold by ROSEMARY SUTCLIFF

In the Valley of the Thrushes, not far from where Dublin stands today, a crowd of men were trying to shift a great boulder from their tilled land, the village headman directing their efforts. The stone had been there as long as any of them could remember, or their grandfathers before them, and always they had grumbled at it because it got in the way of the plowing. But though one or two half-hearted attempts had been made to shift it, it still lay half embedded in the hillside, where it always had lain.

Now at last, they were really set upon getting rid of the thing, and every man in the village had gathered to lend his strength to the task.

But it seemed that their strength was all too little, for there they were heaving and straining and grunting and hauling, their faces crimson and the sweat running off them, and the great boulder not moving so much as a finger's breadth out of its bed.

And as they strained and struggled—and they getting nearer each moment to giving up—they saw riding toward them a horseman such as none of them had ever set eyes on before, save maybe in some glorious dream. Taller and mightier than any man of this world he was, and riding a foam-white stallion as far beyond mortal horses as he was beyond mortal men. His eyes were strangely dark, his fair hair like a sunburst about his head. A mantle of saffron silk flowed back from brooches of yellow gold that clasped it at his shoulders, and at his side hung a great golden-hilted sword.

"It is one of the Fairy Kind!" said an aged villager, making the sign of the horns with the two first fingers of his left hand.

"It is an archangel out of Heaven!" said a young one, and made the sign of the Cross.

The splendid being, man or fairy or angel, reined in his horse, and sat looking down at them with a puzzled pity on his face. "You wanted this shifting?" he said.

The headman drew nearer, greatly daring. "We did so, but it seems 'tis beyond our strength. Would you be lending us the power of your arm, now?"

"Surely," said the rider, and stooping from the saddle, set his hand under the boulder and gave a mighty heave. The boulder came out of the ground and went rolling over and over down the hillside like a shinty ball, and the watching villagers gave a great shout of wonder and admiration. But next moment their shouts turned to fearful and wondering dismay.

For as he heaved at the boulder, the rider's saddle girth had burst, so that he fell headlong to the ground. The moment the white stallion felt himself free, he neighed three times and set off at a tearing gallop toward the coast, and as he went, he seemed not merely to grow small with distance, but to lose shape and substance and fade into the summer air like a wisp of woodsmoke.

And there on the ground, where the splendid stranger had fallen, lay an old, old man, huge still, but with thin white beard and milky half-blind eyes, his silken mantle a patched and tattered cloak of coarsest homespun, his golden-hilted sword a rough ash stick such as a blind old beggar might use to support him and feel his way about the world. He half raised himself and peered about, then with a wild despairing cry, stretched all his length again burying his head in his arms.

In a little, seeing that nothing terrible seemed to have happened to any of themselves, some of the bolder of the villagers came closer and lifted him up and asked him who he was.

"I am Oisin the son of Finn Mac Cool," said the old man.

Then the villagers looked at each other, and the headman said, "If you mean who I think you mean, then you're as crazy as we must have been just now to be taking you for whatever it was we took you for."

"It was the sun in our eyes," said another man.

And they asked the old man a second time who he was.

"Why do you ask again, when I have already told you? I am Oisin the son of Finn Mac Cool, Captain of the Fianna of Erin."

"It is the sun on that bald head of yours," said the headman, kindly enough. "Finn Mac Cool and his heroes we have heard of, yes, but they have been dead these three hundred years."

Then the old man was silent a long while, his face bowed into his hands. At last he said, "How did they die?"

"At the Battle of Gavra, not so far from here at all. There is a green mound up there beside the battleground. I was hearing once it was the grave of one of them, called Osca. A great battle it was, and they do say that there were none but boys and old men left in Erin when the fighting was done."

"But Oisin did not die then," another put in. "No man knows the death of Oisin, but the harpers still sing the songs he made."

"But now Priest Patrick has come into Erin, and told us of the one true God, and Christ His Son, and the old days are done with, and we listen to them only as men listen to old tales that are half forgotten."

The old man seemed half-dazed, like one that has taken a blow between the eyes. Only he cried out once, harshly and near to choking, "Strong and without mercy is your new God! And He has much to answer for if He has slain the memory of Finn and Osca!"

Then the people were angry and cried "Sacrilege!" and some of them picked up the small surface stones of the field to throw at the old man. But the headman bade them let him be until Priest Patrick had seen him and told them what they should do.

So they took him to the old fortress of Drum Derg, where Patrick had at that time made his living place.

And Patrick listened to their account of how he had come to them, and how, with the sun in their eyes they had mistaken him for a young man and asked his aid in moving the great stone from their tilled land, and of what had happened after.

And Patrick was kind to the huge half-blind old beggar, and gave him a place for sleeping and a place for sitting by the fire, among his own Christian brotherhood.

And often the priest of the new God, and the old man who had been Oisin would talk together. And Oisin told wonderful stories of Finn and the Fianna and the High and Far-off Days, which Patrick bade one of his scribes to write down on pages of fair white sheepskin, lest they should be forgotten.

As time went by, Patrick came to believe that the old man was indeed Oisin the son of Finn Mac Cool, and one day he said to him, "It is upward of three hundred years since Finn and Osca and the flower of the Fianna died at Gavra. Tell me then, how is it that you have lived so long beyond your day and the days of your companions?"

So Oisin told him this last story: the story of how he had ridden hunting with the Fianna one summer morning among the lakes of Killarney, and how the Princess Niamh of the Golden Hair had come out of the West, and asked him to return to Tyr-na-nOg with her. And how he had taken leave of Finn and Osca and the rest, and mounted behind her on her white horse, and how they had headed westward again until they came to the sea, and headed westward still, leaving the companions of the Fianna behind them on the shore.

And when he reached that point in his story, Oisin buried his face in his hands and seemed to forget.

Then, to rouse him, and because he was a man of curiosity and interest in all things, Patrick said, "Success and benediction! Tell me what happened after that."

And Oisin raised his head again, and staring with half-blind eyes into the heart of the fire, as though he saw there all things happening again, he went on with his story.

"The white horse galloped across the waves as lightly as he had done across the green hills of Erin, and the wind overtook the waves, and we overtook the wind, and presently we passed into a golden haze through which there loomed half-seen islands with cities on their heights and palaces among leafy gardens. Once a fallow doe fled past us, chased by a milk-white hound with one blood-red ear; and once a maiden fled by on a bay horse, and she carrying a golden apple in her hand, and close behind her in hot pursuit, a young man on a white steed, a purple and crimson cloak flying from his shoulders, and a great sword naked in his hand.

"But the sky began to darken overhead, and the wind rose and began to blow in great gusts that roused the waves to fury and sent the spindrift flying like white birds over our heads, and the lightning leapt between the dark sky and darker sea, while the thunder boomed and crashed all about us. Yet still the white horse sped on, unafraid, as lightly and sweetly as over the summer seas that we had traversed before. And presently the wind died and the darkness rolled away and sunshine touched the racing seas with gold. And ahead of us, under the spreading lake of blue sky, lay the fairest land that ever I had seen. Green plains and distant hills were all bathed in a honey-wash of sunlight that flashed and sparkled from the lakes and streams that met every turn of the eye, and changed to gold the white walls of the beautiful palace which stood close beside the shore. Flowers were everywhere, and butterflies like dancing flames upon the air, and as soon as I saw it, I knew that this could be no place but Tyr-na-nOg, the Land of Youth.

"The white horse skimmed the waves toward the shore, and on the white sand we dismounted, and Niamh turned to me, most sweetly holding out her hands, and said, 'This is my own land. Everything I promised, you shall find here, and above all and before all, the love of Niamh of the Golden Hair.'

"Then there came toward us from the palace a troop of warriors, heroes and champions all, holding their shields reversed in token to me that they came in peace. And after them a gay and beautiful company led by the King of the land himself, in a robe of yellow silk, a golden crown blazing like the midsummer sun upon his head. And behind him came the Queen, most fair to see, and with a hundred maidens clustered all about her.

"They kissed their daughter joyfully and tenderly, and the King took my hand in his saying, 'A hundred thousand welcomes, brave Oisin.' Then turning with me to face all the host, he said, 'This is Oisin, from the far-off land of Erin, he who is to be the husband of Niamh of the Golden Hair. Bid him welcome, as I do.'

"Then all the host, nobles and warriors and maidens alike bade me welcome. And all together, Niamh and myself walking hand in hand in their midst, we went up to the palace, where a great feast was prepared.

"For ten days and nights we feasted, while the harpers made music sweeter than any heard in the world of men. I, Oisin, say that, I who was a harper among harpers of the world of men, in my time—and little birds as brightly colored as flowers flew and fluttered about the banquet house. And on the tenth day, Niamh and I were wed.

"I lived in the Land of Youth three years—I thought it was three years—and I was happy as never man was happy before. But as the third year drew to a close, I began to think more and more of my father and my son, and of all the companions of my youth. Sometimes as we rode hunting, I would fancy that I heard the Fian hunting horn echoing through the woods, and think I recognised the deep baying of Bran and Skolawn among the belling of the milk-white Danann hounds. I began to fall into waking dreams, thinking how they would be hunting the woods of Slieve Bloom, or how the heroes would be telling old stories about the fire, in Almu of the White Walls, until it came to this —that Niamh asked me if I no longer loved her. I told her that she was the very life of my heart, and that I was happy as ever I had been in the Land of Youth, but the restlessness was on me, and I longed to see my father and my friends once more.

"Then Niamh kissed me and clung to me, and tried to turn my thoughts elsewhere. But still I half-heard the Fian hunting horn echoing through my dreams at night, and at last I begged leave of her and of the King her father, to visit my own land once more.

"The King gave me leave, though unwillingly, and Niamh said, 'It's not that I can be holding you while your heart draws you back to Erin, so I give you my leave also, though there's a shadow on my mind, and I fear that I shall never see you again.'

"I said, 'That is a foolish fear, for there's nothing that could keep me long from you. Only give me the white steed, for he knows the way and will bring me back safely to your side.'

"Then she said, 'I will give you the white steed, for indeed he knows the way. But listen now, and keep my words in your mind. Never once dismount from his back all the while you are in the world of men, for if you do, you can never come back to me. If once your feet touch the green grass of Erin, the way back to Tyr-na-nOg will be closed to you forever.'

"I promised that I would never dismount from the white steed, but remember always her words. And seeing her grief, which even my most faithful promise seemed not to touch, I was within a feather-weight of yielding to her and remaining always in Tyr-na-nOg; but the white horse stood ready, and the hunger was still on me, to see my father and my own land.

"So I mounted, and the horse set off at a gallop toward the shore. So again we sped across the sea, and the wind overtook the waves and we overtook the wind, and the shores of the Land of Youth sank into the golden mist behind us.

"Again it drifted all about us, that golden mist, and in the mist the towers and cities of the sea arose once more. And again the maiden with the golden apple in her hand fled past us on her bay horse, and the young horseman riding hard behind, his purple cloak streaming from his shoulders and his sword naked in his hand. And again the fallow doe fled by, hunted by the milk-white hound with one ear red as blood.

"So we came at last to the green shores of Erin.

"Gladly, once we were on land, I turned the horse's head toward Almu of the White Walls and rode on. And as I rode, I looked about me, seeking for familiar scenes and faces, and listening always for the sound of the Fian hunting horn. But all things seemed strangely altered, and nowhere did I hear or see any sign of my companions, and the folk who were tilling the ground were small and puny, so that they did not seem any more like countrymen of mine.

"I came at last through the woods to the open country around the Hill of Almu, and the hill was still there but overgrown with bushes and brambles, and on its broad flat crest, where the white walls of my father's dun had used to rise with its byres and barns and armorers' shops, the women's court and the guest quarters, and Finn's mighty mead-hall rising in the midst of all, were nothing but grassy hummocks grown over with elder and blackthorn and the arched sprays of the brambles, and the heather washing over all.

"Then horror fell upon me—though indeed I believed then that the dun was still there, but hidden from me by some enchantment of the Danann folk. And I flung wide my arms and shouted the names of Finn my father and Osca, and after them, the names of all the old brotherhood, Keelta, and Conan and Dering and the rest. Even Dearmid's name I shouted in that dreadful time. But no one answered, nothing moved save a thrush fluttering among the elder bushes. Then I thought that perhaps the hounds might hear me when men could not, and I shouted to Bran and Skolawn and strained my ears for an answering bark. But no sound came, save the hushing of a little wind through the hilltop grasses.

"So with the horror thick upon me, I wheeled the white horse and rode away from Almu, to search all Erin until I found my friends again, or some way out of the enchantment that held me captive. But everywhere I rode, I met only little puny people who gazed at me in wonder out of the faces of strangers, and in every household of the Fianna the brambles grew and the birds were at their nesting. So at last I came to the Glen of the Thrushes, where often I had hunted with Finn, and saw before me tilled land where I remembered only forest.

"And at the head of the tilled land a knot of these small and puny strangers were striving to shift a great stone that was in the way of the plowing. I rode closer, and they asked me for my help. And that was an easy thing to give, so I stooped in the saddle and set my hand under the stone and sent it rolling down the hillside. But with the strain of the heave my saddle girth broke, and I was flung to the ground, and my feet were on the green grass of Erin.

"Priest Patrick, the rest of my story they have told you!"

The story of Oisin is both a wonderful dream and a horrible nightmare. Tell how the stories of Orpheus, Icarus, Brewster, and Asclepius are also dreams become nightmares. Which story in this unit is a nightmare become a dream? Can you name any other stories or fairy tales which turn a world of nightmare into a world of dreams-come-true? Why do you think people tell both kinds of stories?

What other heroes in this unit do you think would have undertaken the quest for the Land of Youth?

How is a "condition" or a test important in this story, just as a "condition" was important for Orpheus? What do you think is revealed about heroes when they fail to pass such tests? What might such tests represent from actual life?

Do you think the heroes in this unit are trying to be "more than man"? Or are they trying to fulfill their potential and become "most fully human," being and doing all that they can be and do? Do you think these heroes were fools to undertake their quests, or were they wise? Why?

The stories in the first unit tell of a quest for a lost inheritance, a place of freedom and joy and peace which man once possessed, then lost, and now must go on a long journey to recover. In this unit, man's quests are to accomplish something more than human, to reach beyond the limits of the finite and mortal world.

One of the most helpless feelings a man can have during his life is anguish over the death of a loved one. It is not surprising, then, that the imagination creates stories about heroes who make long journeys, even to the land of death itself, in hope of rescuing their loved ones from oblivion. The first three stories in this unit all tell of such a quest, although their endings differ. Orpheus does not succeed, finally, because he is betrayed by his own simple, human anxiety for the well-being of his wife. The speaker in "Annabel Lee" achieves only a partial victory by the strength of his love and his imagination. And only by the force of the prayer of Lemminkainen's mother, and through the power of her magical songs, is that hero returned to life.

Death is a limitation in *time*. Man feels he is limited in *space* also, and there are many stories of heroes who try to free themselves from the limitation of being fixed to the earth in one place. Daedalus has the imagination and skill to make wings, but his son Icarus does not have the wisdom to use them properly. Like Daedalus, Brewster struggles to make wings for himself, but he simply does not have the physical endurance to fly long enough, trapped as he is by the emprisoning structure of the Astrodome. Only the slaves in "All God's Chillen" can fly successfully and escape their oppressor, and that is because of magical words.

The final human limit each person must face is of course his own death. As long as man has told tales he has imagined heroes who went in quest of the secret of eternal life, perhaps because of all the superhuman powers that man dreams of possessing, the power of eternal youth is the one that would make him most like one of the immortal gods. So it is understandable that Hades is jealous of Asclepius' secret, and has him killed. It seems that Gilgamesh may have to hunt all the rest of his life for the same secret. Even Oisin can live in the land of eternal youth for only three hundred years before his longing for his old companions draws him back into the world again, and so to his eventual death. Only the speaker in the poem "Death, Be Not Proud," by drawing on the notion of the miracle of the Christian Resurrection, can envisage a final means by which man may be granted the gift of eternal life, in a world beyond this finite one.

Not all these quests are successful, because their objective lies tantalizingly close to the limits of human desires and powers. In trying to overcome time, space, and death, man seems to be aiming at almost godlike powers. In tragic stories, like those of Orpheus, Icarus, Oisin, and Brewster, the hero seems to be asking for more than he can expect, and he is betrayed by his own human limitations, so that his quest ends in a disastrous fall from the heights of his imaginative desire. In romance stories, however, like the tale of Lemminkainen or "All God's Chillen," the hero finally succeeds in conquering his ultimate human limitation. In romance, magical powers are always available to the hero, and it is by means of these that his final triumph becomes possible. Often these magical powers are related to art: the magic of the songs of Orpheus and of Lemminkainen's mother, the healing art of Asclepius, Daedalus' ingenuity. Somehow, then, man seems to sense that his most godlike power may be his imagination. For in his stories, poems, and dreams, the human imagination can take anything in the world—even the bounds of time, space, and death—and transform them into the images of desire.

92

Alan E. Cober '73

3

TO DO WHAT MUST BE DONE

Heracles

A Greek myth
Retold by PADRAIC COLUM

Heracles, born of Alcmene, a mortal woman, was the son of Zeus. Hera, the spouse of Zeus, bore ill will toward Alcmene and her hero-son, and when Heracles was still an infant in the cradle she sent two great serpents to destroy him. But the child took the serpents and strangled them with his own hands. Then, while he was still a youth, a madness sent by the goddess came upon him, and unwittingly he slew the children of Iphicles, his half-brother. When he came to know what he had done, sleep and rest went from him; he went to Delphi, the shrine of Apollo, to be purified of his crime.

At Delphi, at the shrine of Apollo, the priestess purified him, saying, "Thou shalt go to Eurystheus, thy cousin, in Tiryns, and serve him in all things. When the labors he shall lay upon thee are accomplished, and when the rest of thy life is lived out, thou shalt become one of the immortals." Heracles, on hearing these words, set out for Tiryns.

He stood before his cousin who hated him; he, a towering man, stood before a king who sat there weak and trembling. Heracles said, "I have come to take up the labors that you will lay upon me; speak now, Eurystheus, and tell me what you would have me do."

Eurystheus, that weak king, looking on the young man who stood as tall and as firm as one of the immortals, had a heart that was filled with hatred. He lifted up his head and said with a scowl:

"There is a lion in Nemea that is stronger and more fierce than any lion known before. Kill that lion; bring the lion's skin to me that I may know that you have truly performed your task." So Eurystheus said, and Heracles, with neither shield nor arms, went forth from the king's palace to seek and combat the dread lion of Nemea.

He went on until he came into a country where the fences were overthrown, and the fields wasted, and the houses empty and fallen. He went on until he came to a waste around that land: there he came on the trail of the lion; it led up the side of a mountain, and Heracles, without shield or arms, followed on the trail.

He heard the roar of the lion. Looking up he saw the beast standing at the mouth of a cavern, huge and dark against the sunset. Three times the lion roared, and then went within the cavern.

Around the mouth were strewn the bones of creatures it had killed and carried there. Heracles looked upon the bones when he came to the cavern. He went within. Far into the cavern he went; he came to where the lion lay gorged with the prey it had taken. The breath from its mouth and nostrils came heavily to him. The beast yawned.

Heracles sprang on it; he put his great, knotted hands upon its throat. No growl came out of the mouth, but the great eyes blazed and the terrible paws tore at Heracles. Against the rock Heracles held the beast; strongly he held it, choking it through the skin that was almost impenetrable. Terribly the lion struggled; the strong hands of the hero held its throat until it struggled no more.

Then Heracles stripped off the impenetrable skin from the lion's body; he put it upon himself for a cloak. As he went through the forest he pulled up a young oak-tree and trimmed it to make a club for himself. With the lion's skin over him—that skin that no spear or arrow could pierce—and carrying the club in his hands he journeyed on until he came to the palace of King Eurystheus.

The king, seeing a towering man all covered with the skin of a monstrous lion coming towards him, ran and hid himself in a great jar. He lifted up the cover to ask the servants what was the meaning of that terrible appearance. His servants told him that this was Heracles come back with the skin of the Nemean lion over him. On hearing this Eurystheus hid himself again. He would not speak with Heracles nor have him come near him, so fearful was he. Heracles was content to be left alone. He sat down in the palace and feasted himself.

The servants came to the king, and when Eurystheus lifted the cover of the jar they told him how Heracles was feasting and devouring all the goods in the palace. The king flew into a rage. Still he was fearful of having the hero stand before him. He issued commands through his heralds ordering Heracles to go forth at once and perform the second of his tasks.

It was the task of slaying the great water-snake that made its lair in the swamps of Lerna. Heracles stayed to feast another day; then, with the lion's skin across his shoulders and the great club in his hands, he started off. But this time he did not go alone; the youth Iolaos, his brother's son, went with him.

Heracles and Iolaos went on until they came to the vast swamp of Lerna. Right in the middle of the swamp was the water-snake, the Hydra. Nine heads it had; it raised them out of the water as the hero and his companion came near. They could not cross the swamp to come to the monster, for a man or a beast would sink in it and be lost.

The Hydra remained in the middle of the swamp belching mud at the hero and his companion. Heracles took up his bow and shot flaming arrows at its head. It became more full of rage; it came through the swamp to attack him. Heracles swung his club. As the Hydra came near he knocked head after head off its body.

But for every head knocked off two grew upon the Hydra. And as he struggled with the monster a huge crab came out of the swamp, and, gripping Heracles by the foot, tried to draw him in. The boy Iolaos came; he killed the crab that had come to the Hydra's aid.

Then Heracles laid hands upon the Hydra; he drew it out of its swamp. He knocked off a head; then he had Iolaos put fire to where the head had been, so that two heads might not grow in that place. The life of the Hydra was in its middle head; that head he had not been able to knock off with his club. Now, with his hands he tore it off, and he placed the head under a great boulder so that it could not rise into life again. The Hydra's life was now destroyed. Heracles dipped his arrows into the gall of the monster, making his arrows deadly; afterward, no thing that was struck with these arrows could keep its life.

Again he came to Eurystheus's palace, and Eurystheus, seeing him, ran again and hid himself in the jar. Heracles ordered his servants to tell the king that he had returned and that the second labor was accomplished.

Eurystheus, hearing from the servants that Heracles had spoken mildly to them, came out of the jar. Insolently he spoke. "Twelve labors you have to accomplish for me," he said, "and eleven yet remain to be accomplished."

"How?" said Heracles. "Have I not performed two of the labors? Have I not slain the lion of Nemea and the great water-snake of Lerna?"

"In the killing of the water-snake you were helped by Iolaos," said the king, snapping out his words and looking at Heracles with shifting eyes. "That labor cannot be allowed you."

Heracles would have struck him to the ground. But then he remembered that the crime he had committed in his madness would have to be expiated by labors performed at the order of this man. He looked full upon Eurystheus and he said, "Tell me of the other labors, and I will go forth and accomplish them."

Then Eurystheus bade him go and make clean the stables of King Augeias. Heracles came into the king's country. The smell from the stables was felt for miles around. Countless herds of cattle and goats had been in the stables for years, and because of the uncleanness and the smell that came from the stables the crops were withered all around. Heracles told the king that he would clean the stables if he were given one-tenth of the cattle and the goats for a reward.

The king agreed to give him that reward. Then Heracles drove the cattle and the goats out of the stables; he broke a passage through their foundations and he made channels for the two rivers, Alpheus and Peneus. The waters flowed through the stables, and in a day all the uncleanness was washed away. Then Heracles turned the rivers back into their own courses.

He was not given the reward he had bargained for, however. He went back and told of his labor accomplished. "Ten labors remain for me to do now," he said.

"Eleven," said Eurystheus. "How can I allow the cleaning of King Augeias's stables to you when you did it for a reward?"

Then, while Heracles stood still holding himself back from striking him, Eurystheus ran away and hid himself. Through his heralds he sent word to Heracles, telling him what his other labors would be.

He was to clear the marshes of Stymphalos of the man-eating birds that gathered there; he was to capture and bring to the king the golden-horned deer of Keryneia; he was also to capture and bring back alive the boar of Erymanthos.

Heracles came to the marshes of Stymphalos. The growth of jungle was so dense that he could not cut his way through to where the man-eating birds were; they sat upon low bushes within the jungle, gorging themselves upon the flesh they had carried there.

For days Heracles tried to hack his way through to them. He could not get to where the birds were. Then, thinking that he might not be able to accomplish this labor, he sat upon the ground in despair.

It was then that one of the immortals appeared to him; then, for the first and only time, he was given help by one of the gods. It was Athene who came to him. She stood apart from Heracles; in her hands she held brazen cymbals. These she clashed together. At the sound of the clashing the Stymphalean birds rose up from the low bushes behind the jungle. Heracles shot at them with his unerring arrows. The man-eating birds fell, one after the other, into the marsh.

Then Heracles went north to where the Keryneian deer had her pasture. So swift of foot was she that no hound nor hunter had ever been able to overtake her. For the whole of a year Heracles kept Golden Horns in chase; at last, on the side of Mount Artemision, he caught her. Then Artemis, the Goddess of the Wild Things, would have punished Heracles for capturing the deer. But the hero pleaded with her. She relented and allowed him to bring the deer to Tiryns and show her to King Eurystheus. And Artemis kept charge of Golden Horns while Heracles went off to capture the Erymanthean boar.

He came to the city of Psophis, the inhabitants of which were in deadly fear because of the ravages of the boar. Heracles made his way up the mountain to hunt it. Now, upon this mountain a band of Centaurs lived, and they, knowing Heracles, welcomed him. One of them, Pholos, took Heracles to the great house where the Centaurs stored their wine. Seldom did the Centaurs drink wine; a draught of it made them wild, and so they stored it away, leaving it in the charge of one of their band. Heracles begged Pholos to give him a draught of wine; after he had begged for it again and again the Centaur opened one of his great jars.

Heracles drank wine and spilled it. Then the Centaurs that were without smelled the wine and came hammering at the door, demanding the draughts that would make them wild. Heracles came forth to drive them away. They attacked him. Then he shot at them with his unerring arrows and he drove them away. Up the mountain and away to the far rivers the Centaurs raced, pursued by Heracles with his bow.

One of the band was slain, Pholos, who had entertained the hero. By accident Heracles dropped a poisoned arrow on his foot. Now he took the body of Pholos up to the top of the mountain and he buried the Centaur there. Afterwards, on the snows of Erymanthos, he set a snare for the boar; he caught him there.

Upon his shoulders he carried the boar to Tiryns, and he led the deer there by her golden horns. When Eurystheus had looked upon the boar and upon the deer, the boar was slain and the deer was loosed; she fled back to the Mountain Artemision.

King Eurystheus thought of more terrible labors that he might make Heracles engage in. Now he would send him oversea, and make him strive with fierce tribes there and more terrible monsters. When he had it all thought out he had Heracles brought before him, and he told him of those other labors.

He was to go to savage Thrace and there destroy the man-eating horses of King Diomedes; afterward he was to go amongst the dread women, the Amazons, daughters of Ares, the God of War, and take from their queen, Hippolyte, the girdle that Ares had given her; then he was to go to Crete and take from the keeping of King Minos the bull that Poseidon had given him; afterwards he was to go to the Island of Erytheia, and take away from Geryoneus, the monster that had three bodies instead of one, the herd of red cattle that the two-headed hound Orthos kept guard over; then he was to go to the Garden of the Hesperides, and from that garden he was to take the golden apples that Zeus had given Hera for a marriage-gift—where the Garden of the Hesperides was no mortal knew.

So Heracles set out on this long the perilous quest. First he went to Thrace, that savage land that was ruled by Diomedes, son of Ares, the God of War. Heracles broke into the stable where the horses were; he caught three of them by their heads, and although they kicked, and bit, and trampled, he forced them out of the stable and down to the seashore; his companion Abderos waited for him there. The screams of the fierce horses were heard by the men of Thrace; they, with their king, came after Heracles. He left the horses in charge of Abderos while he fought the Thracians and their savage king. Heracles shot his deadly arrows amongst them. He drove them from the seashore, and he came back to where he had left Abderos with the fierce horses.

They had thrown Abderos upon the ground, and they were trampling upon him. Heracles drew his bow and he shot the horses with his unerring arrows—the arrows that had been dipped in the gall of the Hydra. Screaming, the horses of King Diomedes raced toward the sea; one fell and another fell, and then, as it came to the line of the foam, the third of the fierce horses fell. They were all slain with the unerring arrows.

Then Heracles took up the body of his companion; he was dead. Heracles buried the body with proper rites, and he raised a column over it. Afterwards, around that column a city that bore the name of Heracles's friend was built.

Then toward the Euxine Sea he went. There, where the River Themiskyra flows into the sea, he saw the abodes of the Amazons. And upon the rocks and the steep places he saw the warrior-women;

they were standing there with drawn bows in their hands. Most dangerous did they seem to Heracles. He did not know how to approach them; he might shoot at them with his unerring arrows, but when his arrows were all shot away, the Amazons, from their steep places, might be able to kill him with the arrows from their bows.

While he stood at a distance, wondering what he might do, a horn was sounded, and an Amazon mounted on a white stallion rode toward him. "Heracles," she cried out, "The Queen Hippolyte permits you to come amongst the Amazons. Enter her tent and declare to the queen the thing that has brought you amongst the never-conquered Amazons."

Heracles came to the tent of the queen. There stood tall Hippolyte, an iron crown upon her head and a beautiful girdle of bronze and iridescent glass around her waist. Proud as a fierce mountain eagle looked the queen of the Amazons: Heracles did not know in what way he might conquer her. Outside the Amazons stood; they struck their shields with their spears, keeping up a continuous savage din. "For what has Heracles come to the country of the Amazons?" Queen Hippolyte asked.

"For the girdle you wear," Heracles said, and he held his hands ready for the struggle.

"Is it for the girdle given me by Ares, the God of War, that you have come, braving the Amazons?"

"For that," Heracles said.

"I would not have you enter into strife with the Amazons," said Queen Hippolyte. And so saying she drew off the girdle of bronze and iridescent glass, and gave it into his hands.

Heracles took the beautiful girdle into his hands. He was fearful that some piece of guile was being played upon him. He took the girdle and put it around his great brows. He thanked the queen, but even as he did the din outside became more savage. Hera, the Goddess who was his foe, had appeared amongst the Amazons as an Amazon. She stirred the warrior-women up against him. They fell upon him with their spears. Then Heracles drew his bow. Hippolyte came out of her tent and mounted her stallion to draw her Amazons away from him. She rode toward the River Themiskyra and they rode with her. And now the arrows of Heracles flew amongst them, and as they fled across the river the white flanks of their stallions were stained with the blood of the Amazons.

He went away from that country with Hippolyte's girdle around his brows. He sailed over the sea and he came to Crete. There he found, grazing in a special pasture, the bull that Poseidon had given King Minos. He laid his hands upon the bull's horns and he overthrew the bull. Then he drove the bull down to the seashore.

His next labor was to take away the herd of red cattle that was owned by the monster, Geryoneus. In the Island of Erytheia, in the middle of the Stream of Ocean, lived the monster; his herd was guarded by the two-headed hound Orthos—the hound that was brother to Cerberus, the three-headed hound that kept guard in the Lower-world. As Heracles came near to that island, making Minos's bull swim with him, the sun beat upon him, and drew all his strength away from him; he was dazed and dazzled by the rays of the sun. He drew his bow and shot his arrows upwards. He shouted out against the sun, and in his anger he wanted to strive against the sun. Far, far out of sight the arrows of Heracles went. And the Sun God, Helios, was filled with admiration for Heracles, the man who attempted what was impossible. Then did Helios fling down to Heracles his great golden cup.

Down, and into the Stream of Ocean fell the great golden cup of Helios. It floated there, wide enough to hold all the men who might be in a ship. Heracles put the bull of Minos into the cup of Helios; the cup bore them away, towards the West, and across the Stream of Ocean.

Heracles came to the Island of Erytheia. All over the island straggled the red cattle of Geryoneus, grazing upon the rich pastures. Heracles, leaving the bull of Minos in the cup, went upon the island; he made a club for himself out of a tree, and he went toward the cattle.

The hound Orthos bayed and ran toward him, the two-headed hound sprang upon Heracles with poisonous foam upon his jaws. Heracles swung his club and struck the two heads off the hound. Where the foam of the hound's jaws dropped a poisonous plant sprang up. Heracles took the body of the hound; he swung it around, and he flung it far out into the Ocean.

Then the monster Geryoneus came upon him. Three bodies he had instead of one; he attacked Heracles by hurling great stones at him. Heracles was hurt by the stones. Then the monster beheld the cup of Heracles; he began to hurl stones at the golden thing, striving to sink it in the sea and so leave Heracles without a way of getting from the island. Heracles drew his bow; he shot arrows into the monster, and left him dead in the deep rich grass of the pastures.

He rounded up the red cattle, the bulls and the cows, and he drove

them down to the shore; he put them into the golden cup of Helios where the bull of Minos stayed. Then back across the Stream of Ocean the cup floated. The bull of Crete and the cattle of Erytheia were brought past Sicily and through the straits called the Hellespont. To Thrace, that savage land, they were brought. Then Heracles took the cattle out, and the cup of Helios sank into the sea. Through the wide lands of Thrace he drove the herd of Geryoneus and the bull of Minos, and he came to Tiryns once more.

There he did not stay. He started off to find the Garden of the Hesperides, the Daughters of the Evening Land. Long did he search; he found no one who could tell him where the garden was. At last he came to the Mountain Pelion where the Centaur Cheiron was. And Cheiron told Heracles what journey he would have to make to come to the Hesperides, the Daughters of the Evening Land.

Far did Heracles journey; weary he was when he came to where Atlas stood, bearing the sky upon his weary shoulders. As he came near he felt an undreamed-of perfume being wafted towards him. So weary was he with his journey and all his toils that he was fain to sink down and dream in that Evening Land. But he roused himself, and he journeyed on towards where the perfume came from. Over that place a star seemed always arising.

He came to where a silver lattice fenced a garden that was full of the quiet of evening. Golden bees hummed through the air. How wild and laborious was the world he had come from, Heracles thought! He felt that it would be hard for him to return to that world!

He saw three maidens. They stood with wreaths upon their heads and blossoming branches in their hands. When the maidens saw him, they came towards him, crying out, "O man who has come into the Garden of the Hesperides, go not near the tree that the sleepless dragon guards!" Then they went and stood by a tree as if to keep guard over it. All around were trees that bore flowers and fruit, but this tree had golden apples amongst its bright green leaves.

He saw the guardian of the tree. Beside the trunk a dragon lay. As Heracles drew near, the dragon showed its glittering scales and its deadly claws.

The apples were within reach, but the dragon with its deadly claws stood in the way. Heracles shot an arrow; then a tremor went through the sleepless dragon; it screamed, fell down, and lay stark. The maidens cried in their grief; Heracles went to the tree; he plucked the golden apples and he put them into the pouch he carried. Down on the ground sank the Hesperides, the Daughters of the Evening Land; he heard their laments as he went from the enchanted garden that they guarded.

Back from the ends of the earth came Heracles, back from the place where Atlas stood holding the sky upon his weary shoulders. He went back through Asia and Libya and Egypt, and he came again to Tiryns and to the palace of Eurystheus.

He brought to the king the herd of Geryoneus; he brought to the king the bull of Minos; he brought to the king the girdle of Hippolyte; he brought to the king the golden apples of the Hesperides. And King Eurystheus, with his thin, white face, sat upon his royal throne and looked over all the wonderful things that the hero had brought him. Not pleased was Eurystheus; rather was he angry that one he hated could win such wonderful things.

He took into his hands the golden apples of the Hesperides. But this fruit was not for such as he. An eagle snatched the branch from his hand. The eagle flew and flew until he came to where the Daughters of the Evening Land wept in their garden. There the eagle let fall the branch with the golden apples; the maidens set it back on the tree, and, behold! it grew as it had been growing before Heracles plucked it.

The next day the heralds of Eurystheus came to Heracles and they told him of the last labor that he would have to set out to accomplish — this time he would have to go down into the Underworld and bring up from King Hades's realm Cerberus, the three-headed hound.

Heracles put upon him the impenetrable lion's skin and set forth once more. This might be the last of his life's labors: Cerberus was not an earthly monster, and he who would struggle with Cerberus in the Underworld would have the Gods of the Dead against him.

But Heracles went on. He journeyed to the cavern where there is an entrance to the Underworld. Far into that dismal cavern he went; then he went down, down, down, until he came to that dim river that had beyond it only the people of the dead. Cerberus bayed at him from the place where the dead cross the river. Knowing that this was no shade, the hound Cerberus sprang at Heracles. He could neither bite nor tear through the impenetrable lion's skin. Heracles held him by the neck of his middle head so that Cerberus was neither able to bite nor tear, nor was he able to bellow.

Then Persephone to the brink of that river came. She declared to Heracles that the Gods of the Dead would not strive against him if he promised to bring Cerberus back to the Underworld.

This Heracles promised. He turned around and he carried Cerberus;

his hands were around the monster's neck; from the monster's jaws foam dropped. He carried him on and upward towards the world of men. Out through a cavern that was in the land of Troizen Heracles came, still carrying Cerberus by the neck of his middle head.

From Troizen to Tiryns the hero went; men fled at the sight of the monster he carried. On he went toward the king's palace. Eurystheus was seated outside his palace that day, looking at the great jar he had so often hidden in, and thinking to himself that Heracles would never appear to affright him again. Then Heracles appeared. He called to Eurystheus; he held the Hound of Hell toward him. The three heads grinned at Eurystheus; he gave a cry and scrambled into the jar. But before his feet touched the bottom of it Eurystheus was dead of fear. The jar rolled over, and Heracles looked upon the body that was all twisted with fright. Then he turned around; carrying the hound he made his way back to the Underworld. On the brink of the river he loosed Cerberus, and the bellow of the three-headed hound was heard once more by the River Acheron.

It was then that Heracles was given arms by the gods — the sword of Hermes, the bow of Apollo, the shield made by Hephaestus; it was then that Heracles, coming to the Caucasus, slew the vulture that preyed upon Prometheus' liver, and, at the will of Zeus, liberated the Titan from his bonds. Thereafter Zeus and Prometheus were reconciled, and Zeus, that neither might forget how much the enmity between them had cost gods and men, had a ring made for Prometheus to wear; that ring was made out of the fetter that had been upon him, and in it was set a fragment of the rock that the Titan had been bound to.

Now there was a king who had offered his daughter in marriage to a hero who could excel himself and his sons in shooting with arrows. Heracles had seen the maiden, the blue-eyed and child-like Iole, and he longed to win her. The contest began. The king and his sons shot wonderfully well, and so did the heroes who entered the contest with Heracles. Heracles shot his arrows. No matter how far away they moved the mark, Heracles struck it, and struck the very center of it. The people wondered who the great archer might be. And then a name was guessed at and went round — Heracles!

When the king heard the name of Heracles he would not let him strive in the contest any more. For the maiden Iole would not be given to one who had been mad and whose madness might afflict him again. So the king said, speaking in judgment in the market-place.

Rage came on Heracles when he heard this judgment given. He

would not let his rage master him lest the madness that was spoken of should come with this rage. He left the city, declaring to the king and people that he would return.

In Calydon he saw Deianeira. She was tall, this woman of the mountains; she looked like a priestess, but also like a woman who could cheer camps of men with her counsel, her bravery, and her good companionship; her hair was very dark and she had dark eyes. Straightway she became friends with Heracles; and when they saw each other for a while they loved each other. And Heracles forgot Iole, the childlike maiden whom he had wanted to win. To win Deianeira he strove with Achelous, the River God. Achelous in the form of a bull wrestled with him. Heracles broke off one of his horns. Then, that he might be given the horn back, the River God gave up his claim to Deianeira.

Then a dreadful thing happened in Calydon; by an accident, while using his strength unthinkingly, Heracles killed a lad who was related to Deianeira. He might not marry her now until he had taken punishment for slaying one who was close to her in blood.

As a punishment for the slaying it was judged that Heracles should be sold into slavery for three years. At the end of his three years' slavery he could come back to Calydon and wed Deianeira.

So Heracles and Deianeira were parted. He was sold as a slave in Lydia; the one who bought him was a woman, a widow named Omphale. To her house Heracles went, carrying his armor and wearing his lion's skin. And Omphale laughed to see this tall man dressed in a lion's skin coming to her house to do a servant's tasks for her.

She and all her household had fun with Heracles. They would set him to do housework, to carry water, and set vessels on the tables, and clear the vessels away. Omphale set him to spin with a spindle as the women did. And often she would put on Heracles's lion-skin and go about dragging his club, while he, dressed in woman's garb, washed dishes and emptied pots.

But he would lose patience with these servant's tasks, and then Omphale would let him go away and perform some great exploit. Often he went on long journeys and stayed away long times. It was while he was in slavery to Omphale that he made his journey to Troy. At Troy he helped to repair for King Laomedon the great walls that, years before, Apollo and Poseidon had built around the city. As a reward for his labor he was offered the Princess Hesione in marriage. But Heracles permitted Telamon to take Hesione. On the day they married Heracles showed the pair an eagle in the sky. He said it was sent as an omen for their marriage. And in memory of that omen Telamon named his son "Ajax," that is, "Eagle."

Omphale, the widow, received him mirthfully when he got back to Lydia; she set him to do tasks in the kitchen while she sat and talked to him about Troy and the affairs of King Laomedon. And afterward she put on his lion's skin, and went about in the courtyard dragging the heavy club after her. Mirthfully and pleasantly she made the rest of his time in Lydia pass for Heracles; the last day of his slavery soon came; he bade good-by to Omphale, and he started off to Calydon to claim his bride, Deianeira.

Beautiful, indeed, Deianeira looked now that she had ceased to mourn; the laughter that had been under her grief now flashed out; her dark eyes shone like stars, and her being had the spirit of one who wanders from camp to camp always greeting friends and leaving friends behind her. Heracles wed Deianeira, and they set out for Tiryns.

They came to the River Evenos. Heracles could have crossed the river by himself, but at the part he came to he could not cross carrying Deianeira. He and she went along the river, seeking a ferry that might take them across. They wandered along the side of the river, happy with each other, and they came to a place where they had sight of a Centaur.

Heracles knew this Centaur. He was Nessus, one of the Centaurs whom he had chased up the mountain on the day when he went to hunt the Erymanthean boar. The Centaur spoke to Heracles as if he had friendship for him. He would, he said, carry Heracles's bride across the river.

Heracles crossed the river. He waited on the other side for Nessus and Deianeira. Then Heracles heard screams—the screams of his wife. He saw that the Centaur had attacked her. Heracles leveled his bow. Arrow after arrow he shot in Nessus' body. The Centaur loosed his hold on Deianeira. He lay down on the bank of the river, his life-blood streaming from him.

Nessus, dying, but with his rage against Heracles unabated, thought of a way by which the hero might be made to suffer for the death he had brought upon him. He called to Deianeira; she, seeing he could do her no more hurt, came close to him. He told her that in repentance for his attack upon her he would bestow on her a great gift. She was to gather up some of the blood that flowed from him; his blood, the Centaur said, would be a love-philter, and if ever her husband's love for her waned it would grow fresh again if she gave to him something from her hands that would have this blood upon it.

Deianeira, who had heard from Heracles of the wisdom of the Centaurs, believed what Nessus told her. She took a phial and let the blood poor into it. Then Nessus plunged into the river and died there as Heracles came up to where Deianeira stood.

She did not speak to him about the Centaur's words to her, nor did she tell him that she had hidden the phial that had Nessus' blood in it. They crossed the river at another point; they came after a time to Tiryns, to the kingdom that had been left to Heracles.

There Heracles and Deianeira lived, and a son who was named Hyllus was born to them. And after a time Heracles was led into a war against Oichalia, the kingdom that Iole's father had ruled over.

Word came to Deianeira that Oichalia was conquered by Heracles and that Iole was taken captive by him. Deianeira knew that Heracles had once tried to win Iole for his wife, and she feared that the sight of the maiden would bring his old longing back to him.

She thought upon the words that Nessus had said to her, and even as she thought upon them messengers came from Heracles to ask her to send him a robe—a beautifully woven robe that she had—that he might wear it while making sacrifice. Deianeira took down the robe; through this robe, she thought, the blood of the Centaur could touch Heracles, and then his love for her would revive. Thinking this, she poured Nessus' blood over the robe.

Heracles was in Oichalia when the messengers returned to him. He took the robe that Deianeira sent, and he went to the mountain that overlooked the sea that he might make sacrifice there. Iole went with him. He put on the robe. When it touched his flesh the robe burst into flame. He tried to tear it off; deeper and deeper into his flesh the flames went. The flames burned and none could quench them.

Then Heracles knew that his end was at hand. He would die by fire; knowing this he had a great pile of wood made, and he climbed up on it. There he stayed with the robe burning upon him, and he begged of those who passed to fire the pile that his end might come more quickly.

None would fire the pile. But at last there came that way a young warrior named Philoctetes, and Heracles begged of him to fire the pile. Philoctetes, knowing that it was the will of the gods that Heracles should die that way, lighted the pile. For that Heracles bestowed upon him his great bow and his unerring arrows. And it was this bow and these arrows, brought from Philoctetes, that afterwards helped to take Troy, King Priam's city.

The pile that Heracles stood upon was fired. High up, above the sea, the pile burned. All who had been near fled—all except Iole. She stayed and watched the flames mount up and up. They wrapped the sky, and the voice of Heracles was heard calling upon Zeus. Then a great chariot came, and Heracles was borne away to Olympus. Thus, after many labors, Heracles passed away, a mortal passing into an immortal being, in a great burning high above the sea.

How are the circumstances of Heracles' birth like those of other heroes we have seen?

How are the snakes in this story like the other snakes we have seen? What do you think they represent?

What is Heracles' quest? Why does he take it up?

Why did the god Helios respect Heracles? Do you think this is true of most heroes?

Compare the Garden of the Hesperides with Tyr-na-nOg, the Land of Youth, and with the Golden Age. How are they alike? How are they different? What other garden do these gardens remind you of? Was there a "dragon" in that garden also? In which of these gardens did the hero conquer? In which was he defeated? Do you think it is possible that in the imagination all of these gardens are the same? Why?

Do you think it is true that a hero is both a "master" and a "slave"? How does this apply to other heroes you know? How does this explain the title of this unit?

Using the story of Heracles as a model, draw a line which represents "the life of the hero" and divide it into these major stages and events of the hero's story: mysterious birth, growing up in obscurity, initiation, quest, triumph, death, glorification. How closely does Heracles fit this pattern? Choose another hero and see how his story corresponds.

The Ricksha Puller

In motion, perpetually in motion, are his legs
Running in this world of suffering, like the everflowing water.
He strikes a stance beyond suffering, his sense of pain has long fallen
    asleep.
Despite the passage of time, he still can hold himself erect
As a perfect embodiment of the patience of this ancient land.

Who is racing with him?
Death, death wants to embrace
This Marathon runner racing with life.
If he loses, death will seize him;
If he wins, no triumphal march will be heard.
A breeze stirs on the sea, saying
This is a shameful strange sight;
It must be erased by the ingenuity of man.
Thus, the strength of man's body, an ancient glory,
Has been turned into a modern disgrace.

The storms in the sky, the rugged roads on earth,
The direction of departure in the morning, the route of return at night.
All lie beyond his prediction, his design.
His answer is only an unbreakable silence.
The wishes of the people on the road drive him,
His own wishes are tossed on the roadside.
An aimless man lives to fulfill the wishes of others.

Every time he stops,
Still panting, he stretches out his dirty hands.
(Please reflect, reflect, I beg of you:
Beneath this dirty skin flows clean blood

While in those clean fingers flows dirty blood.
Which is our shame:
The dirty blood, or the dirty hands?)
With his worn feet he opens up for you
The roads leading to innumerable different destinations.
(After having your innumerable purposes fulfilled, would you also
Think of a way out for his purpose that has lain long smothered?)

It's not that there is no way, there is a way,
And it has become the prayer of all men;
It is waiting in the dim distance
For all our hands, all our feet
Both the hungry and the well-fed, to remove
The spreading weeds, and to tread out a smooth road.
In motion, forever in motion are his legs
Running along a road that begins and ends with life.
In the wind of winter, the rain of hunger, and the thunder and lightning
      of death.
Moving, forever moving are his legs.

CHENG MIN

Translated by KAI-YU HSU

Why does the ricksha puller run? How is he, in this way, another Heracles?
How is he different from Heracles?

What quest does this poet say is necessary for us all to undertake?

A Mother's Tale

JAMES AGEE

The calf ran up the hill as fast as he could and stopped sharp. "Mama!" he cried, all out of breath. "What *is* it! What are they *doing!* Where are they *going!*"

Other spring calves came galloping too.

They all were looking up at her and awaiting her explanation, but she looked out over their excited eyes. As she watched the mysterious and majestic thing they had never seen before, her own eyes became even more than ordinarily still, and during the considerable moment before she answered, she scarcely heard their urgent questioning.

Far out along the autumn plain, beneath the sloping light, an immense drove of cattle moved eastward. They went at a walk, not very fast, but faster than they could imaginably enjoy. Those in front were compelled by those behind; those at the rear, with few exceptions, did their best to keep up; those who were locked within the herd could no more help moving than the particles inside a falling rock. Men on horses rode ahead, and alongside, and behind, or spurred their horses intensely back and forth, keeping the pace steady, and the herd in shape; and from man to man a dog sped back and forth incessantly as a shuttle, barking, incessantly, in a hysterical voice. Now and then one of the men shouted fiercely, and this like the shrieking of the dog was tinily audible above a low and awesome sound which seemed to come not from the multitude of hooves but from the center of the world, and above the sporadic bawlings and bellowings of the herd.

From the hillside this tumult was so distant that it only made more delicate the prodigious silence in which the earth and sky were held; and, from the hill, the sight was as modest as its sound. The herd was virtually hidden in the dust it raised, and could be known, in general, only by the horns which pricked this flat sunlit dust like little briars. In one place a twist of the air revealed the trembling fabric of many backs; but it was only along the near edge of the mass that individual animals were discernible, small in a driven frieze, walking fast, stumbling and recovering, tossing their armed heads, or opening their skulls heavenward in one of those cries which reached the hillside long after the jaws were shut.

From where she watched, the mother could not be sure whether there were any she recognized. She knew that among them there must be a son of hers; she had not seen him since some previous spring, and she would not be seeing him again. Then the cries of the young ones impinged on her bemusement: "Where are they going?"

She looked into their ignorant eyes.

"Away," she said.

"Where?" they cried. "Where? Where?" her own son cried again.

She wondered what to say.

"On a long journey."

"But where *to?*" they shouted. "Yes, where *to?*" her son exclaimed, and she could see that he was losing his patience with her, as he always did when he felt she was evasive.

"I'm not sure," she said.

Their silence was so cold that she was unable to avoid their eyes for long.

"Well, not *really* sure. Because, you see," she said in her most reasonable tone, "I've never seen it with my own eyes, and that's the only way to *be* sure; *isn't* it."

They just kept looking at her. She could see no way out.

"But I've *heard* about it," she said with shallow cheerfulness, "from those who *have* seen it, and I don't suppose there's any good reason to doubt them."

She looked away over them again, and for all their interest in what she was about to tell them, her eyes so changed that they turned and looked, too.

The herd, which had been moving broadside to them, was being turned away, so slowly that like the turning of stars it could not quite be seen from one moment to the next; yet soon it was moving directly away from them, and even during the little while she spoke and they all watched after it, it steadily and very noticeably diminished, and the sounds of it as well.

"It happens always about this time of year," she said quietly while they watched. "Nearly all the men and horses leave, and go into the North and the West."

"Out on the range," her son said, and by his voice she knew what enchantment the idea already held for him.

"Yes," she said, "out on the range." And trying, impossibly, to imagine the range, they were touched by the breath of grandeur.

"And then before long," she continued, "everyone has been found, and brought into one place; and then . . . what you see, happens. All of them.

"Sometimes when the wind is right," she said more quietly, "you can hear them coming long before you can see them. It isn't even like a sound, at first. It's more as if something were moving far under the ground. It makes you uneasy. You wonder, why, what in the world can *that* be! Then you remember what it is and then you can really hear it. And then finally, there they all are."

She could see this did not interest them at all.

"But where are they *going?*" one asked, a little impatiently.

"I'm coming to that," she said; and she let them wait. Then she spoke slowly but casually.

"They are on their way to a railroad."

There, she thought; that's for the look you all gave me when I said I wasn't sure. She waited for them to ask; they waited for her to explain.

"A railroad," she told them, "is great hard bars of metal lying side by side, or so they tell me, and they go on and on over the ground as far as the eye can see. And great wagons run on the metal bars on wheels, like wagon wheels but smaller, and these wheels are made of solid metal too. The wagons are much bigger than any wagon you've ever seen, as big as, big as sheds, they say, and they are pulled along on the iron bars by a terrible huge dark machine, with a loud scream."

"Big as *sheds?*" one of the calves said skeptically.

"Big *enough*, anyway," the mother said. "I told you I've never seen it myself. But those wagons are so big that several of us can get inside at once. And that's exactly what happens."

Suddenly she became very quiet, for she felt that somehow, she could not imagine just how, she had said altogether too much.

"Well, *what* happens," her son wanted to know. "What do you mean, *happens.*"

She always tried hard to be a reasonably modern mother. It was probably better, she felt, to go on, than to leave them all full of imaginings and mystification. Besides, there was really nothing at all awful about what happened . . . if only one could know *why*.

"Well," she said, "it's nothing much, really. They just—why, when they all finally *get* there, why there are all the great cars waiting in a long line, and the big dark machine is up ahead . . . smoke comes out of it, they say . . . and . . . well, then, they just put us into the wagons, just as many as will fit in each wagon, and when everybody is in, why . . ." She hesitated, for again, though she couldn't be sure why, she was uneasy.

"Why then," her son said, "the train takes them away."

Hearing that word, she felt a flinching of the heart. Where had he picked it up, she wondered, and she gave him a shy and curious glance. Oh dear, she thought. I should never have even *begun* to explain. "Yes," she said, "when everybody is safely in, they slide the doors shut."

They were all silent for a little while. Then one of them asked thoughtfully, "Are they taking them somewhere they don't want to go?"

"Oh, I don't think so," the mother said. "I imagine it's very nice."

"*I* want to go," she heard her son say with ardor. "I want to go right now," he cried. "Can I, Mama? *Can* I? *Please?*" And looking into his eyes, she was overwhelmed by sadness.

"Silly thing," she said, "there'll be time enough for that when you're grown up. But what I very much hope," she went on, "is that instead of being chosen to go out on the range and to make the long journey, you will grow up to be very strong and bright so they will decide that you may stay here at home with Mother. And you, too," she added, speaking to the other little males; but she could not honestly wish this for any but her own, least of all for the eldest, strongest and most proud, for she knew how few are chosen.

She could see that what she said was not received with enthusiasm.

"But I want to go," her son said.

"Why?" she asked. "I don't think any of you realize that it's a great *honor* to be chosen to stay. A great privilege. Why, it's just the most ordinary ones are taken out onto the range. But only the very pick are chosen to stay here at home. If you want to go out on the range," she said in hurried and happy inspiration, "all you have to do is be ordinary and careless and silly. If you want to have even a chance to be chosen to stay, you have to try to be stronger and bigger and braver and brighter than anyone else, and that takes *hard work. Every day.* Do you see?'' And she looked happily and hopefully from one to another. ''Besides,'' she added, aware that they were not won over, ''I'm told it's a very rough life out there, and the men are unkind.''

''Don't you see,'' she said again; and she pretended to speak to all of them, but it was only to her son.

But he only looked at her. ''Why do you want me to stay home?'' he asked flatly; in their silence she knew the others were asking the same question.

''Because it's safe here,'' she said before she knew better; and realized she had put it in the most unfortunate way possible. ''Not safe, not just that,'' she fumbled. ''I mean . . . because here we *know* what happens, and what's going to happen, and there's never any doubt about it, never any reason to wonder, to worry. Don't you see? It's just *Home*,'' and she put a smile on the word, ''where we all know each other and are happy and well.''

They were so merely quiet, looking back at her, that she felt they were neither won over nor alienated. Then she knew of her son that he, anyhow, was most certainly not persuaded, for he asked the question she most dreaded: ''Where do they go on the train?'' And hearing him, she knew that she would stop at nothing to bring that curiosity and eagerness, and that tendency toward skepticism, within safe bounds.

''Nobody knows,'' she said, and she added, in just the tone she knew would most sharply engage them, ''Not for sure, anyway.''

''What do you mean, *not for sure*,'' her son cried. And the oldest, biggest calf repeated the question, his voice cracking.

The mother deliberately kept silence as she gazed out over the plain, and while she was silent they all heard the last they would ever hear of all those who were going away: one last great cry, as faint almost as a breath; the infinitesimal jabbing vituperation of the dog; the solemn muttering of the earth.

''Well,'' she said, after even this sound was entirely lost, ''there was one who came back.'' Their instant, trustful eyes were too much for her. She added, ''Or so they say.''

They gathered a little more closely around her, for now she spoke very quietly.

''It was my great-grandmother who told me,'' she said. ''She was told it by *her* great-grandmother, who claimed she saw it with her own eyes, though of course I can't vouch for that. Because of course I wasn't even dreamed of then; and Great-grandmother was so very, very old,

you see, that you couldn't always be sure she knew quite *what* she was saying."

Now that she began to remember it more clearly, she was sorry she had committed herself to telling it.

"Yes," she said, "the story is, there was one, *just* one, who ever came back, and he told what happened on the train, and where the train went and what happened after. He told it all in a rush, they say, the last things first and every which way, but as it was finally sorted out and gotten into order by those who heard it and those they told it to, this is more or less what happened:

"He said that after the men had gotten just as many of us as they could into the car he was in, so that their sides pressed tightly together and nobody could lie down, they slid the door shut with a startling rattle and a bang, and then there was a sudden jerk, so strong they might have fallen except that they were packed so closely together, and the car began to move. But after it had moved only a little way, it stopped as suddenly as it had started, so that they all nearly fell down again. You see, they were just moving up the next car that was joined on behind, to put more of us into it. He could see it all between the boards of the car, because the boards were built a little apart from each other, to let in air."

Car, her son said again to himself, Now he would never forget the word.

"He said that then, for the first time in his life, he became very badly frightened, he didn't know why. But he was sure, at that moment, that there was something dreadfully to be afraid of. The others felt this same great fear. They called out loudly to those who were being put into the car behind, and the others called back, but it was no use; those who were getting aboard were between narrow white fences and then were walking up a narrow slope and the men kept jabbing them as they do when they are in an unkind humor, and there was no way to go but on into the car. There was no way to get out of the car, either: he tried, with all his might, and he was the one nearest the door.

"After the next car behind was full, and the door was shut, the train jerked forward again, and stopped again, and they put more of us into still another car, and so on, and on, until all the starting and stopping no longer frightened anybody; it was just something uncomfortable that was never going to stop, and they began instead to realize how hungry and thirsty they were. But there was no food and no water, so they just had to put up with this; and about the time they became resigned to going without their suppers (for now it was almost dark), they heard a sudden and terrible scream which frightened them even more deeply than anything had frightened them before, and the train began to move again, and they braced their legs once more for the jolt when it would stop, but this time, instead of stopping, it began to go fast, and then even faster, so fast that the ground nearby slid past like a flooded creek and the whole country, he claimed, began to move too, turning slowly around a far mountain as if it were all one great wheel. And then there was a strange kind of disturbance inside the car, he said, or even inside his very bones. He felt as if everything in him was *falling*, as if he had been filled full of a heavy liquid that all wanted to flow one way, and all the others were leaning as he was leaning, away from this queer heaviness that was trying to pull them over, and then just as suddenly this leaning heaviness was gone and they nearly fell again before they could stop leaning against it. He could never understand what this was, but it too happened so many times that they all got used to it, just as they got used to seeing the country turn like a slow wheel, and just as they got used to the long cruel screams of the engine, and the steady iron noise beneath them which made the cold darkness so fearsome, and the hunger and the thirst and the continual standing up, and the moving on and on and on as if they would never stop."

"*Didn't* they ever stop?" one asked.

"Once in a great while," she replied. "Each time they did," she said, "he thought, Oh, now *at last! At last* we can get out and stretch our tired legs and lie down! *At last* we'll be given food and water! But they never let them out. And they never gave them food or water. They never even cleaned up under them. They had to stand in their manure and in the water they made."

"Why did the train stop?" her son asked; and with somber gratification she saw that he was taking all this very much to heart.

"He could never understand why," she said. "Sometimes men would walk up and down alongside the cars, and the more nervous and the more trustful of us would call out; but they were only looking around, they never seemed to do anything. Sometimes he could see many houses and bigger buildings together where people lived. Sometimes it was far out in the country and after they had stood still for a long time they would hear a little noise which quickly became louder, and then became suddenly a noise so loud it stopped their breathing, and during this noise something black would go by, very close, and so fast it couldn't be seen. And then it was gone as suddenly as it had appeared, and the noise became small, and then in the silence their train would start up again.

"Once, he tells us, something very strange happened. They were standing still, and cars of a very different kind began to move slowly past. These cars were not red, but black, with many glass windows like those in a house; and he says they were as full of human beings as the car he was in was full of our kind. And one of these people looked into his eyes and smiled, as if he liked him, or as if he knew only too well how hard the journey was.

"So by his account it happens to them, too," she said, with a certain pleased vindictiveness. "Only they were sitting down at their ease, not standing. And the one who smiled was eating."

She was still, trying to think of something; she couldn't quite grasp the thought.

"But didn't they *ever* let them out?" her son asked.

The oldest calf jeered. "Of *course* they did. He came back, didn't he? How would he ever come back if he didn't get out?"

"They didn't let them out," she said, "for a long, long time."

"How long?"

"So long, and he was so tired, he could never quite be sure. But he said that it turned from night to day and from day to night and back again several times over, with the train moving nearly all of this time, and that when it finally stopped, early one morning, they were all so tired and so discouraged that they hardly even noticed any longer, let alone felt any hope that anything would change for them, ever again; and then all of a sudden men came up and put up a wide walk and unbarred the door and slid it open, and it was the most wonderful and happy moment of his life when he saw the door open, and walked into the open air with all his joints trembling, and drank the water and ate the delicious food they had ready for him; it was worth the whole terrible journey."

Now that these scenes came clear before her, there was a faraway shining in her eyes, and her voice, too, had something in it of the faraway.

"When they had eaten and drunk all they could hold they lifted up their heads and looked around, and everything they saw made them happy. Even the trains made them cheerful now, for now they were no longer afraid of them. And though these trains were forever breaking to pieces and joining again with other broken pieces, with shufflings and clashings and rude cries, they hardly paid them attention any more, they were so pleased to be in their new home, and so surprised and delighted to find they were among thousands upon thousands of strangers of their own kind, all lifting up their voices in peacefulness and thanksgiving, and they were so wonderstruck by all they could see, it was so beautiful and so grand.

"For he has told us that now they lived among fences as white as bone, so many, and so spiderishly complicated, and shining so pure, that there's no use trying even to hint at the beauty and the splendor of it to anyone who knows only the pitiful little outfittings of a ranch. Beyond these mazy fences, through the dark and bright smoke which continually turned along the sunlight, dark buildings stood shoulder to shoulder in a wall as huge and proud as mountains. All through the air, all the time, there was an iron humming like the humming of the iron bar after it has been struck to tell the men it is time to eat, and in all the air, all the time, there was that same strange kind of iron strength which makes the silence before lightning so different from all other silence.

"Once for a little while the wind shifted and blew over them straight from the great buildings, and it brought a strange and very powerful smell which confused and disturbed them. He could never quite describe this smell, but he has told us it was unlike anything he had ever known before. It smelled like old fire, he said, and old blood and fear and darkness and sorrow and most terrible and brutal force and something else, something in it that made him want to run away. This sudden uneasiness and this wish to run away swept through every one of them, he tells us, so that they were all moved at once as restlessly as so many leaves in a wind, and there was great worry in their voices. But soon the leaders among them concluded that it was simply the way men must smell when there are a great many of them living together. Those dark buildings must be crowded very full of men, they decided, probably as many thousands of them, indoors, as there were of us, outdoors; so it was no wonder their smell was so strong and, to our kind, so unpleasant. Besides, it was so clear now in every other way that men were not as we had always supposed, but were doing everything they knew how to make us comfortable and happy, that we ought to just put up with their smell, which after all they couldn't help, any more than we could help our own. Very likely men didn't like the way we smelled, any more than we liked theirs. They passed along these ideas to the others, and soon everyone felt more calm, and then the wind changed again, and the fierce smell no longer came to them, and the smell of their own kind was back again, very strong of course, in such a crowd, but ever so homey and comforting, and everyone felt easy again.

"They were fed and watered so generously, and treated so well, and the majesty and the loveliness of this place where they had all come to rest was so far beyond anything they had ever known or dreamed of, that many of the simple and ignorant, whose memories were short, began to wonder whether that whole difficult journey, or even their whole lives up to now, had ever really been. Hadn't it all been just shadows, they murmured, just a bad dream?

"Even the sharp ones, who knew very well it had all really happened, began to figure that everything up to now had been made so full of pain only so that all they had come to now might seem all the sweeter and the more glorious. Some of the oldest and deepest were even of a mind that all the puzzle and tribulation of the journey had been sent us as a kind of harsh trying or proving of our worthiness; and that it was entirely fitting and proper that we could earn our way through to such rewards as these, only through suffering, and through being patient under pain which was beyond our understanding; and that now at the last, to those who had borne all things well, all things were made known: for the mystery of suffering stood revealed in joy. And now as they looked back over all that was past, all their sorrows and bewilderments seemed so little and so fleeting that, from the simplest among them even to the most wise, they could feel only the kind of amused pity we feel toward the very young when, with the first thing that hurts them or they are forbidden, they are sure there is nothing kind or fair in all creation, and carry on accordingly, raving and grieving as if their hearts would break."

She glanced among them with an indulgent smile, hoping the little lesson would sink home. They seemed interested but somewhat dazed. I'm talking way over their heads, she realized. But by now she herself was too deeply absorbed in her story to modify it much. *Let* it be, she thought, a little impatient; it's over *my* head, for that matter.

"They had hardly before this even wondered that they were alive," she went on, "and now all of a sudden they felt they understood *why* they were. This made them very happy, but they were still only beginning to enjoy this new wisdom when quite a new and different kind of restiveness ran among them. Before they quite knew it they were all moving once again, and now they realized that they were being moved, once more, by men, toward still some other place and purpose they could not know. But during these last hours they had been so well that now they felt no uneasiness, but all moved forward calm and sure toward better things still to come; he has told us that he no longer felt as if he were being driven, even as it became clear that they were going toward the shade of those great buildings; but guided.

"He was guided between fences which stood ever more and more narrowly near each other, among companions who were pressed ever more and more closely against one another; and now as he felt their warmth against him it was not uncomfortable, and his pleasure in it was not through any need to be close among others through anxiousness, but was a new kind of strong and gentle delight, at being so very close, so deeply of his own kind, that it seemed as if the very breath and heartbeat of each one were being exchanged through all that multitude, and each was another, and others were each, and each was a multitude, and the multitude was one. And quieted and made mild within this melting, they now entered the cold shadow cast by the buildings, and now with every step the smell of the buildings grew stronger, and in the darkening air the glittering of the fences was ever more queer.

"And now as they were pressed ever more intimately together he could see ahead of him a narrow gate, and he was strongly pressed upon from either side and from behind, and went in eagerly, and now he was between two fences so narrowly set that he brushed either fence with either flank, and walked alone, seeing just one other ahead of him, and knowing of just one other behind him, and for a moment the strange thought came to him, that the one ahead was his father, and that the one behind was the son he had never begotten.

"And now the light was so changed that he knew he must have come inside one of the gloomy and enormous buildings, and the smell was so much stronger that it seemed almost to burn his nostrils, and the swell and the somber new light blended together and became some other thing again, beyond his describing to us except to say that the whole air beat with it like one immense heart and it was as if the beating of this heart were pure violence infinitely manifolded upon violence: so that the uneasy feeling stirred in him again that it would be wise to turn around and run out of this place just as fast and as far as ever he could go. This he heard, as if he were telling it to himself at the top of his voice, but it came from somewhere so deep and so dark inside him that he could only hear the shouting of it as less than a whisper, as just a hot and chilling breath, and he scarcely heeded it, there was so much else to attend to.

"For as he walked along in this sudden and complete loneliness, he tells us, this wonderful knowledge of being one with all his race meant less and less to him, and in its place came something still more wonderful: he knew what it was to be himself alone, a creature separate and different from any other, who had never been before, and would never be again. He could feel this in his whole weight as he walked, and in each foot as he put it down and gave his weight to it and moved above it, and in every muscle as he moved, and it was a pride which lifted him up and made him feel large, and a pleasure which pierced him through. And as he began with such wondering delight to be aware of his own exact singleness in this world, he also began to understand (or so he thought) just why these fences were set so very narrow, and just why he was walking all by himself. It stole over him, he tells us, like the feeling of a slow cool wind, that he was being guided toward some still more wonderful reward or revealing, up ahead, which he could not of course imagine, but he was sure it was being held in store for him alone.

"Just then the one ahead of him fell down with a great sigh, and was so quickly taken out of the way that he did not even have to shift the order of his hooves as he walked on. The sudden fall and the sound of that sigh dismayed him, though, and something within him told him that it would be wise to look up: and there he saw Him.

"A little bridge ran crosswise above the fences. He stood on this bridge with His feet as wide apart as He could set them. He wore spattered trousers but from the belt up He was naked and as wet as rain. Both arms were raised high above His head and in both hands He held an enormous Hammer. With a grunt which was hardly like the voice of a human being, and with all His strength, He brought this Hammer down into the forehead of our friend: who, in a blinding blazing, heard from his own mouth the beginning of a gasping sigh; then there was only darkness."

Oh, this is *enough!* it's *enough!* she cried out within herself, seeing their terrible young eyes. How *could* she have been so foolish as to tell so much!

"What happened then?" she heard, in the voice of the oldest calf, and she was horrified. This shining in their eyes: was it only excitement? no pity? no fear?

"What happened?" two others asked.

Very well, she said to herself. I've gone so far; now I'll go the rest of the way. She decided not to soften it, either. She'd teach them a lesson they wouldn't forget in a hurry.

"Very well," she was surprised to hear herself say aloud.

"How long he lay in this darkness he couldn't know, but when he began to come out of it, all he knew was the most unspeakably dreadful pain. He was upside down and very slowly swinging and turning, for he was hanging by the tendons of his heels from great frightful hooks, and he has told us that the feeling was as if his hide were being torn from him inch by inch, in one piece. And then as he became more clearly aware he found that this was exactly what was happening. Knives would sliver and slice along both flanks, between the hide and the living flesh; then there was a moment of most precious relief; then red hands seized his hide and there was a jerking of the hide and a tearing of tissue which it was almost as terrible to hear as to feel, turning his whole body and the poor head at the bottom of it; and then the knives again.

"It was so far beyond anything he had ever known unnatural and amazing that he hung there through several more such slicings and jerkings and tearings before he was fully able to take it all in: then, with a scream, and a supreme straining of all his strength, he tore himself from the hooks and collapsed sprawling to the floor and, scrambling right to his feet, charged the men with the knives. For just a moment they were so astonished and so terrified they could not move. Then they moved faster than he had ever known men could—and so did all the other men who chanced to be in his way. He ran down a glowing floor of blood and down endless corridors which were hung with the bleeding carcasses of our kind and with bleeding fragments of carcasses, among blood-clothed men who carried bleeding weapons, and out of that vast room into the open, and over and through one fence after another, shoving aside many an astounded stranger and shouting out warnings as he ran, and away up the railroad toward the West.

"How he ever managed to get away, and how he ever found his way home, we can only try to guess. It's told that he scarcely knew, himself, by the time he came to this part of his story. He was impatient with those who interrupted him to ask about that, he had so much more important things to tell them, and by then he was so exhausted and so far gone that he could say nothing very clear about the little he did know. But we can realize that he must have had really tremendous strength, otherwise he couldn't have outlived the Hammer; and that strength such as his—which we simply don't see these days, it's of the olden time—is capable of things our own strongest and bravest would sicken to dream of. But there was something even stronger than his strength. There was his righteous fury, which nothing could stand up against, which brought him out of that fearful place. And there was his high and burning and heroic purpose, to keep him safe along the way, and to guide him home, and to keep the breath of life in him until he could warn us. He did manage to tell us that he just followed the railroad, but how he chose one among the many which branched out from that place, he couldn't say. He told us, too, that from time to time he recognized shapes of mountains and other landmarks, from his journey by train, all reappearing backward and with a changed look and hard to see, too (for he was shrewd enough to travel mostly at night), but still recognizable. But that isn't enough to account for it. For he has told us, too, that he simply *knew* the way; that he didn't hesitate one moment in choosing the right line of railroad, or even think of it as choosing; and that the landmarks didn't really guide him, but just made him the more sure of what he was already sure of; and that whenever he *did* encounter human beings—and during the later stages of his journey, when he began to doubt he would live to tell us, he traveled day and night—they never so much as moved to make him trouble, but stopped dead in their tracks, and their jaws fell open.

"And surely we can't wonder that their jaws fell open. I'm sure yours would, if you had seen him as he arrived, and I'm very glad I wasn't there to see it, either, even though it is said to be the greatest and most momentous day of all the days that ever were or shall be. For we have the testimony of eyewitnesses, how he looked, and it is only too vivid, even to hear of. He came up out of the East as much staggering as galloping (for by now he was so worn out by pain and exertion and loss of blood that he could hardly stay upright), and his heels were so piteously torn by the hooks that his hooves doubled under more often than not, and in his broken forehead the mark of the Hammer was like the socket for a third eye.

"He came to the meadow where the great trees made shade over the water. 'Bring them all together!' he cried out, as soon as he could find breath. 'All!' Then he drank; and then he began to speak to those who were already there: for as soon as he saw himself in the water it was as clear to him as it was to those who watched him that there was no time left to send for the others. His hide was all gone from his head and his neck and his forelegs and his chest and most of one side and a part of the other side. It was flung backward from his naked muscles by the wind of his running and now it lay around him in the dust like a ragged garment. They say there is no imagining how terrible and in some way how grand the eyeball is when the skin has been taken entirely from around it: his eyes, which were bare in this way, also burned with pain, and with the final energies of his life, and with his desperate concern to warn us while he could; and he rolled his eyes wildly while he talked, or looked piercingly from one to another of the listeners, interrupting himself to cry out, *'Believe* me! Oh, *believe* me!' For it had evidently never occurred to him that he might not be believed, and must make this last great effort, in addition to all he had gone through for us, to *make* himself believed; so that he groaned with sorrow and with rage and railed at them without tact or mercy for their slowness to believe.

He had scarcely what you could call a voice left, but with this relic of a voice he shouted and bellowed and bullied us and insulted us, in the agony of his concern. While he talked he bled from the mouth, and the mingled blood and saliva hung from his chin like the beard of a goat.

"Some say that with his naked face, and his savage eyes, and that beard and the hide lying off his bare shoulders like shabby clothing, he looked almost human. But others feel this is an irreverence even to think; and others, that it is a poor compliment to pay the one who told us, at such cost to himself, the true ultimate purpose of Man. Some did not believe he had ever come from our ranch in the first place, and of course he was so different from us in appearance and even in his voice, and so changed from what he might ever have looked or sounded like before, that nobody could recognize him for sure, though some were sure they did. Others suspected that he had been sent among us with his story for some mischievous and cruel purpose, and the fact that they could not imagine what this purpose might be, made them, naturally, all the more suspicious. Some believed he was actually a man, trying — and none too successfully, they said — to disguise himself as one of us; and again the fact that they could not imagine why a man would do this, made them all the more uneasy. There were quite a few who doubted that anyone who could get into such bad condition as he was in, was fit even to give reliable information, let alone advice, to those in good health. And some whispered, even while he spoke, that he had turned lunatic; and many came to believe this. It wasn't only that his story was so fantastic; there was good reason to wonder, many felt, whether anybody in his right mind would go to such trouble for others. But even those who did not believe him listened intently, out of curiosity to hear so wild a tale, and out of the respect it is only proper to show any creature who is in the last agony.

"What he told, was what I have just told you. But his purpose was away beyond just the telling. When they asked questions, no matter how curious or suspicious or idle or foolish, he learned, toward the last, to answer them with all the patience he could and in all the detail he could remember. He even invited them to examine his wounded heels and the pulsing wound in his head as closely as they pleased. He even begged them to, for he knew that before everything else, he must be believed. For unless we could believe him, wherever could we find any reason, or enough courage, to do the hard and dreadful things he told us we must do!

"It was only these things he cared about. Only for these, he came back."

Now clearly remembering what these things were, she felt her whole being quail. She looked at the young ones quickly and as quickly looked away.

"While he talked," she went on, "and our ancestors listened, men came quietly among us; one of them shot him. Whether he was shot in kindness or to silence him is an endlessly disputed question which will probably never be settled. Whether, even, he died of the shot, or through his own great pain and weariness (for his eyes, they say, were glazing for some time before the men came), we will never be sure. Some suppose even that he may have died of his sorrow and his concern for us. Others feel that he had quite enough to die of, without that. All these things are tangled and lost in the disputes of those who love to theorize and to argue. There is no arguing about his dying words, though; they were very clearly remembered:

" 'Tell them! Believe!' "

After a while her son asked, "What did he tell them to do?"

She avoided his eyes. "There's a great deal of disagreement about that, too," she said after a moment. "You see, he was so very tired."

They were silent.

"So tired," she said, "some think that toward the end, he really *must* have been out of his mind."

"Why?" asked her son.

"Because he was so tired out and so badly hurt."

They looked at her mistrustfully.

"And because of what he told us to do."

"What did he tell us to do?" her son asked again.

Her throat felt dry. "Just . . . things you can hardly bear even to think of. That's all."

They waited. "Well, *what?*" her son asked in a cold, accusing voice.

" '*Each one is himself,*' " she said shyly. " '*Not of the herd. Himself alone.*' That's one."

"What else?"

" '*Obey nobody. Depend on none.*' "

"What else?"

She found that she was moved. " '*Break down the fences,*' " she said less shyly. " '*Tell everybody, everywhere.*' "

"Where?"

"Everywhere. You see, he thought there must be ever so many more of us than we had ever known."

They were silent. "What else?" her son asked.

" '*For if even a few do not hear me, or disbelieve me, we are all betrayed.*' "

"Betrayed?"

"He meant, doing as men want us to. Not for ourselves, or the good of each other."

They were puzzled.

"Because, you see, he felt there was no other way." Again her voice altered: " '*All who are put on the range are put onto trains. All who are put onto trains meet the Man With The Hammer. All who stay home are kept there to breed others to go onto the range, and so betray themselves and their kind and their children forever.*

" '*We are brought into this life only to be victims; and there is no other way for us unless we save ourselves.*' "

"Do you understand?"

Still they were puzzled, she saw; and no wonder, poor things. But now the ancient lines rang in her memory, terrible and brave. They made her somehow proud. She began actually to want to say them.

" '*Never be taken,*' " she said. " '*Never be driven. Let those who can, kill Man. Let those who cannot, avoid him.*' "

She looked around at them.

"What else?" her son asked, and in his voice there was a rising valor.

She looked straight into his eyes. " '*Kill the yearlings,*' " she said very gently. " '*Kill the calves.*' "

She saw the valor leave his eyes.

"Kill us?"

She nodded, " 'So long as Man holds dominion over us,' " she said. And in dread and amazement she heard herself add, " 'Bear no young.' "

With this they all looked at her at once in such a way that she loved her child, and all these others, as never before; and there dilated within her such a sorrowful and marveling grandeur that for a moment she was nothing except her own inward whisper, "Why, *I* am one alone. And of the herd, too. Both at once. All one."

Her son's voice brought her back: "Did they do what he told them to?"

The oldest one scoffed, "Would we be here, if they had?"

"They say some did," the mother replied. "Some tried. Not all."

"What did the men do to them?" another asked.

"I don't know," she said. "It was such a very long time ago."

"Do you believe it?" asked the oldest calf.

"There are some who believe it," she said.

"Do *you?*"

"I'm told that far back in the wildest corners of the range there are some of us, mostly very, very old ones, who have never been taken. It's said that they meet, every so often, to talk and just to think together about the heroism and the terror of two sublime Beings, The One Who Came Back, and The Man With The Hammer. Even here at home, some of the old ones, and some of us who are just old-fashioned, believe it, or parts of it anyway. I know there are some who say that a hollow at the center of the forehead — a sort of shadow of the Hammer's blow — is a sign of very special ability. And I remember how Great-grandmother used to sing an old, pious song, let's see now, yes, 'Be not like dumb-driven cattle, be a hero in the strife.' But there aren't many. Not any more."

"Do *you* believe it?" the oldest calf insisted; and now she was touched to realize that every one of them, from the oldest to the youngest, needed very badly to be sure about that.

"Of course not, silly," she said; and all at once she was overcome by a most curious shyness, for it occurred to her that in the course of time, this young thing might be bred to her. "It's just an old, old legend." With a tender little laugh she added, lightly, "We use it to frighten children with."

By now the light was long on the plain and the herd was only a fume of gold near the horizon. Behind it, dung steamed, and dust sank gently to the shattered ground. She looked far away for a moment, wondering.

Something—it was like a forgotten word on the tip of the tongue. She felt the sudden chill of the late afternoon and she wondered what she had been wondering about. "Come, children," she said briskly, "it's high time for supper." And she turned away; they followed.

The trouble was, her son was thinking, you could never trust her. If she said a thing was so, she was probably just trying to get her way with you. If she said a thing wasn't so, it probably was so. But you never could be sure. Not without seeing for yourself. I'm going to go, he told himself; I don't care *what* she wants. And if it isn't so, why then I'll live on the range and make the great journey and find out what *is* so. And if what she told was true, why then I'll know ahead of time and the one *I* will charge is The Man With The Hammer. I'll put Him and His Hammer out of the way forever, and that will make me an even better hero than The One Who Came Back.

So, when his mother glanced at him in concern, not quite daring to ask her question, he gave her his most docile smile, and snuggled his head against her, and she was comforted.

The littlest and youngest of them was doing double skips in his efforts to keep up with her. Now that he wouldn't be interrupting her, and none of the big ones would hear and make fun of him, he shyly whispered his question, so warmly moistly ticklish that she felt as if he were licking her ear.

"What is it, darling?" she asked, bending down.

"What's a train?"

"A Mother's Tale" is an allegory, a story in which the characters and things are really symbols, standing for other characters and things. What do you think the herd is supposed to represent? The One Who Came Back? The Man With The Hammer? The journey on the train? Staying at home with Mother?

What characters have you seen so far in this book who could also be called "The One Who Came Back"? Where have they all come back from?

In what ways is the Mother in this story like the mothers of Richard and Kamau in unit one and the mother of Lemminkainen in unit two? How is she different? What do mothers represent in these stories? Why do you think the imagination has given certain roles to mothers, fathers, and to sons in quest stories? What, in general, are their roles?

In unit one, Richard's battle with the gang provides his initiation from the security of his mother to the violence of the world of men. What is the initiation in this story?

Is there always an element of sacrifice in an initiation? What is sacrificed? What is gained?

What time of the year does the story take place? Why is it an appropriate setting?

Do you think The One Who Came Back ever really existed? Or did some of the ancient members of the herd make him up? Why would they? Do you think Heracles ever existed? Why? Why do you think people tell stories about heroes? Do you think the Golden Age ever existed? Why? Do any of these characters lose any of their power if they did not actually exist? What kind of power do they have?

The strength of The One Who Came Back is said to be "of the olden time," far greater than that of anyone living now. What characters in units one and two share this mythical quality? Why do you think stories set in modern times have more believable heroes, people who are more like us?

The One Who Came Back did what he had to do. And, as with all heroes, this action raised him to a level beyond himself and beyond all others of his kind. In other words, he became like a god. This is the final stage of the true hero's life, his glorification or *apotheosis*. What was Heracles' apotheosis? What other heroes can you name, from literature or history, who are revered as godlike by a people?

Many hero stories have religious connotations. What religious beliefs do you think could come into being out of this story? What religious systems are founded on the quest and return of a great hero? What does this tell you about one of the possible reasons that men tell hero stories?

A Ritual

From The Golden Bough
SIR JAMES FRAZER

Some tribes of Northern New Guinea—the Yabim, Bukaua, Kai, and Tami—like many Australian tribes, require every male member of the tribe to be circumcised before he ranks as a full-grown man; and the tribal initiation, of which circumcision is the central feature, is conceived by them, as by some Australian tribes, as a process of being swallowed and disgorged by a mythical monster, whose voice is heard in the humming sound of the bull-roarer. Indeed the New Guinea tribes not only impress this belief on the minds of women and children, but enact it in a dramatic form at the actual rites of initiation, at which no woman or uninitiated person may be present. For this purpose a hut about a hundred feet long is erected either in the village or in a lonely part of the forest. It is modelled in the shape of the mythical monster; at the end which represents his head it is high, and it tapers away at the other end. A betel-palm, grubbed up with the roots, stands for the backbone of the great being and its clustering fibres for his hair; and to complete the resemblance the butt end of the building is adorned by a native artist with a pair of goggle eyes and a gaping mouth. When after a tearful parting from their mothers and women folk, who believe or pretend to believe in the monster that swallows their dear ones, the awe-struck novices are brought face to face with this imposing structure, the huge creature emits a sullen growl, which is in fact no other than the humming note of bull-roarers swung by men concealed in the monster's belly. The actual process of deglutition* is variously enacted. Among the Tami it is represented by causing the candidates to defile

* swallowing

past a row of men who hold bull-roarers over their heads; among the Kai it is more graphically set forth by making them pass under a scaffold on which stands a man, who makes a gesture of swallowing and takes in fact a gulp of water as each trembling novice passes beneath him. But the present of a pig, opportunely offered for the redemption of the youth, induces the monster to relent and disgorge his victim; the man who represents the monster accepts the gift vicariously, a gurgling sound is heard, and the water which had just been swallowed descends in a jet on the novice. This signifies that the young man has been released from the monster's belly. However, he has now to undergo the more painful and dangerous operation of circumcision. It follows immediately, and the cut made by the knife of the operator is explained to be a bite or scratch which the monster inflicted on the novice in spewing him out of his capacious maw. While the operation is proceeding, a prodigious noise is made by the swinging of bull-roarers to represent the roar of the dreadful being who is in the act of swallowing the young man.

When, as sometimes happens, a lad dies from the effect of the operation, he is buried secretly in the forest, and his sorrowing mother is told that the monster has a pig's stomach as well as a human stomach, and that unfortunately her son slipped into the wrong stomach, from which it was impossible to extricate him. After they have been circumcised the lads must remain for some months in seclusion, shunning all contact with women and even the sight of them. They live in the long hut which represents the monster's belly. When at last the lads, now ranking as initiated men, are brought back with great pomp and ceremony to the village, they are received with sobs and tears of joy by the women, as if the grave had given up its dead.

The basic components of an initiation are: a youthful hero, separation from mother and the world of women, death (symbolized by passing through a monster or tunnel or underworld), and rebirth (symbolized by emerging fully mature from a womb or darkness or obscurity). Tell what aspects of initiation you can find in the following stories: "The Street," "The Return," "Orpheus," "A Mother's Tale."

Why is an initiation—or what it symbolizes—something that "must be done"?

Losses

It was not dying: everybody died.
It was not dying: we had died before
In the routine crashes—and our fields
Called up the papers, wrote home to our folks,
And the rates rose, all because of us.
We died on the wrong page of the almanac,
Scattered on mountains fifty miles away;
Diving on haystacks, fighting with a friend,
We blazed up on the lines we never saw.
We died like ants or pets or foreigners.
(When we left high school nothing else had died
For us to figure we had died like.)

In our new planes, with our new crews, we bombed
The ranges by the desert or the shore,
Fired at towed targets, waited for our scores—
And turned into replacements and woke up
One morning, over England, operational.
It wasn't different: but if we died
It was not an accident but a mistake
(But an easy one for anyone to make).
We read our mail and counted up our missions—
In bombers named for girls, we burned
The cities we had learned about in school—
Till our lives wore out; our bodies lay among
The people we had killed and never seen.
When we lasted long enough they gave us medals;
When we died they said, "Our casualties were low."
They said, "Here are the maps"; we burned the cities.

It was not dying—no, not ever dying;
But the night I died I dreamed that I was dead,
And the cities said to me: "Why are you dying?
We are satisfied, if you are; but why did I die?"

RANDALL JARRELL

Like The One Who Came Back, these young soldiers journeyed from the known into the unknown. But The One Who Came Back had a profound insight at the end of his quest. What did the soldiers find?

What qualities do you think these young pilots have in common with Heracles and with The One Who Came Back? What do they have in common with the ricksha puller?

Antigone

A Greek myth
Retold by REX WARNER

Creon became King of Thebes at a time when the city had lost half its army and at least half of its best warriors in civil war. The war was over. Eteocles, the king, was dead; dead also was his brother Polynices, who had come with the army of the Argives to fight for his own right to the kingdom.

Creon, as the new king, decided first of all to show his people how unforgivable it was to make war upon one's own country. To Eteocles, who had reigned in Thebes, he gave a splendid burial; but he ordered that, upon pain of death, no one was to prepare for funeral or even sprinkle earth upon the body of Polynices. It was to lie as it had fallen in the plain for birds and beasts to devour. To make certain that his orders should be carried out Creon set a patrol of men to watch the body night and day.

Antigone and Ismene, sisters of Polynices, heard the king's orders with alarm and shame. They had loved both their brothers, and hated the thought that one of them should lie unburied, unable to join the world of the ghosts, mutilated and torn by the teeth of dogs and jackals and by the beaks and talons of birds. Ismene, in spite of her feelings, did not dare oppose the king; but Antigone stole out of the city by night, and, after searching among the piled-up bodies of those who had died in the great battle, found the body of her brother. She lightly covered it with dust, and said for it the prayers that ought to be said for the dead.

Next day it was reported to Creon that someone (the guards did not know whom) had disobeyed the king's orders and scattered earth over the body of Polynices. Creon swore an oath that if the guilty person should be found, even though that person was a member of his own family, he or she should die for it. He threatened the guards also with death if they failed to find the criminal, and told them immediately to uncover the body and leave it to the birds and beasts of prey.

That day a hot wind blew from the south. Clouds of dust covered the plain, and Antigone again stole out of the city to complete her work of burying her brother. This time, however, the guards kept better watch. They seized her and brought her before King Creon.

Creon was moved by no other feelings than the feelings of one whose orders have been disobeyed. "Did you know," he asked Antigone, "the law that I made and the penalty that I laid down for those who broke the law?"

"I knew it," Antigone replied, "but there are other laws, made not by men but by the gods. There is a law of pity and of mercy. That law is to be obeyed first. After I have obeyed that, I will, if I may, obey the laws that are made by men"

"If you love your brother," said Creon, "more than the established laws of your country and your king, then you must bear the penalty of the laws, loving your brother in the world of the dead."

"You may kill me with your laws," Antigone replied, "but to me death is, in all these sufferings, less of an evil than would be treachery to my brother or cowardice when the time came to help him."

Her confident and calm words stirred Creon to even greater anger. Now her sister Ismene, who had at first been too frightened to help Antigone in her defiance of the law, came forward and asked to be allowed to share in Antigone's punishment; but Antigone would not permit her to claim a share with her in the deed or in its results. Nor would Creon listen to any appeal for mercy. Not wishing to have the blood of his niece upon his own hands, he gave orders that she should be put into an underground chamber, walled up from the light and then left to die.

So Antigone was carried away to a slow and lingering death, willing to suffer it, since she had obeyed the promptings of her heart. She had been about to marry Haemon, the king's son, but, instead of the palace that she would have entered as a bride, she was now going to the house of death.

Haemon himself came to beg his father to be merciful. He spoke mildly, but let it clearly be understood that neither he nor the rest of the people of Thebes approved of so savage a sentence. It was true that Antigone had broken the law; but it was also true that she had acted as a sister ought to act when her brother was unburied. And, Haemon said, though most people did not dare oppose the king in his anger, nevertheless most people in their hearts felt as *he* did.

Haemon's love for Antigone and even his good will toward his father only increased the fury of the king. With harsh words he drove his son from him.

Next came the blind prophet Tiresias to warn King Creon that the gods were angry with him both for his merciless punishment of Antigone and for leaving the body of Polynices to be desecrated by the wild beasts and birds. Creon might have remembered how often in the past the words of Tiresias had been fulfilled, but now, in his obstinate rage, he merely insulted the prophet. "You have been bribed," he said, "either by Haemon or by some traitor to try and save the life of a criminal by dishonest threats that have nothing to do with the gods at all."

Tiresias turned his sightless eyes on the king. "This very day," he said, "before the sun sets, you will pay twice, yes, with two dead bodies, for the sin which you could easily have avoided. As for me, I shall keep far away from one who, in his own pride, rejects the gods and is sure to suffer."

Tiresias went away, and now Creon for the first time began to feel that it was possible that his punishments had been too hard. For the first time, but too late, he was willing to listen to the advice of his council, who begged him to be merciful, to release Antigone and to give burial to the body of Polynices.

With no very good grace Creon consented to do as he had been advised. He gave orders for the burial of Polynices and went himself to release Antigone from the prison in which she had been walled away from the light. Joyfully his son Haemon went ahead of the rest with pickaxes and bars for breaking down the wall. But when they broke the stones of the wall they found that Antigone had made a noose out of the veil which she was wearing and had hanged herself. Haemon could not bear to outlive her. He drew his sword and plunged it into his heart before the eyes of his father. Then he fell forward dead on the body of the girl whom he had wished to be his wife.

As for Creon he had scarcely time to lament for his son when news reached him of another disaster. His wife had heard of Haemon's death and she too had taken her own life. So the words of Tiresias were fulfilled.

Antigone is driven by an intense inner purpose. What force decrees that she must defy the king? What other characters in this book follow their hearts instead of the herd? What is the value of acting in a way that brings punishment and death?

The Song of Wandering Aengus

I went out to the hazel wood,
Because a fire was in my head,
And cut and peeled a hazel wand,
And hooked a berry to a thread;
And when white moths were on the wing,
And moth-like stars were flickering out,
I dropped the berry in a stream
And caught a little silver trout.

When I had laid it on the floor
I went to blow the fire aflame,
But something rustled on the floor,
And some one called me by my name:
It had become a glimmering girl
With apple blossom in her hair
Who called me by my name and ran
And faded through the brightening air.

Though I am old with wandering
Through hollow lands and hilly lands,
I will find out where she has gone,
And kiss her lips and take her hands;
And walk among long dappled grass,
And pluck till time and times are done
The silver apples of the moon,
The golden apples of the sun.

WILLIAM BUTLER YEATS

What is Aengus' quest? Why does he undertake it? Who else searched for golden apples? Do you think that such objects might be symbols of something larger and greater? What?

"Wart," the boy who would someday be King Arthur,
is lost. But the wonders he discovers in that
unknown forest are beautiful to him — especially
the wonder of a real questing knight.

The Questing Beast

From The Once and Future King

T. H. WHITE

The sun finished the last rays of its lingering good-by, and the moon rose in awful majesty over the silver treetops, before he dared to stand. Then he got up, and dusted the twigs out of his jerkin, and wandered off forlorn, taking the easiest way and trusting himself to God. He had been walking like this for about half an hour, and sometimes feeling more cheerful — because it really was very cool and lovely in the summer forest by moonlight — when he came upon the most beautiful thing that he had seen in his short life so far.

There was a clearing in the forest, a wide sward of moonlit grass, and the white rays shone full upon the tree trunks on the opposite side. These trees were beeches, whose trunks are always more beautiful in a pearly light, and among the beeches there was the smallest movement and a silvery clink. Before the clink there were just the beeches, but immediately afterward there was a knight in full armor, standing still and silent and unearthly, among the majestic trunks. He was mounted on an enormous white horse that stood as rapt as its master, and he carried in his right hand, with its butt resting on the stirrup, a high, smooth jousting lance, which stood up among the tree stumps, higher and higher, till it was outlined against the velvet sky. All was moonlit, all silver, too beautiful to describe.

The Wart did not know what to do. He did not know whether it would be safe to go up to this knight, for there were so many terrible things in the forest that even the knight might be a ghost. Most ghostly he looked, too, as he hoved meditating on the confines of the gloom. Eventually the boy made up his mind that even if it were a ghost, it would be the ghost of a knight, and knights were bound by their vows to help people in distress.

"Excuse me," he said, when he was right under the mysterious figure, "but can you tell me the way back to Sir Ector's castle?"

At this the ghost jumped, so that it nearly fell off its horse, and gave out a muffled baaa through its visor, like a sheep.

"Excuse me," began the Wart again, and stopped, terrified, in the middle of his speech.

For the ghost lifted up its visor, revealing two enormous eyes frosted like ice; exclaimed in an anxious voice, "What, what?"; took off its eyes—which turned out to be horn-rimmed spectacles, fogged by being inside the helmet; tried to wipe them on the horse's mane—which only made them worse; lifted both hands above its head and tried to wipe them on its plume; dropped its lance; dropped the spectacles; got off the horse to search for them—the visor shutting in the process; lifted its visor; bent down for the spectacles; stood up again as the visor shut once more, and exclaimed in a plaintive voice, "Oh, dear!"

The Wart found the spectacles, wiped them, and gave them to the ghost, who immediately put them on (the visor shut at once) and began scrambling back on its horse for dear life. When it was there it held out its hand for the lance, which the Wart handed up, and, feeling all secure, opened the visor with its left hand, and held it open. It peered at the boy with one hand up—like a lost mariner searching for land—and exclaimed, "Ah-hah! Whom have we here, what?"

"Please," said the Wart, "I am a boy whose guardian is Sir Ector."

"Charming fellah," said the knight. "Never met him in me life."

"Can you tell me the way back to his castle?"

"Faintest idea. Stranger in these parts meself."

"I am lost," said the Wart.

"Funny thing that. Now I have been lost for seventeen years.

"Name of King Pellinore," continued the Knight. "May have heard of me, what?" The visor shut with a pop, like an echo to the What, but was opened again immediately. "Seventeen years ago, come Michaelmas, and been after the Questing Beast ever since. Boring, very."

"I should think it would be," said the Wart, who had never heard of King Pellinore, nor of the Questing Beast, but he felt that this was the safest thing to say in the circumstances.

"It is the Burden of the Pellinores," said the King proudly. "Only a Pellinore can catch it—that is, of course, or his next of kin. Train all the Pellinores with that idea in mind. Limited eddication, rather. Fewmets, and all that."

"I know what fewmets are," said the boy with interest. "They are the droppings of the beast pursued. The harborer keeps them in his horn, to show to his master, and can tell by them whether it is a warrantable beast or otherwise, and what state it is in."

"Intelligent child," remarked the King. "Very. Now I carry fewmets about with me practically all the time.

"Insanitary habit," he added, beginning to look dejected, "and quite pointless. Only one Questing Beast, you know, so there can't be any question whether she is warrantable or not."

Here his visor began to droop so much that the Wart decided he had better forget his own troubles and try to cheer his companion, by asking questions on the one subject about which he seemed qualified to speak. Even talking to a lost royalty was better than being alone in the wood.

"What does the Questing Beast look like?"

"Ah, we call it the Beast Glatisant, you know," replied the monarch, assuming a learned air and beginning to speak quite volubly. "Now the Beast Glatisant, or, as we say in English, the Questing Beast—you may call it either," he added graciously—"this Beast has the head of a serpent, ah, and the body of a libbard, the haunches of a lion, and he is footed like a hart. Wherever this beast goes he makes a noise in his belly as it had been the noise of thirty couple of hounds questing.

"Except when he is drinking, of course," added the King.

"It must be a dreadful kind of monster," said the Wart, looking about him anxiously.

"A dreadful monster," repeated the King. "It is the Beast Glatisant."

"And how do you follow it?"

This seemed to be the wrong question, for Pellinore began to look even more depressed.

"I have a brachet," he said sadly. "There she is, over there."

The Wart looked in the direction which had been indicated with a despondent thumb, and saw a lot of rope wound round a tree. The other end of the rope was tied to King Pellinore's saddle.

"I do not see her very well."

"Wound herself round the other side, I dare say. She always goes the opposite way from me."

The Wart went over to the tree and found a large white dog scratching herself for fleas. As soon as she saw the Wart, she began wagging her whole body, grinning vacuously, and panting in her efforts to lick his face, in spite of the cord. She was too tangled up to move.

"It's quite a good brachet," said King Pellinore, "only it pants so, and gets wound round things, and goes the opposite way. What with that and the visor, what, I sometimes don't know which way to turn."

"Why don't you let her loose?" asked the Wart. "She would follow the Beast just as well like that."

"She goes right away then, you see, and I don't see her sometimes for a week.

"Gets a bit lonely without her," added the King, "following the Beast about, and never knowing where one is. Makes a bit of company, you know."

"She seems to have a friendly nature."

"Too friendly. Sometimes I doubt whether she is really chasing the Beast at all."

"What does she do when she sees it?"

"Nothing."

"Oh, well," said the Wart. "I dare say she will get to be interested in it after a time."

"It is eight months, anyway, since we saw the Beast at all."

The poor fellow's voice had grown sadder and sadder since the beginning of the conversation, and now he definitely began to snuffle. "It is the curse of the Pellinores," he exclaimed. "Always mollocking about after that beastly Beast. What on earth use is she, anyway? First you have to stop to unwind the brachet, then your visor falls down, then you can't see through your spectacles. Nowhere to sleep, never know where you are. Rheumatism in the winter, sunstroke in the summer. All this horrid armor takes hours to put on. When it is on it's either frying or freezing, and it gets rusty. You have to sit up all night polishing the stuff. Oh, how I do wish I had a nice house of my own to live in, a house with beds in it and real pillows and sheets. If I was rich that's what I would buy. A nice bed with a nice pillow and a nice sheet that you could lie in, and then I would put this beastly horse in a meadow and tell that beastly brachet to run away and play, and throw all this beastly armor out of the window, and let the beastly Beast go and chase himself—that I would."

"If you could show me the way home," said the Wart craftily, "I am sure Sir Ector would put you up in a bed for the night."

"Do you really mean it?" cried the King. "In a bed?"

"A feather bed."

King Pellinore's eyes grew round as saucers. "A feather bed?" he repeated slowly. "Would it have pillows?"

"Down pillows."

"Down pillows!" whispered the King, holding his breath. And then, letting it out in one rush, "What a lovely house your gentleman must have!"

"I do not think it is more than two hours away," said the Wart, following up his advantage.

"And did this gentleman really send you out to invite me in?" (He had forgotten about the Wart being lost.) "How nice of him, how very nice of him, I do think, what?"

"He will be pleased to see us," said the Wart truthfully.

"Oh, how nice of him," exclaimed the King again, beginning to bustle about with his various trappings. "And what a lovely gentleman he must be, to have a feather bed!

"I suppose I should have to share it with somebody?" he added doubtfully.

"You could have one of your own."

"A feather bed of one's very own, with sheets and a pillow—perhaps even two pillows, or a pillow and a bolster—and no need to get up in time for breakfast! Does your guardian get up in time for breakfast?"

"Never," said the Wart.

"Fleas in the bed?"

"Not one."

"Well!" said King Pellinore. "It does sound too nice for words, I must say. A feather bed and none of those fewmets for ever so long. How long did you say it would take us to get there?"

"Two hours," said the Wart—but he had to shout the second of these words, for the sounds were drowned in his mouth by a noise which had that moment arisen close beside them.

"What was that?" exclaimed the Wart.

"Hark!" cried the King.

"Mercy!"

"It is the Beast!"

And immediately the loving huntsman had forgotten everything else, but was busied about his task. He wiped his spectacles upon the seat of his trousers, the only accessible piece of cloth about him, while the belling and bloody cry arose all round. He balanced them on the end of his long nose, just before the visor automatically clapped to. He clutched his jousting lance in his right hand, and galloped off in the direction of the noise. He was brought up short by the rope which was wound round the tree—the vacuous brachet meanwhile giving a melancholy yelp—and fell off his horse with a tremendous clang. In a second he was up again—the Wart was convinced that the spectacles must be broken—and hopping round the white horse with one foot in the stirrup. The girths stood the test and he was in the saddle somehow, with his jousting lance between his legs, and then he was galloping round and round the tree, in the opposite direction to the one in which the brachet had wound herself up. He went round three times too often, the brachet meanwhile running and yelping the other way, and then, after four or five back casts, they were both free of the obstruction. "Yoicks, what!" cried King Pellinore, waving his lance in the air, and swaying excitedly in the saddle. Then he disappeared into the gloom of the forest, with the unfortunate hound trailing behind him at the other end of the cord.

How is the Questing Beast humorously described as a combination of the monsters that heroes traditionally fight?

What are the perils of Pellinore's journey?

Why does Pellinore continue his quest? Is he driven by some inner purpose or by some outer force? What drives each of the other characters in this unit?

Shooting the Sun

Four horizons cozen me
To distances I dimly see.

Four paths beckon me to stray,
Each a bold and separate way.

Monday morning shows the East
Satisfying as a feast.

Tuesday I will none of it,
West alone holds benefit.

Later in the week 'tis due
North that I would hurry to.

While on other days I find
To the South content of mind.

So I start, but never rest
North or South or East or West.

Each horizon has its claim
Solace to a different aim.

Four-souled like the wind am I,
Voyaging an endless sky,
Undergoing destiny.

AMY LOWELL

What is this poet's quest? Why does she voyage the endless sky? Do you think she might be chasing what Aengus called his "glimmering girl"?

List the other characters in this book you would say were "undergoing destiny."

The Bear

WILLIAM FAULKNER

He was ten. But it had already begun, long before that day when at last he wrote his age in two figures and he saw for the first time the camp where his father and Major de Spain and old General Compson and the others spent two weeks each November and two weeks again each June. He had already inherited then, without ever having seen it, the tremendous bear with one trap-ruined foot which, in an area almost a hundred miles deep, had earned for itself a name, a definite designation like a living man.

He had listened to it for years: the long legend of corncribs rifled, of shoats and grown pigs and even calves carried bodily into the woods and devoured, of traps and deadfalls overthrown and dogs mangled and slain, and shotgun and even rifle charges delivered at point-blank range and with no more effect than so many peas blown through a tube by a boy—a corridor of wreckage and destruction beginning back before he was born, through which sped, not fast but rather with the ruthless and irresistible deliberation of a locomotive, the shaggy tremendous shape.

It ran in his knowledge before he ever saw it. It looked and towered in his dreams before he even saw the unaxed woods where it left its crooked print, shaggy, huge, red-eyed, not malevolent but just big— too big for the dogs which tried to bay it, for the horses which tried to ride it down, for the men and the bullets they fired into it, too big for the very country which was its constricting scope. He seemed to see it entire with a child's complete divination before he ever laid eyes on either—the doomed wilderness whose edges were being constantly and punily gnawed at by men with axes and plows who feared it because it was wilderness, men myriad and nameless even to one another in the land where the old bear had earned a name, through which ran not even a mortal animal but an anachronism, indomitable and invincible, out of an old dead time, a phantom, epitome and apotheosis of the old wild life at which the puny humans swarmed and hacked in a fury of abhorrence and fear, like pygmies about the ankles of a drowsing elephant; the old bear solitary, indomitable and alone, widowered, childless and absolved of mortality—old Priam reft of his old wife and having outlived all his sons.

Until he was ten, each November he would watch the wagon containing the dogs and the bedding and food and guns and his father and Tennie's Jim, the Negro, and Sam Fathers, the Indian, son of a slave woman and a Chickasaw chief, depart on the road to town, to Jefferson, where Major de Spain and the others would join them. To the boy, at seven and eight and nine, they were not going into the Big Bottom to hunt bear and deer, but to keep yearly rendezvous with the bear which they did not even intend to kill. Two weeks later they would return, with no trophy, no head and skin. He had not expected it. He had not even been afraid it would be in the wagon. He believed that even after he was ten and his father would let him go too, for those two November weeks, he would merely make another one, along with his father and Major de Spain and General Compson and the others, the dogs which feared to bay it and the rifles and shotguns which failed even to bleed it, in the yearly pageant of the old bear's furious immortality.

Then he heard the dogs. It was in the second week of his first time in the camp. He stood with Sam Fathers against a big oak beside the faint crossing where they had stood each dawn for nine days now, hearing the dogs. He had heard them once before, one morning last week—a murmur, sourceless, echoing through the wet woods, swelling presently into separate voices which he could recognize and call by name. He had raised and cocked the gun as Sam told him and stood motionless again while the uproar, the invisible course, swept up and past and faded; it seemed to him that he could actually see the deer, the buck, blond, smoke-colored, elongated with speed, fleeing, vanishing, the woods, the gray solitude, still ringing even when the cries of the dogs had died away.

"Now let the hammers down," Sam said.

"You knew they were not coming here too," he said.

"Yes," Sam said. "I want you to learn how to do when you didn't shoot. It's after the chance for the bear or the deer has done already come and gone that men and dogs get killed."

"Anyway," he said, "it was just a deer."

Then on the tenth morning he heard the dogs again. And he readied the too-long, too-heavy gun as Sam had taught him, before Sam even spoke. But this time it was no deer, no ringing chorus of dogs running strong on a free scent, but a moiling yapping an octave too high, with something more than indecision and even abjectness in it, not even moving very fast, taking a long time to pass completely out of hearing, leaving even then somewhere in the air that echo, thin, slightly hysterical, abject, almost grieving, with no sense of a fleeing, unseen, smoke-colored, grass-eating shape ahead of it, and Sam who had taught him first of all to cock the gun and take position where he could see everywhere and then never move again, had himself moved up beside him; he could hear Sam breathing at his shoulder and he could see the arched curve of the old man's inhaling nostrils.

"Hah," Sam said. "Not even running. Walking."

"Old Ben!" the boy said. "But up here!" he cried. "Way up here!"

"He do it every year," Sam said. "Once. Maybe to see who in camp this time, if he can shoot or not. Whether we got the dog yet that can bay and hold him. He'll take them to the river, then he'll send them back home. We may as well go back, too; see how they look when they come back to camp."

When they reached the camp the hounds were already there, ten of them crouching back under the kitchen, the boy and Sam squatting to peer back into the obscurity where they huddled, quiet, the eyes luminous, glowing at them and vanishing, and no sound, only that effluvium of something more than dog, stronger than dog and not just animal, just beast, because still there had been nothing in front of that abject and almost painful yapping save the solitude, the wilderness, so that when the eleventh hound came in at noon and with all the others watching—even old Uncle Ash, who called himself first a cook—Sam daubed the tattered ear and the raked shoulder with turpentine and axle grease, to the boy it was still no living creature, but the wilderness which, leaning for the moment down, had patted lightly once the hound's temerity.

"Just like a man," Sam said. "Just like folks. Put off as long as she could having to be brave, knowing all the time that sooner or later she would have to be brave once to keep on living with herself, and knowing all the time beforehand what was going to happen to her when she done it."

That afternoon, himself on the one-eyed wagon mule which did not mind the smell of blood nor, as they told him, of bear, and with Sam on the other one, they rode for more than three hours through the rapid, shortening winter day. They followed no path, no trail even that he could see; almost at once they were in a country which he had never seen before. Then he knew why Sam had made him ride the mule which would not spook. The sound one stopped short and tried to whirl and bolt even as Sam got down, blowing its breath, jerking and wrenching at the rein while Sam held it, coaxing it forward with his voice, since he could not risk tying it, drawing it forward while the boy got down from the marred one.

Then, standing beside Sam in the gloom of the dying afternoon, he looked down at the rotted overturned log, gutted and scored with claw marks and, in the wet earth beside it, the print of the enormous warped two-toed foot. He knew now what he had smelled when he peered under the kitchen where the dogs huddled. He realized for the first time that the bear which had run in his listening and loomed in his dreams since before he could remember to the contrary, and which, therefore, must have existed in the listening and dreams of his father and Major de Spain and even old General Compson, too, before they began to remember in their turn, was a mortal animal, and that if they had departed for the camp each November without any actual hope of bringing its trophy back, it was not because it could not be slain, but because so far they had no actual hope to.

"Tomorrow," he said.

"We'll try tomorrow," Sam said. "We ain't got the dog yet."

"We've got eleven. They ran him this morning."

"It won't need but one," Sam said. "He ain't here. Maybe he ain't nowhere. The only other way will be for him to run by accident over somebody that has a gun."

"That wouldn't be me," the boy said. "It will be Walter or Major or—"

"It might," Sam said. "You watch close in the morning. Because he's smart. That's how come he has lived this long. If he gets hemmed up and has to pick out somebody to run over, he will pick out you."

"How?" the boy said. "How will he know—" He ceased. "You mean he already knows me, that I ain't never been here before, ain't had time to find out yet whether I—" He ceased again, looking at Sam, the old man whose face revealed nothing until it smiled. He said humbly, not even amazed. "It was me he was watching. I don't reckon he did need to come but once."

The next morning they left the camp three hours before daylight. They rode this time because it was too far to walk, even the dogs in the wagon; again the first gray light found him in a place which he had never seen before, where Sam had placed him and told him to stay and then departed. With the gun which was too big for him, which did not even belong to him, but to Major de Spain, and which he had fired only once — at a stump on the first day, to learn the recoil and how to reload it — he stood against a gum tree beside a little bayou whose black still water crept without movement out of a canebrake and crossed a small clearing and into cane again, where, invisible, a bird — the big woodpecker called Lord-to-God by Negroes — clattered at a dead limb.

It was a stand like any other, dissimilar only in incidentals to the one where he had stood each morning for ten days; a territory new to him, yet no less familiar than that other one which, after almost two weeks, he had come to believe he knew a little — the same solitude, the same loneliness through which human beings had merely passed without altering it, leaving no mark, no scar, which looked exactly as it must have looked when the first ancestor of Sam Fathers' Chickasaw predecessors crept into it and looked about, club or stone ax or bone arrow drawn and poised; different only because, squatting at the edge of the kitchen, he smelled the hounds huddled and cringing beneath it and saw the raked ear and shoulder of the one who, Sam said, had had to be brave once in order to live with herself, and saw yesterday in the earth beside the gutted log the print of the living foot.

He heard no dogs at all. He never did hear them. He only heard the drumming of the woodpecker stop short off and knew that the bear was looking at him. He never saw it. He did not know whether it was in front of him or behind him. He did not move, holding the useless gun, which he had not even had warning to cock and which even now he did not cock, tasting in his saliva that taint as of brass which he knew now because he had smelled it when he peered under the kitchen at the huddled dogs.

Then it was gone. As abruptly as it had ceased, the woodpecker's dry, monotonous clatter set up again, and after a while he even believed he could hear the dogs — a murmur, scarce a sound even, which he had probably been hearing for some time before he even remarked it, drifting into hearing and then out again, dying away. They came nowhere near him. If it was a bear they ran, it was another bear. It was Sam himself who came out of the cane and crossed the bayou, followed by the injured bitch of yesterday. She was almost at heel, like a bird dog,

making no sound. She came and crouched against his leg, trembling, staring off into the cane.

"I didn't see him," he said. "I didn't, Sam!"

"I know it," Sam said. "He done the looking. You didn't hear him neither, did you?"

"No," the boy said. "I—"

"He's smart," Sam said. "Too smart." He looked down at the hound, trembling faintly and steadily against the boy's knee. From the raked shoulder a few drops of fresh blood oozed and clung. "Too big. We ain't got the dog yet. But maybe someday. Maybe not next time. But someday."

So I must see him, he thought. *I must look at him.* Otherwise, it seemed to him that it would go on like this forever, as it had gone on with his father and Major de Spain, who was older than his father, and even with old General Compson, who had been old enough to be a brigade commander in 1865. Otherwise, it would go on so forever, next time and next time, after and after and after. It seemed to him that he could see the two of them, himself and the bear, shadowy in the limbo from which time emerged, becoming time; the old bear absolved of mortality and himself partaking, sharing a little of it, enough of it. And he knew now what he had smelled in the huddled dogs and tasted in his saliva. He recognized fear. *So I will have to see him,* he thought, without dread or even hope. *I will have to look at him.*

It was in June of the next year. He was eleven. They were in camp again, celebrating Major de Spain's and General Compson's birthdays. Although the one had been born in September and the other in the depth of winter and in another decade, they had met for two weeks to fish and shoot squirrels and turkey and run coons and wildcats with the dogs at night. That is, he and Boon Hoggenbeck and the Negroes fished and shot squirrels and ran the coons and cats, because the proved hunters, not only Major de Spain and old General Compson, who spent those two weeks sitting in a rocking chair before a tremendous iron pot of Brunswick stew, stirring and tasting, with old Ash to quarrel with about how he was making it and Tennie's Jim to pour whisky from the demijohn into the tin dipper from which he drank it, but even the boy's father and Walter Ewell, who were still young enough, scorned such, other than shooting the wild gobblers with pistols for wagers on their marksmanship.

Or, that is, his father and the others believed he was hunting squirrels. Until the third day he thought that Sam Fathers believed that too. Each morning he would leave the camp right after breakfast. He had his own gun now, a Christmas present. He went back to the tree beside the little bayou where he had stood that morning. Using the compass which old General Compson had given him, he ranged from that point; he was teaching himself to be a better-than-fair woodsman without knowing he was doing it. On the second day he even found the gutted log where he had first seen the crooked print. It was almost completely crumbled now, healing with unbelievable speed, a passionate and almost visible relinquishment, back into the earth from which the tree had grown.

He ranged the summer woods now, green with gloom; if anything, actually dimmer than in November's gray dissolution, where, even at noon, the sun fell only in intermittent dappling upon the earth, which never completely dried out and which crawled with snakes—moccasins and water snakes and rattlers, themselves the color of the dappled gloom, so that he would not always see them until they moved, returning later and later, first day, second day, passing in the twilight of the third evening the little log pen enclosing the log stable where Sam was putting up the horses for the night.

"You ain't looked right yet," Sam said.

He stopped. For a moment he didn't answer. Then he said peacefully, in a peaceful rushing burst as when a boy's miniature dam in a little brook gives way, "All right. But how? I went to the bayou. I even found that log again. I—"

"I reckon that was all right. Likely he's been watching you. You never saw his foot?"

"I," the boy said—"I didn't—I never thought—"

"It's the gun," Sam said. He stood beside the fence, motionless—the old man, the Indian, in the battered faded overalls and the frayed five-cent straw hat which in the Negro's race had been the badge of his enslavement and was now the regalia of his freedom. The camp—the clearing, the house, the barn and its tiny lot with which Major de Spain in his turn had scratched punily and evanescently at the wilderness—faded in the dusk, back into the immemorial darkness of the woods. *The gun*, the boy thought. *The gun.*

"Be scared," Sam said. "You can't help that. But don't be afraid. Ain't nothing in the woods going to hurt you unless you corner it, or it smells that you are afraid. A bear or a deer, too, has got to be scared of a coward the same as a brave man has got to be."

The gun, the boy thought.

"You will have to choose," Sam said.

He left the camp before daylight, long before Uncle Ash would wake in his quilts on the kitchen floor and start the fire for breakfast. He had only the compass and a stick for snakes. He could go almost a mile before he would begin to need the compass. He sat on a log, the invisible compass in his invisible hand, while the secret night sounds, fallen still at his movements, scurried again and then ceased for good, and the owls ceased and gave over to the waking of day birds, and he could see the compass. Then he went fast yet still quietly; he was becoming better and better as a woodsman, still without having yet realized it.

He jumped a doe and a fawn at sunrise, walked them out of the bed, close enough to see them—the crash of undergrowth, the white scut, the fawn scudding behind her faster than he had believed it could run. He was hunting right, upwind, as Sam had taught him; not that it mattered now. He had left the gun; of his own will and relinquishment he had accepted not a gambit, not a choice, but a condition in which not only the bear's heretofore inviolable anonymity but all the old rules and balances of hunter and hunted had been abrogated. He would not even be afraid, not even in the moment when the fear would take him completely—blood, skin, bowels, bones, memory from the long time before it became his memory—all save that thin, clear, quenchless, immortal lucidity which alone differed him from this bear and from all the other bear and deer he would ever kill in the humility and pride of his skill and endurance, to which Sam had spoken when he leaned in the twilight on the lot fence yesterday.

By noon he was far beyond the little bayou, farther into the new and alien country than he had ever been. He was traveling now not only by the compass but by the old, heavy, biscuit-thick silver watch which had belonged to his grandfather. When he stopped at last, it was for the first time since he had risen from the log at dawn when he could see the compass. It was far enough. He had left the camp nine hours ago; nine hours from now, dark would have already been an hour old. But he didn't think that. He thought, *All right. Yes. But what?* and stood for a moment, alien and small in the green and topless solitude, answering his own question before it had formed and ceased. It was the watch, the compass, the stick—the three lifeless mechanicals with which for nine hours he had fended the wilderness off; he hung the watch and compass carefully on a bush and leaned the stick beside them and relinquished completely to it.

He had not been going very fast for the last two or three hours. He went no faster now, since distance would not matter even if he could have gone fast. And he was trying to keep a bearing on the tree where he had left the compass, trying to complete a circle which would bring him back to it or at least intersect itself, since direction would not matter now either. But the tree was not there, and he did as Sam schooled him — made the next circle in the opposite direction, so that the two patterns would bisect somewhere, but crossing no print of his own feet, finding the tree at last, but in the wrong place — no bush, no compass, no watch — and the tree not even the tree, because there was a down log beside it and he did what Sam Fathers had told him was the next thing and the last.

As he sat down on the log he saw the crooked print — the warped, tremendous, two-toed indentation which, even as he watched it, filled with water. As he looked up, the wilderness coalesced, solidified — the glade, the tree he sought, the bush, the watch and the compass glinting where a ray of sunlight touched them. Then he saw the bear. It did not emerge, appear; it was just there, immobile, solid, fixed in the hot dappling of the green and windless noon, not as big as he had dreamed it, but as big as he had expected it, bigger, dimensionless against the dappled obscurity, looking at him where he sat quietly on the log and looked back at it.

Then it moved. It made no sound. It did not hurry. It crossed the glade, walking for an instant into the full glare of the sun; when it reached the other side it stopped again and looked back at him across one shoulder while his quiet breathing inhaled and exhaled three times.

Then it was gone. It didn't walk into the woods, the undergrowth. It faded, sank back into the wilderness as he had watched a fish, a huge old bass, sink and vanish back into the dark depths of its pool without even any movement of its fins.

He thought, *It will be next fall.* But it was not next fall, nor the next nor the next. He was fourteen then. He had killed his buck, and Sam Fathers had marked his face with the hot blood, and in the next year he killed a bear. But even before that accolade he had become as competent in the woods as many grown men with the same experience; by his fourteenth year he was a better woodsman than most grown men with more. There was no territory within thirty miles of the camp that he did not know—bayou, ridge, brake, landmark tree and path. He could have led anyone to any point in it without deviation, and brought them out again. He knew game trails that even Sam Fathers did not know; in his thirteenth year he found a buck's bedding place, and unbeknown to his father he borrowed Walter Ewell's rifle and lay in wait at dawn and killed the buck when it walked back to the bed, as Sam had told him how the old Chickasaw fathers did.

But not the old bear, although by now he knew its footprint better than he did his own, and not only the crooked one. He could see any one of the three sound ones and distinguish it from any other, and not only by its size. There were other bears within those thirty miles which left tracks almost as large, but this was more than that. If Sam Fathers had been his mentor and the back-yard rabbits and squirrels at home his kindergarten, then the wilderness the old bear ran was his college, the old male bear itself, so long unwifed and childless as to have become its own ungendered progenitor, was his alma mater. But he never saw it.

He could find the crooked print now almost whenever he liked, fifteen or ten or five miles, or sometimes nearer the camp than that. Twice while on stand during the three years he heard the dogs strike its trail by accident; on the second time they jumped it seemingly, the voices high, abject, almost human in hysteria, as on that first morning two years ago. But not the bear itself. He would remember that noon three years ago, the glade, himself and the bear fixed during that moment in the windless and dappled blaze, and it would seem to him that it had never happened, that he had dreamed that too. But it had happened. They had looked at each other, they had emerged from the wilderness old as earth, synchronized to that instant by something more than the blood that moved the flesh and bones which bore them, and touched, pledged something, affirmed something more lasting than the frail web of bones and flesh which any accident could obliterate.

Then he saw it again. Because of the very fact that he thought of nothing else, he had forgotten to look for it. He was still-hunting with Walter Ewell's rifle. He saw it cross the end of a long blow-down, a corridor where a tornado had swept, rushing through rather than over the tangle of trunks and branches as a locomotive would have, faster than he had ever believed it could move, almost as fast as a deer even, because a deer would have spent most of that time in the air, faster than he could bring the rifle sights up to it, so that he believed the reason he never let off the shot was that he was still behind it, had never caught up with it. And now he knew what had been wrong during all the three years. He sat on a log, shaking and trembling as if he had never seen the woods before nor anything that ran them, wondering with incredulous amazement how he could have forgotten the very thing which Sam Fathers had told him and which the bear itself had proved the next day and had now returned after three years to reaffirm.

And he now knew what Sam Fathers had meant about the right dog, a dog in which size would mean less than nothing. So when he returned alone in April—school was out then, so that the sons of farmers could help with the land's planting, and at last his father had granted him permission, on his promise to be back in four days—he had the dog. It was his own, a mongrel of the sort called by Negroes a fyce, a ratter, itself not much bigger than a rat and possessing that bravery which had long since stopped being courage and had become foolhardiness.

It did not take four days. Alone again, he found the trail on the first morning. It was not a stalk; it was an ambush. He timed the meeting almost as if it were an appointment with a human being. Himself holding the fyce muffled in a feed sack and Sam Fathers with two of the hounds on a piece of plowline rope, they lay down wind of the trail at dawn of the second morning. They were so close that the bear turned without even running, as if in surprised amazement at the shrill and frantic uproar of the released fyce, turning at bay against the trunk of a tree, on its hind feet; it seemed to the boy that it would never stop rising, taller and taller, and even the two hounds seemed to take a sort of desperate and despairing courage from the fyce, following it as it went in.

Then he realized that the fyce was actually not going to stop. He flung, threw the gun away, and ran; when he overtook and grasped the frantically pinwheeling little dog, it seemed to him that he was directly under the bear.

He could smell it, strong and hot and rank. Sprawling, he looked up to where it loomed and towered over him like a cloudburst and colored like a thunderclap, quite familiar, peacefully and even lucidly familiar, until he remembered: This was the way he had used to dream about it. Then it was gone. He didn't see it go. He knelt, holding the frantic fyce with both hands, hearing the abased wailing of the hounds drawing farther and farther away, until Sam came up. He carried the gun. He laid it down quietly beside the boy and stood looking down at him.

"You've done seed him twice now with a gun in your hands," he said. "This time you couldn't have missed him."

The boy rose. He still held the fyce. Even in his arms and clear of the ground, it yapped frantically, straining and surging after the fading uproar of the two hounds like a tangle of wire springs. He was panting a little, but he was neither shaking nor trembling now.

"Neither could you!" he said. "You had the gun! Neither did you!"

"And you didn't shoot," his father said. "How close were you?"

"I don't know, sir," he said. "There was a big wood tick inside his right hind leg. I saw that. But I didn't have the gun then."

"But you didn't shoot when you had the gun," his father said. "Why?"

But he didn't answer, and his father didn't wait for him to, rising and crossing the room, across the pelt of the bear which the boy had killed two years ago and the larger one which his father had killed before he was born, to the bookcase beneath the mounted head of the boy's first buck. It was the room which his father called the office, from which all the plantation business was transacted; in it for the fourteen years of his life he had heard the best of all talking. Major de Spain would be there and sometimes old General Compson, and Walter Ewell and Boon Hoggenbeck and Sam Fathers and Tennie's Jim, too, because they, too, were hunters, knew the woods and what ran them.

He would hear it, not talking himself but listening—the wilderness, the big woods, bigger and older than any recorded document of white man fatuous enough to believe he had bought any fragment of it or Indian ruthless enough to pretend that any fragment of it had been his to convey. It was of the men, not white nor black nor red, but men, hunters with the will and hardihood to endure and the humility and skill to survive, and the dogs and the bear and deer juxtaposed and reliefed against it, ordered and compelled by and within the wilderness in the ancient and unremitting contest by the ancient and immitigable rules which voided all regrets and brooked no quarter, the voices quiet and weighty and deliberate for retrospection and recollection and exact remembering, while he squatted in the blazing firelight as Tennie's Jim squatted, who stirred only to put more wood on the fire and to pass the bottle from one glass to another. Because the bottle was always present, so that after a while it seemed to him that those fierce instants of heart and brain and courage and wiliness and speed were concentrated and distilled into that brown liquor which not women, not boys and children, but only hunters drank, drinking not of the blood they had spilled but some condensation of the wild immortal spirit, drinking it moderately, humbly even, not with the pagan's base hope of acquiring thereby the virtues of cunning and strength and speed, but in salute to them.

His father returned with the book and sat down again and opened it. "Listen," he said. He read the five stanzas aloud, his voice quiet and deliberate in the room where there was no fire now because it was already spring. Then he looked up. The boy watched him. "All right," his father said. "Listen." He read again, but only the second stanza this time, to the end of it, the last two lines, and closed the book and put it on the table beside him. " 'She cannot fade, though thou has not thy bliss, for ever wilt thou love, and she be fair,' " he said.

"He's talking about a girl," the boy said.

"He had to talk about something," his father said. Then he said, "He was talking about truth. Truth doesn't change. Truth is one thing. It covers all things which touch the heart—honor and pride and pity and justice and courage and love. Do you see now?"

He didn't know. Somehow it was simpler than that. There was an old bear, fierce and ruthless, not merely just to stay alive, but with the fierce pride of liberty and freedom, proud enough of that liberty and freedom to see it threatened without fear or even alarm; nay, who at times even seemed deliberately to put that freedom and liberty in jeopardy in order to savor them, to remind his old strong bones and flesh to keep supple and quick to defend and preserve them. There was an old man, son of a Negro slave and an Indian king, inheritor on the one side of the long chronicle of a people who had learned humility through suffering, and pride through the endurance which survived the suffering and injustice, and on the other side, the chronicle of a people even longer in the land than the first, yet who no longer existed in the land at all save in the solitary brotherhood of an old Negro's alien blood and the wild and invincible spirit of an old bear. There was a boy who wished to learn humility and pride in order to become skillful and worthy in the woods, who suddenly found himself becoming so skillful so rapidly that he feared he would never become worthy because he had not learned humility and pride, although he had tried to, until one day and as suddenly he discovered that an old man who could not have defined either had led him, as though by the hand, to that point where an old bear and a little mongrel dog showed him that, by possessing one thing other, he would possess them both.

And a little dog, nameless and mongrel and many-fathered, grown, yet weighing less than six pounds, saying as if to itself, "I can't be dangerous, because there's nothing much smaller than I am; I can't be fierce, because they would call it just noise; I can't be humble, because I'm already too close to the ground to genuflect; I can't be proud, because I wouldn't be near enough to it for anyone to know who was casting that shadow, and I don't even know that I'm not going to heaven, because they have already decided that I don't possess an immortal soul. So all I can be is brave. But it's all right. I can be that, even if they still call it just noise."

That was all. It was simple, much simpler than somebody talking in a book about a youth and a girl he would never need to grieve over, because he could never approach any nearer her and would never have to get any farther away. He had heard about a bear, and finally got big enough to trail it, and he trailed it four years and at last met it with a gun in his hands and he didn't shoot. Because a little dog—But he could have shot long before the little dog covered the twenty yards to where the bear waited, and Sam Fathers could have shot at any time during that interminable minute while Old Ben stood on his hind feet over them. He stopped. His father was watching him gravely across the spring-rife twilight of the room; when he spoke, his words were as quiet as the twilight, too, not loud, because they did not need to be because they would last, "Courage, and honor, and pride," his father said, "and pity, and love of justice and of liberty. They all touch the heart, and what the heart holds to becomes truth, as far as we know truth. Do you see now?"

Sam, and Old Ben, and Nip, he thought. And himself too. He had been all right too. His father had said so. "Yes, sir," he said.

Some heroes discover their quests, some never do. Some people have heroism forced upon them, some never find out "what must be done." What other characters have we seen, like the hero of this story, who "inherit" their quests?

In a sense, this is a monster-slaying story turned upside down. What happens to the boy because he does *not* slay the bear?

What does this story have in common with "The Street" in unit one? How does each boy change? What does each become?

Is there an Underworld in this story? What is it?

What do the bear, the Questing Beast, and the glimmering girl have in common? The goals of these quests are not ordinary creatures. What do you think they are?

Do you think that a quest may be its own goal? How?

One writer once said that we tell these tales of heroes so that we may all become the heroes of our own lives. How could reading about these heroes affect your own life? What kinds of models of action do such stories provide?

In the first two units of this book, men took quests upon themselves voluntarily. Like the boy in the canoe, they chose to set off in search of "places never dreamed of." Or like Brewster or Icarus, they chose to defy human limitations.

But there is a kind of quest that can demand an even greater courage than these. This is the quest to do something that a man must do, whether he wants to or not. Things happen to some men and women that do not seem to happen to others, and their quest in life becomes finding a way of dealing with the special destinies that have been thrust upon them. In the myth of Heracles, the hero killed the children of his brother Iphicles "unwittingly," when "the madness of the goddess Hera fell upon him." But even though a god indirectly committed this crime, Heracles becomes responsible for it, and the rest of his life must consist of a search for a way to lift its curse from his shoulders. The degree of responsibility, courage, and endurance such a quest demands is testified to by the long life of labors that he must endure before he has expiated his "crime."

In a more realistic setting, the ricksha puller is cursed with the poverty of his birth, which compels him to become "a marathon runner with life," where "the wishes of the people of the road drive him," and "his own wishes are tossed on the roadside." "The Bear" relates that at age ten, the boy "had already inherited then, without ever having seen it, the tremendous bear." For the next several years of his life he must pursue it like the others, "to keep yearly rendezvous with the bear which they did not even intend to kill." In a lighter vein, King Pellinore has been pursuing the Questing Beast which he calls "the burden of the Pellinores," almost against his will, for seventeen years.

Sometimes such a quest becomes a matter of simple survival. In "A Mother's Tale," the cow tells her offspring "we are brought into this life to be victims; and there is no other way for us, unless we save ourselves." The flyers in "Losses" find themselves in this situation — forced to kill and destroy in order to avoid being killed themselves. Even though war is to them a mad mistake, they must still head deliberately towards death.

Sometimes, however, death must be faced because it is right. This is Antigone's dilemma. She is caught between two laws, and cannot avoid making a choice. Either way she loses something, but she tells Creon, "My death is less of an evil than would be treachery to my brother and cowardice when the time had come to help him."

In most quests of this kind the hero is forced by destiny to endure unusual suffering, injustice, and even death. These stories, therefore, tend to be tragic. Tragedy is a form of literature that places alongside suffering and loss a sense of the dignity and grandeur of the hero's character. In the end, most of these individuals could have run away from the challenge, had they been people with less pride and honor. But they are what they are, and that is part of what makes them heroic. For this kind of quest is ultimately a quest for the possession of one's self. So the mother in "A Mother's Tale" tells her calves that The One Who Came Back "knew what it meant to be himself alone, a creature separate and different from any other, who had never been before and would never be again." Aengus wandered all his life because the girl with the gleaming hair had called his name. And the boy in "The Bear" learns about the little dog that "sooner or later she would have to be brave once to keep on living with herself." If this is "undergoing destiny, voyaging an endless sky," then it is what makes every man both "one with the race" and also "himself alone." "To do what must be done" is to be completely the person you know you are.

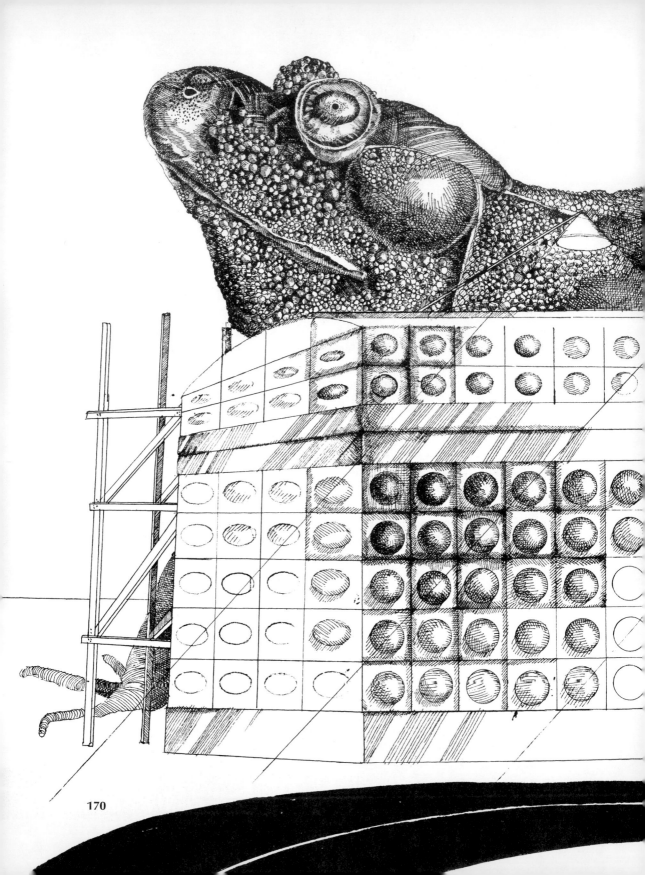

4

THE GOLDEN CUP

Alan E. Cober '73

Jason

A Greek myth
Retold by W. T. JEWKES

In ancient days, the throne of the city of Iolcus was seized from its rightful heir. Aeson, the true successor was forced from the throne by the cruel Pelias. There followed a period of great fear and tension, since Pelias, consulting the oracle about his act, had received this warning:

> The throne you get by force, O king,
> You'll hold by force until one night
> The seed of him whose land it is by right
> Wind-blown from far your death shall bring.

Like all words from the oracle, these were shrouded in enigma, but Pelias knew that they pointed to trouble from the family of Aeson. Accordingly, he began a period of persecution that was to last for a long time.

Because Aeson was his half-brother, Pelias did not dare kill him, but he assassinated as many members of the rightful king's family as he could track down. But vigilant as his spies were, in the course of time they reported that Aeson's wife Polymele had given birth to a boy. The child appeared to have been still-born, however, for a spy had heared the women of the household wailing and lamenting shortly after the birth. Relieved, Pelias returned to the oracle to seek further advice. These were the troubling words he heard:

> Pelias, although it seems you may have found
> Security, and think you've sidestepped Fate,
> Beware the stranger passing through your gate
> Whose single bare heel touches sandy ground.

What the oracle didn't tell Pelias was that the wailing of the women was a trick that Polymele had adopted to put his spy off the trail. As soon as the boy was weaned, Aeson sent him out of Iolcus to Mount Pelion, where the famous schoolmaster Cheiron, the Centaur, was given the responsibility of raising the young prince. There young Jason lived in safety until he had grown to a strong young man.

As the years went by, Pelias began to feel more secure. That is how things stood in Iolcus when one fine spring day young Jason said good-by to Cheiron and set off on foot to return to his native land and claim the throne. He wore a tunic of leather, over which he had flung the mottled skin of a great leopard that he had slain, and in his hand he carried two spears of gleaming bronze. Marching stoutly on his way, he arrived at length at a wide and muddy river. There on the bank he found a wrinkled old woman.

"Young man," she croaked, "your shoulders are broad and your back is straight and strong. And you see that I am old and weak and haven't the strength to get across that swift current. Will you put me on your back and carry me across to the other side?"

Though Jason did not know it, this crone was the goddess Hera in disguise. Hera used this ruse to test the good will of travelers.

"Old mother," said Jason heartily, "climb on my back. I'll have you across in no time, and not even the hem of your garments will become wet."

So Jason, with the goddess on his back, stepped down into the swirling water. For a moment he almost regretted his offer, for no sooner had he put his foot on the bottom of the river than he felt the astonishing weight that he had to bear. It took him much longer to stagger to the other side than he had anticipated, and he lost one of his leather sandals in the strong current. Eventually he struggled up the opposite bank and set the old woman down. Thanking him kindly, she set off in the opposite direction from Jason. Hera had decided not to reveal her identity, but she vowed to keep a friendly eye on the fortunes of the young man who had been so obliging.

Jason stepped out boldly on his way to Iolcus and it was not long before he was walking along the seashore that swept eastward to where the many-walled city of Iolcus stood on the edge of a cliff. A large number of people had gathered at the edge of the sea to perform sacrificial rites to the god Poseidon. Jason marched up to them and demanded to know where he might find Pelias.

"I am Pelias," declared the most richly dressed of the group. "Who are you, and what might your business be with me?"

"My name is Jason and I have come from Mount Pelion." Jason stepped forward. "There the Centaur Cheiron was my foster father. He told me that I am the son of Aeson, and that the throne of Iolcus rightfully belongs to me. So, Uncle, I have come back to claim it from you."

Pelias hardly heard these words, however, for his attention was fixed on the young man's left foot. It was bare and its heel touched the sand. From years back, the strange words of the oracle came to his mind. This man with only one sandal was the one he had been warned about.

The king ignored Jason's demand; rather, he asked, "Can you advise a king? How might you act if an oracle warned you of a threat to your life by a stranger?"

Jason was taken aback by this sudden request, but he tried to think of a difficult task that would remove a threatened assassin.

"Well," he declared, "I would send that man to the distant city of Colchis with instructions to bring back the Golden Fleece that hangs there in the sacred grove."

These words were put into Jason's mouth by the goddess Hera, who had been angered at Pelias for withholding her customary sacrifices. She knew that Jason was the one man who could succeed in a quest that had been impossible for every mortal who attempted it: to gain the fleece of the Golden Ram of Zeus. In the same way, Hera sealed the fate of Pelias by bringing these words into his mouth:

"That is an excellent suggestion," declared Pelias. "But it's for yourself that you have set the task. For," he went on, pointing at Jason's foot, "the oracle warned me against a man who wore only one sandal. That means you, Jason; you are the one who must get the Golden Fleece. If, and when, you bring it back, then I will turn over Iolcus to you."

The journey to Colchis was long and dangerous; so Jason commissioned the famous shipwright Argus to build the largest and strongest ship ever made. The massive craft, named the *Argo,* sat fifty oarsmen, and the goddess Athene herself contributed a great piece of wood for the prow—a bough from a sacred oak tree that had the power of prophecy.

Jason sent a messenger to all the cities of Greece to ask for companions to join him on his great quest. Hera herself sped before the messenger and filled the hearts of some of the greatest heroes in the land with a longing for adventure. From all over they came to join Jason, the noblest warriors in Greece: Castor and Polydeuces, twin sons of Zeus; Peleus, the father of Achilles; Oileus, the father of Ajax; Mopsus, the soothsayer; Orpheus, the harper; Tiphys, the navigator; Calais and Zetes, sons of the North Wind; and even Heracles himself, along with his armor-bearer Hylas. And they called themselves the Argonauts, "sailors of the Argo."

The whole city of Iolcus turned out to bid them farewell. Citizens lined the cliffs and watched as the greatest ship the world had ever known leapt into the bay. Everyone wished the heroes a prosperous voyage and a safe return; everyone, that is, but Pelias, who prayed that they were going to their deaths.

As it grew dark on the first day out, the heroes beached the ship and prepared for their evening meal. Heracles, who had snapped his oar in the mighty effort to launch the ship, went off to find a tree that he could carve into a new oar. His armor-bearer, Hylas, took the great water-pitcher and went into a wood in search of a clear spring for drinking water. Heracles soon found a long, straight fir tree and dragged it down to the ship, but when he got there he found that the boy had not returned. Anxiously he set off once again in the direction of the forest.

But Hylas had vanished. As he had leaned over a pool to fill his pitcher, a nymph had caught sight of the handsome lad. Reaching up her lovely arms from the pool, she had clasped him around the neck and drawn him down into her underwater world. Heracles did not know this, of course, and all that night he ranged through the forest, calling Hylas' name. Even after the first pale streaks of dawn tinted the eastern sky, Heracles still searched on, grieving.

With daylight, however, a favorable breeze and tide urged the Argonauts to reload their gear onto the *Argo,* and they dispatched some of their number to search for Heracles. But there was no trace of him. Unwilling to miss the tide, Jason gave orders to leave Heracles behind.

For some days they sailed safely along the shore of Thrace, toward Salmydessus. At the start of the expedition, Heracles had advised Jason to visit King Phineus who reigned over that cold and wind-swept land. Phineus was blessed with the gift of prophecy, and Heracles had thought that he might be able to give them good advice about the dangerous trip that lay ahead in the Black Sea. Landing safely at Salmydessus, Jason at once presented himself before the king.

"Jason," said Phineus, "everyone wants my advice, but I am the one who must pay for it! For as you can see, the gods are jealous of my gift of prophecy, and out of spite they have blinded me. Worse, I am tormented by two Harpies, monsters with the bodies of women and the wings of hawks. Every time my table is spread and I and my guests sit down to eat, these foul creatures swoop down and steal the food, leaving their vile filth behind. You cannot restore my sight, but if you can rid me of these creatures, I will tell you everything I know about the perils you will encounter, and where you must put ashore to get the Fleece."

So Jason directed Phineus to spread a feast for him and his men in the great banquet hall of the palace. Hardly were they seated when the shrieking Harpies swooped in through the window and dived for the food. At a signal from Jason, however, Calais and Zetes, the winged sons of the North Wind, soared high into the air. Brandishing their swords, they put the Harpies to rapid flight across the waters of the Black Sea, where some say they are to be seen yet.

In gratitude, Phineus showed Jason and his men the course to take through the treacherous Bosphorus, and he predicted what kind of weather they might encounter, where they might meet with hospitality, and what fortunes would befall them as they crossed the Black Sea to Colchis.

The Argonauts reached the entrance to this vast sea without mishap, but there they faced the perils of the Symplegades, twin blue rocks, cloaked in mist, that guarded the entrance to the sea. As ships tried to pass there, the rocks clashed together and crushed vessels and crews. Phineus had warned them about the Symplegades and had told Jason how passage into the sea might be gained. As they approached the dreaded rocks, Jason set free a dove to fly between them. White waves were tossed up as the rocks heaved together, clipping feathers from the tail of the dove. When the thundering rocks began to part and the sea to settle, the Argonauts urged their sleek vessel into the shadow of the great walled passage. The yellow oars bowed like saplings in a gale as the *Argo* leapt through the swirling current and landed safely in the Black Sea.

For many days the Argonauts sailed on around the southern shore of the Black Sea, warily avoiding all the mishaps that Phineus had told them of, until at last they came in sight of the white towers of Colchis. There they beached their travel-scarred ship in an inlet, and on foot

Jason and his companions set off for the palace of Aietes, which stood glistening in the bright sunshine on top of a hill sacred to Aietes' father, the sun-god Helios. Boldly marching through the main gate of the palace, Jason confronted Aietes as the king stood on the steps of the inner court. With him stood his wife and his two daughters, Chalciope and Medea, the witch-priestess.

"Who are you, stranger?" called out Aietes. "It's a bold man who ventures here without my leave."

"I am Jason from Iolcus," replied the young hero courteously, looking straight into the eyes of the angry king. "I have come on a long journey to gain the Golden Fleece and take it to Iolcus, the land that I will rightfully rule."

Aietes cared little about Jason's desires, however, and was enraged at the thought that someone had come to take away the sacred Fleece. But he thought it best to hide his anger.

"It is brave of you to come so far," he said. "But I have sworn to give the Fleece away only if certain terms are met. Come with me." He led Jason to an enclosure at the far side of the court. In the enclosure were two huge brazen bulls, who pawed the ground impatiently. From their mouths flicked long tongues of flame.

"Those bulls were made for me by Hephaestus," went on Aietes. "If you can yoke them, plow with them till sundown in the war-god's field outside the city, and sow in the furrows a crop of dragon's teeth, then I shall give you the Golden Fleece."

When Jason heard Aietes' terms for yielding up the Fleece, his heart sank. The task that the king had set seemed an impossible one, and yet now that he had brought his brave companions on such a long journey, he could not reject the challenge. There was no choice but to accept, but it was a sad man who retraced his way to the ship that evening. Jason did not know that up on Olympus help was being mustered. The goddesses Hera and Aphrodite were consulting about how they could help Jason.

"Medea is the key," declared Hera. "She will know how to use her magic to protect Jason from the bulls. Now how to persuade her to deceive her father; that is the question."

"That won't be as hard as you think," said Aphrodite. "I have influence with Eros. If I give him a pretty present, he will shoot one of his arrows into Medea's breast. There is no cure for one of his love wounds, and once she has been struck, she will do anything for Jason."

So Aphrodite convinced Eros to make his way swiftly down to the palace of Aietes. He found Medea thinking of the handsome stranger who had been so bold with her father that morning. Quickly Eros fitted a love bolt to his bow and shot it straight into the heart of Medea. It was not long before the priestess was inflamed with a desire for Jason.

"I must have him for a husband," she mused. "But first I'll have to arm him against tomorrow."

So she sent her sister Chalciope secretly to Jason at the ship, bidding him come back with her. Quickly Jason donned his cloak and, following Chalciope's lead, he entered the palace by a secret door and soon found himself before Medea. The priestess looked most beautiful, for she had put on a bright saffron robe and her long black hair sparkled with jewels.

"Jason," Medea said, "I can tell you how to succeed tomorrow, but you must agree to my terms."

"Priestess," declared Jason eagerly, "if you can help me to yoke those bulls, I will do anything you wish."

"If I help you, Jason, you must swear by all the gods of Olympus that you will take me back with you to Iolcus and make me your wife."

Though he was startled by Medea's boldness, Jason was willing enough to take the oath. After he had sworn to keep faith with Medea forever, she revealed her strategy.

"You must not go back to the ship tonight, Jason. Instead, when you leave here, you must spend the night at the shrine of the goddess Hecate. It is not a pleasant place by night, and you will hear strange noises, groans and cries and the baying of hounds, and the eerie sighing of the wind. But whatever happens, you must stay there until dawn. Take with you this ointment, and when day dawns smear it over your body. It will protect you from the fiery breath of the bulls. When you sow the dragon's teeth in the furrows, a crop of armed men will spring up. But if you throw a boulder into their midst, they will turn on each other and leave you alone. The rest you must accomplish with your own strength. And if you prevail, remember your promise to me."

So Jason did as Medea had told him. He found the shrine of Hecate in the dark corner of a lonely field. There he dug a pit, killed a sheep, and sacrificed it to Hecate, letting the sheep's blood soak into the ground. All night he saw torches flitting about the hillside and heard the howling of the hounds of Hades. But he stayed in the shrine through it all, and when the first pink streaks of dawn tinted the eastern sky, he poured the ointment over his body and rubbed it in. Then he set off for the bulls' enclosure.

Waiting beside the enclosure with a large crowd of his people was King Aietes, dressed in his bronze armor, with a golden helmet on his head. The king's herdsman, seeing Jason approach, let up the gate of the pen and the great brazen creatures charged out in a cloud of black smoke, with flames of fire shooting from their huge muzzles. Everyone fled in terror, but Jason stood his ground. The magic lotion protected him from the great heat, and with his shield he warded off the horns until he got the advantage of the first bull. Grasping it firmly by the horns, he forced it to its knees. It was soon followed by the other, and then, holding them both down with one hand, with the other he slipped over their necks the unbreakable yoke. Then he let them up, and as they plunged and reared like ships in a storm, he drove them to the fields. All that day Jason plowed the field, and into the furrows he cast the dragon's teeth.

By late afternoon, the harvest had begun to spring up: first the gleam of helmets broke through the soil, then whole bodies of armed men sprouted and faced Jason. Remembering Medea's advice, he quickly seized a great boulder from the edge of the field and threw it in among the warriors. At once they turned fiercely on one another, slashing and cutting with their swords, until a din like thunder shook the field. In and out Jason ran among the warriors, tripping them up, giving a blow here and a slash there to keep the fight stirred up. By nightfall the furrows of the field were soaked in blood as the last warrior fell dead. Wearily, Jason dragged his blood-soaked body back to the ship. Meanwhile, Aietes, who had quit the field when he saw that Jason would fulfill his task, sat moodily at his supper.

Well did Medea know the mood her father was in. Putting on a dark cloak and a heavy veil, the priestess took a last look at her home; then, accompanied only by her maids and by her young brother Absyrtus, she swiftly sneaked past the palace guards and ran toward the *Argo*. The lookouts brought her before their leader.

"Jason," she cried, "there is no time yet to rest. My father is plotting to massacre all of you. You must get away before dawn."

"Not before I have the Fleece," insisted Jason.

"I will have to guide you to where it hangs, and I must deal with the dragon that guards it. Come! There is little time!"

Swiftly and silently, Jason and a party of his men followed Medea some six miles inland to where the Fleece was hung in a grove sacred to the war-god Ares. In front of the tree on which it hung loomed the huge shape of the dragon. Singing softly and sweetly, Medea approached the great beast as it lay there hissing and weaving its huge head from side to side. When she had hypnotized the dragon, she sprinkled a sleeping potion on its eyelids. In great haste, Jason seized the Fleece from the tree, and while the dragon still lay drugged, the party sped off for their ship. During the time they had been away, the ship had been prepared for a speedy departure, and as soon as all the Argonauts had scrambled aboard, they turned to the dawn-light and pushed off. Jason stood in the stern clutching the Golden Fleece, and Medea was at his side.

But meanwhile, one of Medea's women had discovered the absence of her mistress. Quickly she gave the alarm, and by the time that the *Argo* was starting down the river toward the sea, Aietes knew what had happened.

"O Zeus, father of gods!" he cried, raising his hands to the skies. "Help me take revenge on this wicked guest who has stolen my daughter and the Fleece. And you," he yelled, turning on his trembling courtiers, "send men to the ships at once! If they return without Medea and the Fleece, you all lose your lives."

Aietes had a fleet of light boats, and urged on by the angry king's threats, his sailors soon were within sight of the massive *Argo*. Then Medea turned to her young brother Absyrtus. Without a moment's hesitation she seized a sword, and before the stunned gaze of Jason, she cut off the boy's head and threw it into the *Argo's* wake. Then, still working skillfully and intently, she carved the headless trunk into small pieces and scattered them also into the wake of the ship. Medea had found the only means of avoiding capture. The lookout on the lead Colchian ship spied the head of the king's son floating by, and the captain knew he must stop to retrieve it for sacred burial. In moments the whole fleet was stalled, busy picking up the bloody fragments of Absyrtus that swirled by them. By the time they had retrieved them all, the *Argo* was out of sight.

But a price would be paid for Medea's unholy act. Trouble began before the Argonauts had even left the Black Sea. Near the mouth of the Danube river, a wild storm stirred the waves so that the ship could barely resist the current. The skies grew black as pitch, and the thunder and lightning were so terrifying that the men scarcely had courage to keep to their oars. They had tossed about this way for some hours and were near exhaustion, when the thunder suddenly died down, the lightning trailed off to a few quick flashes, and a great eerie calm settled over the water. Then, out of the gloom the Argonauts heard a strange human sound issue from the oaken prow of the ship. With a booming hollow note, it told them that Zeus was dreadfully offended by Medea's crime.

"This foul ship shall go no farther," said the oaken prow. "I will not carry those stained with the blood of slaughtered kin until they have been purified of their deed. Jason and Medea must leave the ship and make their way to the home of the enchantress Circe, who alone has the power to cleanse them of their crime."

Circe was Medea's aunt and her island lay at the mouth of the Tiber River off the western coast of Italy. It would be a long and weary journey by land. That same afternoon Jason and Medea left the *Argo* at the mouth of the Danube. There the couple found a small boat, and for many months they made their laborious way up the great inland rivers until at last they arrived at Circe's island.

There Jason and Medea were led to the enchantress on her golden throne. At once Circe recognized her niece, for those of the race of Helios are known by the golden gleam that shines from their eyes.

"You come in a troubled hour, Medea," said Circe, as she came forward to embrace her niece. "Last night I had a terrible dream in which the walls and chambers of this palace seemed to run with blood. Such a dream portends evil near at hand. Nevertheless, you are welcome, and this strong man who comes with you."

But Jason and Medea remained on their knees as suppliants before the queen-enchantress. It was Jason who finally spoke.

"Queen Circe," he said, "your dream was indeed a portent of trouble—for we bring a curse with us." Drawing from his belt the sword still red with Absyrtus's blood, he continued: "With this sword Medea slew her brother Absyrtus in order to put her angry father off our track. For this deed Zeus has condemned us to cross many painful miles to your island, for only by you may we be cleansed of the blood."

"For such a deed I should have you slain," responded Circe. "But since Medea is my kinswoman, and Zeus has chosen me to purify her, you may stay until I have offered sacrifice and burned cakes for atonement. But then you must leave this island at once."

When the rites of purification were done, Jason and Medea went back to the mainland, where they found the *Argo* waiting for them in the estuary of the Tiber.

In fine weather, they sailed on round the tip of Italy, until they came to the island of Scheria, where the kindly Alcinous ruled. But when they put into the harbor, they were dismayed to see several Colchian ships at anchor. Aietes' crew, afraid to go home and face the wrath of their king, had kept up the pursuit. But the Argonauts were out of food and water, and their ship had to be reprovisioned before they could set sail again. Seeing the situation, Medea called Jason and his men to her.

"I know what my countrymen want," she announced bitterly. "They want me, and already they must have laid claim to me before the king of this land. Swear now not to give me up to them, and I will see to it that we get our provisions and depart in safety."

So Jason and his men swore once again to stand by the witch-maiden Medea. Then they disembarked and were well received by the hospitable Alcinous.

"You are welcome to my land," said the king, "and tonight I will entertain you as a king should. But tomorrow I must render judgment on the woman you have with you, for her countrymen have come to me with a request that she be returned to her father."

At the great feast that night, Medea sat next to Alcinous' beautiful wife Arete. So touched was the queen by this strange girl's pleading that before she went to sleep she spoke to her husband.

"Sweet husband," Arete coaxed as she stroked his hair, "do not permit that beautiful girl to be returned to her father. He is enraged, and punishment lies in wait for her if you allow her countrymen to take her back. What she did was for love of Jason, and it would be cruel to punish her for that."

"Ah, Arete," replied Alcinous, "you know it would be easy for me to send the Colchians away; even by force, if need be. But what if Zeus intends her to be returned? Such an action would give offense to the father of the gods, and I would suffer punishment in my turn."

"But if she is married to Jason," insisted his wife, "surely she belongs by right to him, and not to her father."

"That is true," agreed Alcinous. "In the morning I will inquire if she is married to him. If she is, she shall remain with him, and if not, she must go back to Colchis and her father."

When the king drifted off to sleep, Arete sent a messenger to Medea with news of the king's decision. In haste and in darkness, a marriage took place. The Golden Fleece covered the marriage couch, and Orpheus sang songs of love to celebrate the event. In the morning when Alcinous sent to inquire, he found that Jason and Medea were indeed man and wife. The Argonauts were sent on their way with festivities, and a joyful crowd brought wedding gifts to the ship. Jason thus bound himself more surely to Medea, while the Colchians, still afraid to return home, settled in Phaecia.

One evening in autumn, the weather-worn and barnacled ship was beached on the shore near Iolcus. It was a weary group of survivors that disembarked. They had aged greatly since that day they left Iolcus so many years ago. On that day they had sailed off to the sounds of men cheering and women weeping. Now they could walk the streets unknown, unrecognized. Everything seemed to have altered. Taking Medea with him, Jason set off to seek out his father Aeson. You can imagine the joy of the old man as he was reunited with his son, whom he had long since given up for dead. But Jason's joy was mingled with sorrow, for his mother Polymele was dead, and his father was so worn and emaciated with worry and hardship that he looked twice his age. Full of pity at how Pelias' harsh treatment had wasted his father, Jason asked Medea to invoke a magic spell and restore the old man's youth.

That afternoon Medea spent on the hillside searching for potent and rare herbs that she alone knew of, and when darkness had fallen, she brewed these herbs in a cauldron, all the while reciting incantations to Hecate, the dark queen of the underworld. Finally, she made Aeson lie down, and while she drained blood from a vein in his ankle, she infused her brew into a vein in his arm. Almost immediately the old man's flesh filled out and became firm and rosy, and his white hair grew as black again as it had been when Jason was a boy.

It was a cause for great rejoicing, but still a cloud was cast over the joy. For old Pelias still ruled in Iolcos, and although all the Argonauts agreed that he deserved death, they were reluctant to try an assault on the palace with such a small company. But once again Medea offered her services. Once again Jason accepted.

The next morning Medea set off carrying a statue of the goddess Artemis, one of the few possessions she had brought with her from Colchis. She had changed her own appearance to that of a withered old woman, and Pelias' guard, thinking she could do no harm, let her enter. Once inside the court, Medea demanded an audience with Pelias, claiming that she had been sent by Artemis to bring him good luck.

"King Pelias," she declared in a quavery voice, as she was led before the old tyrant, "I have come to give you back your youth, so that you may reign many more years in this beautiful city."

"Old crone," replied Pelias, "don't talk nonsense. Do you think I would let you practice magic on me, just on your word alone?"

"Not on my word alone," replied Medea, smiling at the king and showing her toothless gums. "Have your men fetch me an old ram, the oldest you can find among your flocks."

While Pelias' men were off searching for the old ram, Medea set up a table and on it placed a kettle of boiling water, into which she sprinkled herbs. When the old ram was brought, the men held it for her while she drew a long knife across its throat. Catching its blood in a pitcher, she added it to the steaming mixture in the pot. Then she cut up the ram into small pieces and as she recited her spells in the Colchian tongue, she dropped the pieces of flesh into the pot. At once a healthy young lamb leapt from the cauldron.

"See," she chuckled, "see for yourself the power that Artemis has given me. Will you take advantage of my offer?"

"Amazing!" replied the gaping Pelias. "Indeed I will try you. What must I do?"

"Bring your daughters here, Pelias," cackled the crone. "For it is they who must do to you what I did to the ram, while I prepare the cauldron and pronounce the magic words."

When Pelias' three daughters had been brought to the chamber, and Medea had explained to them what she wanted them to do, one of them refused. But the other two were more gullible. Willingly enough they laid their father down and cut his throat while Medea held a basin for the blood. When the last drop had drained into the basin, Medea poured it into the cauldron. Then, while the two daughters proceeded to cut their sire into small pieces, Medea seized a torch that hung on the wall, left the room, and raced to the palace roof. From the rooftop she waved the torch to and fro, for that was the signal for Jason and his party to storm the palace. By the time they arrived at the gates, the whole palace was in turmoil at the bloody death of King Pelias, and the Argonauts took control without a blow.

With one more murder added to their crimes, Jason and Medea were soon driven out of Iolcus by the populace, who discovered that the foreign priestess had murdered their king. From Iolcus, the couple set sail in the old *Argo* for Corinth, where they were accepted by the kindly king. There they lived for some time in peace.

But Jason grew to hate the woman who had led him into so many terrible crimes, and at last he decided to divorce her in favor of the

young Corinthian princess, the daughter of his host. Medea thought of all she had done out of devotion to Jason, and her heart turned to stone when she learned that he no longer wanted her for his wife. While preparations for the wedding were under way, Media sent her children to the young princess with a wedding gift, a beautiful robe trimmed with pearls. The princess was overjoyed with the gift and she tried it on at once, but before she had time to turn even once before her mirror, the robe began to burn her as fiercely as Heracles' shirt had burned him, and the girl fell dead before her astounded maids. When word of this treacherous act reached him, Jason ran in blind rage to his home. But he was only across the threshold when he saw a terrible sight: there before him lay the bodies of his children, murdered by their mother. There was not a trace of Medea in Corinth; she fled the city in a dragon-borne chariot which Hecate had sent at her command.

From the day that Jason broke faith with Medea, the faith that he had sworn so many times in the name of the gods, he was haunted by ill fortune. Now no one would shelter him, and he spent the last part of his life as a homeless wanderer. One day at sunset he came back to the seashore near Corinth, and there he saw the old hulk of the *Argo*. The storms had battered the ship until only her skeleton remained, and it was now silhouetted against the dying sun. In great weariness and bitterness, he sank down in the shadow of his ship. And in a moment that the Fates had awaited, the rotting hull, decaying as Jason's glory and honor had decayed, collapsed upon him. Jason was dead.

Long afterward, it is said, the hulk of the *Argo* disappeared mysteriously from its resting place. Years later, men saw it reappear in the heavens where Poseidon had set it as a constellation.

It is said that Medea never died, but was taken by the gods to be one of the immortals, to live forever in the Elysian fields.

The quests of heroes often overlap. In what other unit might this story fit? Why?

Why do you think Jason's quest failed?

We have seen women characterized as goddesses, mothers, lovers, and witches. The story of Jason happens to include them all. Classify the women in this myth according to these types.

Ex-Basketball Player

Pearl Avenue runs past the high school lot,
Bends with the trolley tracks, and stops, cut off
Before it has a chance to go two blocks,
At Colonel McComsky Plaza. Berth's Garage
Is on the corner facing west, and there,
Most days, you'll find Flick Webb, who helps Berth out.

Flick stands tall among the idiot pumps—
Five on a side, the old bubble-head style,
Their rubber elbows hanging loose and low.
One's nostrils are two S's, and his eyes
An E and O. And one is squat, without
A head at all—more of a football type.

Once, Flick played for the high school team, the Wizards.
He was good: in fact, the best. In '46,
He bucketed three hundred ninety points,
A county record still. The ball loved Flick.
I saw him rack up thirty-eight or forty
In one home game. His hands were like wild birds.

He never learned a trade; he just sells gas,
Checks oil, and changes flats. Once in a while,
As a gag, he dribbles an inner tube,
But most of us remember anyway.
His hands are fine and nervous on the lug wrench.
It makes no difference to the lug wrench, though.

Off work, he hangs around Mae's Luncheonette.
Grease-gray and kind of coiled, he plays pinball,
Sips lemon cokes, and smokes those thin cigars;
Flick seldom speaks to Mae, just sits and nods
Beyond her face towards the bright applauding tiers
Of Necco Wafers, Nibs, and Juju Beads.

JOHN UPDIKE

What was Flick's "golden cup"? Would you call his quest a success? Why?

Make a scale of action-power and place some of the heroes you know on it. What do the ones at the top have in common? The ones in the middle? At the bottom? Where would you rank Flick?

Success Is Counted Sweetest

Success is counted sweetest
By those who ne'er succeed.
To comprehend a nectar
Requires sorest need.

Not one of all the purple host
Who took the flag to-day
Can tell the definition,
So clear, of victory,

As he, defeated, dying,
On whose forbidden ear
The distant strains of triumph
Break, agonized and clear.

EMILY DICKINSON

What was Jason's definition of success? What was Medea's? Do you think their definition of victory was different from Heracles' or Antigone's?

Do you agree with this poet? What insight accompanies defeat? What did Orpheus learn, or Oisin? Would you be able to believe in a hero who never lost a battle? Would you believe in a hero who never won a battle?

The Princess and
the Tin Box

JAMES THURBER

Once upon a time, in a far country, there lived a king whose daughter was the prettiest princess in the world. Her eyes were like the corn-flower, her hair was sweeter than the hyacinth, and her throat made the swan look dusty.

From the time she was a year old, the princess had been showered with presents. Her nursery looked like Cartier's window. Her toys were all made of gold or platinum or diamonds or emeralds. She was not permitted to have wooden blocks or china dolls or rubber dogs or linen books, because such materials were considered cheap for the daughter of a king.

When she was seven, she was allowed to attend the wedding of her brother and throw real pearls at the bride instead of rice. Only the nightingale, with his lyre of gold, was permitted to sing for the prin-cess. The common blackbird, with his boxwood flute, was kept out of the palace grounds. She walked in silver-and-samite slippers to a sapphire-and-topaz bathroom and slept in an ivory bed inlaid with rubies.

On the day the princess was eighteen, the king sent a royal ambas-sador to the courts of five neighboring kingdoms to announce that he would give his daughter's hand in marriage to the prince who brought her the gift she liked the most.

The first prince to arrive at the palace rode a swift white stallion and laid at the feet of the princess an enormous apple made of solid gold which he had taken from a dragon who had guarded it for a thousand years. It was placed on a long ebony table set up to hold the gifts of the princess's suitors. The second prince, who came on a gray charger, brought her a nightingale made of a thousand diamonds, and it was placed beside the golden apple. The third prince, riding on a black horse, carried a great jewel box made of platinum and sapphires, and it was placed next to the diamond nightingale. The fourth prince, astride a fiery yellow horse, gave the princess a gigantic heart made of rubies and pierced by an emerald arrow. It was placed next to the platinum-and-sapphire jewel box.

Now the fifth prince was the strongest and handsomest of all the five suitors, but he was the son of a poor king whose realm had been overrun by mice and locusts and wizards and mining engineers so that there was nothing much of value left in it. He came plodding up to the palace of the princess on a plow horse and he brought her a small tin box filled with mica and feldspar and hornblende which he had picked up on the way.

The other princes roared with disdainful laughter when they saw the tawdry gift the fifth prince had brought to the princess. But she examined it with great interest and squealed with delight, for all her life she had been glutted with precious stones and priceless metals, but she had never seen tin before or mica or feldspar or hornblende. The tin box was placed next to the ruby heart pierced with an emerald arrow.

"Now," the king said to his daughter, "you must select the gift you like best and marry the prince that brought it."

The princess smiled and walked up to the table and picked up the present she liked the most. It was the platinum-and-sapphire jewel box, the gift of the third prince.

"The way I figure it," she said, "is this. It is a very large and expensive box, and when I am married, I will meet many admirers who will give me precious gems with which to fill it to the top. Therefore, it is the most valuable of all the gifts my suitors have brought me and I like it the best."

The princess married the third prince that very day in the midst of great merriment and high revelry. More than a hundred thousand pearls were thrown at her and she loved it.

Moral: All those who thought the princess was going to select the tin box filled with worthless stones instead of one of the other gifts will kindly stay after class and write one hundred times on the blackboard "I would rather have a hunk of aluminum silicate than a diamond necklace."

This is the quest for gold turned upside down. If it were a real fairytale, what would the princess have had to do to live happily ever after?

Cup of Gold

From the novel by
JOHN STEINBECK

Ten years of fighting and plundering and burning, and he was thirty. His graying hair seemed to coil more closely to his head. Henry Morgan was successful, the most luck-followed freebooter the world had known, and the men of his profession gave him that admiration he had craved. His enemies—and any man of Spain who had money was his enemy—shuddered at the metnion of his name. They had placed him in their fears beside Drake and L'Ollonais.

He had gone out with Grippo in the *Ganymede,* assured that when his guns roared into a Spanish hull, when he stood embattled on a Spanish deck with cries and clash of iron weapons about him, there would come that flaming happiness his heart desired. These things he had experienced, and there was not even content. The nameless craving in him grew and flexed its claws against his heart. He had thought the adulation of the Brotherhood might salve the wound of his desire; that when the pirates saw the results of his planning and marveled at them, he would be pleased and flattered. And this thing happened. The men fairly fawned on him, and he found that he despised them for it and considered them fools to be taken with such simple things.

Henry had grown lonely in his glory. Old Merlin had spoken truth so long ago, for Captain Morgan had come to his success, and he was alone in his success, with no friend anywhere. The craving of his heart must lie crouched within him. All his fears and sorrows and conceits, his failures and little weaknesses, must be concealed. These, his followers, had gathered to the cry of his success; they would leave him at the first small sign of weakness.

While he was engaged in winning plunder, a little rumor had come stealthily across the isthmus, had floated among the islands and stolen aboard the ships. Men caught the whispered name and listened carefully.

"There is a woman in Panama and she is lovely as the sun. They call her the Red Saint in Panama. All men kneel to her." Thus said the whispering. The voice grew and grew until men in the taverns drank to La Santa Roja. Young seamen whispered of her in the dog watch. "There is a woman in the Cup of Gold and all men fall before her as heathen kneel before the sun." They spoke softly of her in the streets of Goaves. No one had seen her; no one could tell the tint of her cheeks or the color of her hair. Yet, in a few years, every man in the wide, wild Main had drunk to the Red Saint, had dreamed of her; many had prayed to La Santa Roja. She became to every man the quest of his heart, bearing the image of some fair young girl left on a European beach to be gloriously colored by the years. And Panama was to every man the nest of his desire. It was a curious thing. In time, no speech among gathered men could end without mention of La Santa Roja. She was become a queer delirium in the minds of the rough pirates, a new virgin for their worship. Many said she was Mary come to live on earth again, and they added her name in their prayers.

Now, when Captain Morgan had taken Puerto Bello, the Governor of Panama was filled with admiration and wonder that such a ragged band of ill-ordered men, and without uniforms, could capture such a city. He sent a messenger asking for a small sample of the weapons which had made this thing possible. Captain Morgan took the runner to a small room that had escaped the general fire.

"Have you seen the woman whom they call the Red Saint in Panama?" he asked.

"I have not seen her, no; but I have heard of her. The young men put only the Blessed Virgin before her in their worship. It is said that she is lovely as the sun."

"What is her name besides La Santa Roja?"

"I do not know. I have only heard that she is lovely as the sun. They tell in Panama that she came from Cordova and has been to Paris. It is said her family is noble. They tell how she rides great horses, sitting astride, in a meadow guarded with a thick hedge. It is said that in her hand a rapier is a living thing, and that she can fence more skillfully than any man. These things she does in secret that no one may see the crime against her modesty."

"Ah, well!" said Captain Morgan, "if she be beautiful enough what need has she of modesty. This modesty is only a kind of beauty patch which is put on when there are visitors—an enthralling gesture. I should like to see her ride. And do you know nothing more of her?"

"Only what they say in the taverns, sir—that she has stolen worship from the Blessed Saints."

Captain Morgan dreamed long in his chair while the runner waited silently. At last Henry shook his head, as though to disengage it of cloying thoughts. He drew a pistol from his belt and gave it to the messenger.

"Take this to Don Juan Perez de Guzman, and say that this is a sample of the weapons we have used in laying Puerto Bello in the dust. But my other weapons are the strong hearts of my followers. I will not send him one of these, but I will bring him a great number. And tell him to keep the pistol for a year, when I myself will come to Panama to receive it from his own hands. Do you understand?"

"I do, sir."

And in a few days the runner came again, bringing the pistol back, and a large square emerald set in a ring.

"My master begs that you accept this stone as a token of his regard. He begs that you do not give yourself the trouble to come to Panama, for then his duty would overwhelm his admiration and force him to hang you to a tree."

"It is a good message," said the captain; "a good, brave message. I should like to meet with Don Juan if only at swords' points. It has been long since any one defied me. And did you learn more of La Santa Roja?"

"Only what they tell in the streets, sir. I inquired closely for your benefit. I was told that in the streets she wears a thick veil that none may see her face. Some think she does this so that the poor men who meet her will not kill themselves for love. That is all I could learn. Have you further messages, sir?"

"Only repeat that I will go to the Cup of Gold within the year."

Through all his life his will had been like an iron weathervane, steadfastly pointing, always, but never long in one direction. The Indies and the sea and pillage and glory all seemed to have failed him. He had touched all things and watched them pale and shrivel at his touch. And he was lonely. His men regarded him with respect and sullen awe. They were afraid of him, and this state did not feed his vanity as once it had.

He wondered if he might not make a friend among his followers, but the time he had dwelt alone in the castle of himself had been so long that this thought filled him with a curious, boyish embarrassment. Who among his followers might be his friend? He considered them, remembering their sullen scowls, their gleaming, avaricious eyes at the division of spoil. He felt nothing but contempt for them.

But there was one whom he had noticed, a young Frenchman who was called Cœur de Gris. Captain Morgan had seen him in action, leaping about the deck like a supple animal while his rapier flicked out in lithe tongues of silver fire. He scorned a cutlass for the long thin blade. And this young man answered his orders with a smile at Captain Morgan. There was respect in his eyes, surely, but no fear, no jealousy, and no suspicion.

"I wonder if this Cœur de Gris would be my friend," mused Henry Morgan. "It is said that he has left a trail of broken hearts from Cuba to Saint Kit's, and somehow, for this, I fear him a little."

Captain Morgan sent for the young man, and when he was come, found difficulty in speaking to him.

"Ah—how are you, Cœur de Gris?"

The young man was overwhelmed by any show of warmth from this captain.

"Why, sir, I am very well. Have you orders for me?"

"Orders? No; I—I thought I would like to talk with you—that is all."

"To talk with me, sir? But to talk of what?"

"Well—How are the many little loves you are reputed to have?" the captain asked in an uneasy effort at joviality.

"Repute is kinder to me than nature, sir."

Henry Morgan plunged to his purpose.

"Listen to me, Cœur de Gris! Can you not imagine that I may need a friend? Can you not think of me as a lonely man? Consider how all my followers are afraid of me. They come for orders, but never to pass a quiet time of day. I know I made this so. It was necessary once, for I had to build up respect before I could command obedience. But now there are times when I should like to be telling my thoughts and talking of something besides war and spoil. For ten years I have ravaged the seas like a silent wolf, and I have no friend anywhere.

"I have chosen you to be my friend; first, because I like you, and second, because you have not a thing on earth you might be thinking I want to steal. Thus you may like me without fear. It is a strange thing how my men suspect me. I have given a strict accounting for every voyage, yet, if I spoke to them as friends, they would beat their brains to discover my plot. And will you be my friend, Cœur de Gris?"

"Why, certainly, I will, my Captain, and had I known of such a thing in your mind, I would have been for long. How may I serve you, sir?"

"Oh, just by talking with me now and then, and by trusting me a little. I have no motive save my loneliness. But you speak and act like a gentleman, Cœur de Gris. May I ask of your family? or do you draw this name about you like a cape, as so many do here on the Main?"

"It is very simple to tell you of my family. It is said that my father was the great Bras de Fer, and who he was no one ever knew. The people gave me my name, remembering his. My mother is one of the free women of Goaves. She was sixteen when I was born. Hers was a very ancient family, but Huguenot in worship. Their holdings were destroyed in the murders of St. Bartholomew. Thus it came about that they were penniless when my mother was born. And she was picked up by the watch in Paris streets one day and sent to Goaves with a shipload of women vagrants. Bras de Fer found her soon afterwards."

"But you say she is a free woman," said Henry Morgan, scandalized at this young man's apparent lack of shame. "Surely she has given up this—this practice, now you are successful on the sea. You are taking home enough for both of you, and more."

"I know I am, but she continues. I do not mention it, for why should I interfere with what she considers a serious work. She is proud of her position, proud that her callers are the best people in the port. And it pleases her that, although she is nearly forty, she can more than compete with the young, unseasoned squabs who come in every year. Why should I change the gentle course of her ways, even if I could? No, she is a dear, lovely woman, and she has been a good mother to me. Her only fault is that she is filled with over-many little scruples. She nags at me when I am at home, and cries so when I leave. She is dreadfully afraid that I may find some woman who may do me harm."

"That is strange, is it not?—considering her life," said Henry Morgan.

"Why is it strange? Must they have a different brain in that ancient profession? No, sir; I assure you that her life is immaculate—prayers thrice a day, and there is no finer house in all Goaves than hers. Why, sir, when last I went there, I took with me a scarf which fell to my lot in the division, a glorious thing of gossamer and gold. She would not have it. It belonged about the neck of some woman who put her faith in the Romish church, she said, and it would not be decent for a good

Huguenot to wear it. Ah! she worries so about me when I am off to sea. She is terribly afraid I may be hurt, but far more afraid of the tainting of my soul. Such is all my knowledge of my family, sir."

Captain Morgan had stepped to a cupboard and brought out some queer little jugs with wine of Peru. There were two necks on each jug, and when the wine was poured out from one, a sweet, whistling sound came from the other.

"I took these from a Spanish ship," he said. "Will you drink with me, Cœur de Gris?"

"I should be very much honored, sir."

They sat a long time sipping the wine, then Captain Morgan spoke dreamily.

"I suppose, Cœur de Gris, that you will one day be stricken with the Red Saint, and then we shall have the bees of Panama buzzing out upon us. I have no doubt she is as jealously guarded as was Helen. You have heard of the Red Saint, have you not?"

The young man's eyes were glowing with the wine.

"Heard of her!" he said softly. "Sir, I have dreamed of her and called to her in my sleep. Who has not? Who in all this quarter of the world has not heard of her, and yet who knows any single thing about her? It is a strange thing, the magic of this woman's name. La Santa Roja! La Santa Roja! It conjures up desire in the heart of every man — not active, possible desire, but the 'if I were handsome, if I were a prince' kind of desire. The young men make wild plans; some to go disguised to Panama, others to blow it up with quantities of powder. They daydream of carrying the Red Saint off with them. Sir, I have heard a seaman all rotten with disease whispering to himself in the night, 'If this thing were not on me, I would go adventuring for La Santa Roja.'

"My mother frets and frets there in Goaves, lest I go mad and run to her. She is terrified by this strange woman. 'Go not near to her, my son,' she says. 'This woman is wicked; she is a devil; besides, she is without doubt a Catholic.' And no one has ever seen her that we know of. We do not know certainly that there exists such a woman as the Red Saint in the Cup of Gold. Ah! She has spread the sea with dreams — with longing dreams. I have been thinking, sir, that perhaps, sometime, the Cup of Gold may go the way of Troy town on account of her."

Henry Morgan had filled the glasses again and again. He was slumped forward in his chair, and a little crooked smile was on his mouth.

"Yes," he said rather thickly, "she is a danger to the peace of nations and to the peace of men's minds. The matter is wholly ridiculous, of course. She is probably a shrewish bitch who takes her bright features from the legend. But how might such a legend be started? Your health, Cœur de Gris. You will be a good friend to me and true?"

"I will, my Captain."

And again they sat silently, drinking the rich wine.

"But there is much suffering bound up in women." Henry Morgan began, as though he had just finished speaking. "They seem to carry pain about with them in a leaking package. You have loved often, they say, Cœur de Gris. Have you not felt the pain they carry?"

"No, sir, I do not think I have. Surely I have been assailed by regrets and little sorrows—everyone has; but mostly I have found only pleasure among women."

"Ah, you are lucky," the captain said. "You are filled with luck not to have know the pain. My own life was poisoned by love. This life I lead was forced on me by lost love."

"Why, how was that, sir? Surely, I had not thought that you—"

"I know; I know how I must have changed so that even you laugh a little at the thought of my being in love. I could not now command the affection of the daughter of an Earl."

"The daughter of an Earl, sir?"

"Yes, an Earl's daughter. We loved too perfectly—too passionately. Once she came to me in a rose garden and lay in my arms until the dark was gone. I thought to run away with her to some new, lovely country, and sink her title in the sea behind us. Perhaps even now I might be living safe in Virginia, with little joys crowding my footstool."

"It is a great pity, sir." Cœur de Gris was truly sorry for this man.

"Ah, well; her father was informed. On one dark night my arms were pinned to my sides, and she—oh, dear Elizabeth!—was torn away from me. They placed me, still bound, in a ship, and sold me in Barbados. Can you not see, Cœur de Gris, the bitterness that lies restlessly in my heart? During these years, her face has followed me in all my wanderings. Somehow I feel that I might have made some later move—but her father was a powerful lord."

"And did you never go back for her, after your imprisonment was done?"

Henry Morgan looked down at the floor.

"No, my friend—I never did."

The legend of the Red Saint grew in his brain like a powerful vine, and a voice came out of the west to coax and mock, to jeer and cozen Henry Morgan. He forgot the sea and his idling ships. The buccaneers were penniless from their long inactivity. They lay about the decks and cursed their captain for a dreaming fool. He struggled madly against the folding meshes of his dream and argued with the voice.

"May God damn La Santa Roja for sowing the world with an insanity. She has made cutthroats bay the moon like lovesick dogs. She is making me crazy with this vain desire. I must do something—anything—to lay the insistent haunting of this woman I have never seen. I must destroy the ghost. Ah, it is a foolish thing to dream of capturing the Cup of Gold. It would seem that my desire is death."

And he remembered the hunger which had drawn him from Cambria, for it was duplicated and strengthened now. His thoughts were driving sleep away. When drowsiness crept in on the heels of exhaustion, La Santa Roja came in, too.

"I will take Maracaibo," he cried in desperation. "I will drown this lusting in a bowl of horror. I will pillage Maracaibo, tear it to pieces, and leave it bleeding in the sand."

(There is a woman in the Cup of Gold, and they worship her for unnamable beauties.)

"Make the gathering at the Isle de la Vaca! Call in true hearts from the corners of the sea! We go to riches!"

His ships flew out to the bay of Maracaibo and the town was frantic in defense.

"Run into this bottle harbor! Yes, under the guns!"

Cannon balls cried through the air and struck up clouds of dirt from the walls, but the defense held ground.

"It will not fall? Then take it in assault!"

Powder pots flew over the walls, tearing and maiming the defenders in their burst.

"Who are these wolves?" they cried. "Ah, brothers! we must fight until we die! We must ask no clemency, brothers. If we fall, our dear city—"

Ladders rose against the fort, and a wave of roaring men swarmed over the walls.

"Ah, San Lorenzo! hide us! bear us away! These are no men, but devils. Hear me! Hear me! Quarter! Ah, Jesus! where art thou now?"

"Throw down the walls! Let no two stones stand together!"

(There is a woman in the Cup of Gold, and she is lovely as the sun.)

"Grant no quarter! Kill the Spanish rats! Kill all of them!"

And Maracaibo lay pleading at his feet. Doors were torn from the houses, and the rooms gutted of every movable thing. They herded the women to a church and locked them in. Then the prisoners were brought to Henry Morgan.

"Here is an old man, sir. We are sure he has riches, but he has hidden them away and we can never find any."

"Then put his feet in the fire—why, he is a brazen fool! Break his arms!—He will not tell? Put the whip-cord about his temples—Oh, kill him! kill him and stop his screaming—Perhaps he had no money—"

(There is a woman in Panama—)

"Have you scratched out every grain of gold? Place the city at ransom! We must have riches after pain."

A fleet of Spanish ships came sailing to the rescue.

"A Spanish squadron coming? We will fight them! No, no; we shall run from them if we can get away. Our hulls lag in the water with their weight of gold. Kill the prisoners!"

(—she is lovely as the sun.)

And Captain Morgan sailed from broken Maracaibo. Two hundred and fifty thousand pieces of eight were in his ships, and rolls of silken stuffs and plates of silver and sacks of spices. There were golden images from the Cathedral, and vestments crusted with embroidery of pearls. And the city was a fire-swept wreck.

"We are richer than we could have hoped. There will be joy in Tortuga when we come. Every man a hero! We shall have a mad riot of a time."

(La Santa Roja is in Panama.)

"Ah, God! then if I must, I must. But I fear I go to my death. It is a dreadful thing to be attempting. If this is my desire, I must, though I die." He called young Cœur de Gris to him.

"You have distinguished yourself in this fight, my friend."

"I have done what was necessary, sir."

"But you fought finely. I saw you when we engaged. Now I have made you my lieutenant in the field, my second in command. You are brave, you are sagacious, and you are my friend. I can trust you, and who among my men will bear this trust if it be worth his while to fail?"

"It is a great honor, sir. I will pay you, surely, with my fidelity. My mother will be very pleased."

"Yes," said Captain Morgan; "you are a young fool, and that is a virtue in this business as long as one has a leader. Now the men are straining to get back that they may spend their money. If it were possible they would be pushing the ships to hurry them. What will you do with your money, Cœur de Gris?"

"Why, I shall send half to my mother. The remaining sum I shall divide in two. Part I shall put away, and on the other I expect to be drunk for a few days, or perhaps a week. It is good to be drunk after fighting."

"Drunkenness has never been a pleasure to me," the captain said. "It makes me very sad. But I have a new venture turning in my brain. Cœur de Gris, what is the richest city of the western world? What place has been immune from the slightest gesture of the Brotherhood? Where might we all make millions?"

"But, sir, you do not think—Surely you cannot consider it possible to take—"

"I will take Panama—even the Cup of Gold."

"How may you do this thing? The city is strongly guarded with walls and troops, and the way across the isthmus is nigh impassable but for the burro trail. How will you do this thing?"

"I must take Panama. I must capture the Cup of Gold." The captain's jaw set fiercely.

Now Cœur de Gris was smiling quietly.

"Why do you grin at me?" demanded Captain Morgan.

"I was thinking of a chance remark I made a little time ago, that Panama was like to go the way of Troy town."

"Ah! this nameless woman is in your mind. Dismiss her! It may be there exists no such woman."

"But then, sir, we are rich enough of this last spoil."

"It would be no evil thing to grow richer. I am tired of plundering. I would rest securely."

Cœue de Gris hesitated a time, while his eyes were covered with a soft veil.

"I am thinking, sir, that when we come to Panama every man will be at his friend's throat over the Red Saint."

"Oh, you may trust me to keep order among my men—strict order— though I hang half of them to do it. A while ago I sent word to Panama that I would go there, but I did it as a joke. And I wonder, now, whether they have been fortifying themselves. Perhaps they, too, thought it a joke. Go, now, Cœur de Gris, and speak to no man of this. I make you my ambassador. Let the men throw their gold away. Encourage gambling — here — now — on the ship. Give them an example at the taverns — an expensive example. Then they will be driven to go out with me. I must have an army this time, my friend, and even then we may all die. Perhaps that is the chief joy of life — to risk it. Do my work well, Cœur de Gris, and it may one day you will be richer than you can think."

Young Cœur de Gris stood musing by the mast.

"Our captain, our cold captain, has been bitten by this great, nebulous rumoring. How strange this pattern is! It is as though the Red Saint had been stolen from my arms. My dream is violated. I wonder, then, when they know, if every man will carry this feeling of a bitter loss — will hate the captain for stealing his desire."

Was Henry Morgan *of* the people, or *above* them? Can there be heroes of both kinds? Name some of each. Why do you think each kind of hero is accepted by his people?

What was "the wound of his desire"? In what other unit do you think this story might fit? Why? What do you think Morgan's quest really was?

"He was alone in his success." Do you think this is true of all heroes? Why?

This story, too, contains a goddess, a mother, a lover, and a witch. Who are they? List the qualities of each. Compare them to the characters in the Jason story. What do they have in common? How are they like other female characters in this book, Lemminkainen's mother, for instance, or Orpheus' Eurydice?

"It would seem that my desire is death." Why does Morgan say this? What other heroes in this book might have felt the same way? What heroes would have said, "My desire is life"?

Remembering the quests of the other characters in this unit, do you think Morgan will find success at the end of his journey? Why?

A Man Saw a Ball of Gold in the Sky

A man saw a ball of gold in the sky.
He climbed for it,
And eventually he achieved it—
It was clay.

Now this is the strange part:
When the man went to earth
And looked again,
Lo, there was the ball of gold.
Now this is the strange part:
It was a ball of gold.
Ay, by the heavens it was a ball of gold.

STEPHEN CRANE

Tell how this poem could be a fitting conclusion to Henry Morgan's quest.

A quest can be based on a dream, a hope, or an illusion. Which is the source of the quests in this unit? How are they different from those in other units?

Up to now most of the quests in this book have been successful. Even though many of the stories have ended in the tragic destruction of the hero, the values he has sought and fought for have been upheld. But what happens when a quest goes wrong? What happens when the desire of the hero is focused on an unworthy object?

In literature there are many stories of failed quests. For a quest may be for a real inheritance, or it may be for an illusion, and it is important for the hero to know the difference. The stories and poems in this unit all follow the pattern of failed quests.

One of the most difficult things a hero must do is choose the right means for his task. Jason has all the qualities that a romance hero should have—noble birth, good education, courage, wisdom, and perseverance. He is a born leader. And yet, to obtain the object of his quest, he allies himself with evil powers. Medea is a witch, as her first advice to Jason demonstrates: he must pray to the goddess of the Underworld, Hecate. Subsequently, to get the Fleece, he must promise to marry Medea. To escape pursuit he must be party to a brutal murder, and then go through with his promise of marriage. To bring back his father's youth, he must consent to a foul butchery. When he finally gains his kingdom, it is only to lose it again because of the means he had employed. And when he tries to break his bond with Medea, the worse horror of all is in store for him, and he ends his life as a homeless wanderer. Everything went wrong for Jason from the moment the object of his quest became more important than the means he used to get it.

The story of Jason's failed quest is tragic because his original goal was a good one. More ironic are stories of men whose quest has been for the wrong thing from the start. Sometimes this may mean not aiming high enough. Flick Webb had his moment of glory early, but unprepared for the most significant quest of all—his own life—he wastes away like the wandering Jason.

Often the wrong goal for a heroic quest is seen as mere material gain. The poem "Success Is Counted Sweetest" suggests that those who win do not often realize the true value of victory. Frequently in literature, the goal of material success is associated with gold—a quest that almost always ends in failure. So it does for Jason, searching for the Golden Fleece. The parody in "The Princess and the Tin Box" implies that, although the Princess acts very worldly wise in choosing the jewelled box, she is not likely to live happily ever after. The "ball of gold" in the sky turns out to be clay when it is possessed. The Cup of Gold and the Red Saint, in quest of which Henry Morgan has laid waste to half the Caribbean, may indeed be just an illusion, and will probably lose Morgan the loyalty of his men.

The ironic or failed quest turns out to be a parody of the successful romantic quest. And it can be taken in three different ways. It may be taken to suggest that the goal of a quest will always be a disappointment when it is obtained, that only the perilous journey itself is worthwhile. Or, it may make a mockery of the whole notion of quest, suggesting that the goal of a quest, the supposed kingdom the hero wishes to regain, is a mere illusion. Or, finally, it may signify that the important thing for a hero is to distinguish between the true dream of his inheritance, and a false illusion that will lead to his failure. Whichever interpretation the imagination chooses, the Golden Cup stands within it as a bright and shining emblem of destruction.

210

5

MIGHT FOR RIGHT

alan E. Cober '73

The Story of Theseus

A Greek myth
Retold by REX WARNER

Not far across the sea from Athens lies the city of Troizen. To this city once came Aegeus, King of Athens, and there he and Aethra, daughter of the King of Troizen, had a child who was called Theseus.

Aegeus returned to Athens but, before leaving, he took his sword with its ivory sheath and put it under a great rock. Then he said to Aethra: "When the boy is strong enough to lift this rock, let him take his father's sword and come to me in Athens."

By the time that Theseus was sixteen, he was not only strong but intelligent and ambitious. When his mother showed him the rock, he easily lifted it up and took from beneath it the sword, still bright and shining in its close-fitting ivory scabbard. His next task was to visit his father in Athens. Instead of going there by sea, which was the safe and easy way, he decided to travel by land. This meant a journey through narrow mountain passes and rough ways, through a country infested with robbers and wild beasts. Not for a long time had anyone from Troizen dared to go this way.

The first part of the road lay along the seashore, and Theseus had not gone far before he met a giant called Periphetes or "Famous," who was the son of Vulcan, the god of fire, and carried a huge iron club with which he would beat out the brains of all travelers who attempted to pass him. Like his father Vulcan, he limped in one foot, but he was immensely strong and quite without mercy. Theseus was well trained in the use of the sword, and, being nimble on his feet, avoided the great swinging blows of the giant's club, thrusting his sword over and over again into his enemy's body. So he slew him and went on his way along the solitary road, carrying with him as a trophy the great club.

The road to Athens went north to the Isthmus of Corinth, where two seas are separated by a narrow strip of land. Near here lived the brigand Sinis, called "the Pine-bender," because, when he seized upon a traveler, he would bend down two pine trees and, after tying their tops to the arms or legs of his miserable victims, would let the trees go, thus tearing limb from limb the men or women who had fallen into his power. This notable robber attempted to overpower Theseus so that he could treat him in the same way as he had treated so many others. But Theseus smote him to the ground half stunned with his club and, bending down two pine trees himself, fastened them to Sinis' own limbs. Then he released the trees, and the criminal met the same death that he had so often inflicted on innocent people. Henceforward the road to the Isthmus from the south was open to all travelers.

Theseus now turned eastward. Ahead of him on his right was the island of Salamis and on his left the two rounded citadels of Megara. Near here, on cliffs that towered above the sea, lived Sciron, another brigand of the most evil fame. First he would plunder travelers and then force them to wash his feet in a bronze bowl. While they were doing this, he would suddenly, from where he sat, kick them over the cliff into the sea. There their bodies were devoured by a large tortoise who for many years had swum around the base of the cliffs, fed continually on human flesh.

Theseus had heard of this cruel murderer, and when he met him in the narrow pathway over the rocks, he pretended to be willing to wash his feet. But, just as Sciron was preparing, with one blow of his foot, to hurl him into the sea, Theseus gripped his foot firmly, swung him round and, grasping him by the shoulder, threw him into the sea himself. Far below he saw the sea turn white as the body fell, and then he saw the back and head of the monstrous tortoise coming to the surface for his last meal of men's flesh.

There was yet another wicked enemy to strangers whom Theseus treated in the same way as he had treated others. This was the strong man Procrustes who wrestled with all travelers and, when he had overcome them, would make them lie down on his bed. If their bodies were too short for the bed, he would rack their arms and legs with weights or hammer them out until they were long enough to fit. If they were too tall to lie on it, he would chop pieces off their limbs until they fitted exactly. At last this cruel robber had met his match. Theseus, after wrestling for long with him, threw him to the ground.

Then he bound him to his own bed and, though here his body was exactly the right length, he cut off his head.

Theseus was now close to Athens and had conquered all the human enemies whom he would meet on his way. What he met with next was a monstrous sow, which for long had terrorized the villagers in the country districts near Athens itself. Some say that this sow had been the mother of the great boar that Meleager killed in Calydon. At all events she was an immense animal, strong and savage, and used to root up the crops with her snout, drag down the vines from their supports and kill and eat young children and defenseless old people. Theseus went out alone to hunt this sow. He avoided the animal's furious charges and each time she swept past him he planted a hunting spear in her back. Finally, with a blow of the club he had taken from Periphetes he killed the sow and enabled the country people to continue unmolested their work in the fields.

Soon afterwards from the top of a hill he saw below him the city of Athens which poets have called "violet crowned," because, as the sun sets, the ring of rocky hills that surround the city turns from shade to shade of violet and amethyst. He drew nearer and came to the great stone walls of the citadel, or Acropolis, where his father's palace stood. Having accomplished such brave deeds on his journey, he was confident that his father Aegeus would receive him kindly.

As it happened, however, he very nearly met his death at his father's hands. The enchantress Medea had fled to Athens after her cruel murder of her own children and of the royal house of Corinth. In Athens Aegeus had protected her, had made use of her magic powers and by her had had a child. Medea, by her enchantments, knew that Theseus was now on his way to Athens. She was jealous of the fame that he had won already and she wished her own son to have the throne of Athens after Aegeus's death. She therefore pretended that she had discovered by her magic arts that the stranger who would shortly arrive in Athens was a criminal who had come to murder the king. She instructed Aegeus to give him, as soon as he arrived and without getting into conversation with him, a cup of wine into which she had put deadly poisons. Aegeus believed her, and, when Theseus arrived and stood before him, he himself handed to his son the poisoned cup. Theseus raised it to his lips and was about to drink when, at the last moment, Aegeus noticed at Theseus's side the ivory scabbard of the sword he had left long ago under the rock in Troizen. He dashed the cup from the young man's lips and folded him in his arms. Then he turned in anger upon Medea who had so nearly made him the murderer of his own son. But Medea, knowing that this time no excuses could save her, had mounted into her winged chariot and disappeared through the air. This was the last of her wicked deeds. Some say that she returned to her country of Colchis and became reconciled with her family, but nothing really certain is known about this.

Even now Theseus and his father were not entirely secure in the land of Athens. First there was the hero Pallas who, with his fifty sons, tried to seize the kingdom from Aegeus. They made a treacherous attack on Theseus, but he, fighting back at them with a small company of friends, killed every one of them.

Then, at the time when Theseus reached Athens, the whole plain to the north, the plain of Marathon, where later the great army of the Persians was destroyed, was ravaged by a great bull. The people of the district had turned in vain to their king for help. No man or body of men dared encounter this fierce tremendous animal. Theseus went out to Marathon alone. He captured the bull alive, bound it with ropes and brought it back to Athens. There, after a triumphant procession through the streets, he sacrificed it to Minerva, the goddess of the city. The joyful throngs of people acclaimed him gladly as their future king and as a hero who had driven from their country and its surroundings both robbers and wild beasts. No one in the world, they said, except Hercules, had done such deeds.

Athens was now safe and peaceful within the borders of her own land, but still every year she had to make a cruel sacrifice to a foreign power. At this time Minos, King of Crete, ruled the sea with his fleet of ships. Once he had made war on Athens because his son, a famous wrestler, had been murdered by the Athenians. He refused to make peace except on the condition that every year the Athenians should send him seven young men and seven girls. These, when they arrived in Crete, were to be put inside the famous labyrinth which the great artist Daedalus had built, and then they were to be devoured by the monstrous creature, half man, half bull, which was known as the Minotaur. The Athenians were forced to accept these conditions. Every year the youths and maidens were chosen by lot, and every year, among the lamentations of the whole people, they set out for Crete in a ship which carried black sails as a sign of mourning.

When Theseus heard of this cruel custom he resolved to be himself one of the seven young men who were handed over to Minos. "Either

I shall save my people," he said, "or I shall die with them. In any case I shall have done what I can."

His old father Aegeus was reluctant to let him go, but Theseus insisted on the plan which he had made. "Go then," said his father, "and may the gods preserve you! When the time comes I shall watch every day for your return. If you are successful and come back alive, change the sails of your ship to white, so that I may know at once what has happened."

Theseus promised to do as his father had asked him. Then he and the other thirteen victims, girls and young men, said farewell to their city, their friends and their relations and embarked in a black ship with black sails which was to take them to Crete.

When they arrived at the great city of King Minos they looked in astonishment at the huge buildings decorated with paintings in all kinds of colors. There were paintings of bullfights, at which the Cretans were particularly expert, of sea creatures, octopuses, dolphins and twining seaweeds. There were other paintings showing the life of the country—pictures of Cretan officers with their hired Negro troops, of priestesses, naked above the waist, with outstretched arms round which coiled sacred serpents. There were high halls and galleries, enormous buildings; and at the seaport thronged the ships of Egypt and of Asia doing trade with the kingdom of Minos.

Theseus and his companions were, according to the custom, entertained for one night at the palace of the king. On the next day they were to be sent into the intricate mazes of the labyrinth. It was known that there was no escape from this place. The most that anyone could hope for was to die of hunger while wandering in the countless passages before meeting the monstrous Minotaur who would devour any human creature whom he met.

Theseus, as he sat at dinner and told King Minos of the exploits which he had already achieved, won not only the attention but also the love of the king's daughter Ariadne. She could not bear the thought that so beautiful and distinguished a young man should perish miserably on the next day and she determined to help him.

When, therefore, the fourteen young Athenians were led to the entrance of the labyrinth, Ariadne took Theseus aside and put into his hands a ball of wool. "Fasten one end of this wool," she said to him, "inside the doors, and, as you go, unwind the rest. Then, if you are successful in killing the monster, you will be able to find your way back again. I shall be waiting for you. In return for helping you I want

you to take me back with you to Greece and make me your wife."

Theseus readily agreed to do as she said. As well as the ball of wool she had brought him a sword, and, hiding this underneath his cloak, he went forward into the labyrinth. The girls and the other young men waited for him inside the gates, while he picked his way along passages which turned and twisted and linked up with other passages, winding in and out, turning abruptly, or sweeping in long or short curves. As he went he unwound the ball of wool and listened carefully for any noise that might tell him of the whereabouts of the strange monster with whom he was to fight. For long he wandered in complete silence and then, as he approached a part of the labyrinth where the walls turned at right angles, he heard the noise of heavy breathing, a noise that might have been made by an animal or might almost have been made by a man. He put down the ball of wool, gripped his sword in his hand, and advanced cautiously to the corner. Looking round it he saw a monstrous shape. Standing, with his head lowered, was the figure of a giant, but, on the massive neck and shoulders was not a human head but the swinging dewlaps, blunt muzzle and huge horns of a bull. For a moment Theseus and the Minotaur gazed at each other. Then, after pawing the ground with his feet, the monster lowered his head and plunged forward. In the narrow passage Theseus had no room to step aside. With his left hand he seized one of the creature's horns and violently threw the head back while he buried his sword in the thick muscles of its neck. With a roar of pain the Minotaur shook his head and fell backwards. Theseus clung to the beast's throat, avoiding the blows of the great horns, and, stabbing with his sword, soon drenched the floors and walls with blood. The struggle was soon over. Theseus left the great body on the ground and, picking up what was left of the ball of wool, he began to rewind it and so retrace his steps to the place where he had left his companions. Seeing him safe, with the blood upon his hands, they knew that he had been victorious and crowded round him to press his hand and congratulate him upon his victory.

But there was no time to lose. Ariadne was waiting for them and she hid them until nightfall. In the dark they reached their ship, hoisted the sails and escaped. Never more would Athens have to pay the abominable tribute to the King of Crete.

On their return voyage they stopped for the night at the island of Naxos. Here some god put into the hearts and minds of Theseus and his companions a strange and cruel forgetfulness. They rose at dawn and sailed away, leaving Ariadne asleep on the seashore. When she woke and saw the ship far away on the horizon and realized that she had been deserted, she wept and tore her hair, calling all the gods to witness how treacherously she had been treated by the man whose life she had saved. Alone and miserable she wandered on the rocky shore, frightened of wild beasts, but grieving most of all for the loss of her lover.

Here, in her terror, misery and loneliness, she was saved by the god Bacchus. Tigers and lynxes drew the chariot in which he rode. Behind him came, riding on a mule, his drunken old companion Silenus, with a band of fauns, satyrs and dancing worshipers waving their ivy wands, their loose hair wreathed in ivy or in myrtle. The sand and rocks of the deserted shore grew green with sprouting vines as the procession passed. Ariadne, too, felt the joy of the god's presence. Bacchus loved her and made her his wife. He took the crown that she wore upon her head and set it in the sky as a constellation among the stars.

Meanwhile Theseus sailed on to Athens. The joy and glory of his return was spoiled by another act of forgetfulness. His father Aegeus had told him that, if he returned safe, he was to change the black sails of the ship and hoist white sails as a sign of victory. This Theseus forgot to do, and when his old father, watching from the cliffs, saw a vessel with black sails coming from the south, believing that his son was dead, he threw himself down into the sea. So the day of Theseus's return was a day not only of triumph but of mourning.

On the death of Aegeus, Theseus became king of Athens and the surrounding country. His government, both in peace and war, was strong and just, and, though at the end of his life the Athenians showed themselves ungrateful to him, long after his death they gave him the honors due to gods and heroes.

During his reign he saved Athens from two great invasions. First the warlike nation of the Amazons swept over the northern passes and reached the walls of Athens itself. The Amazons were women who spent their lives in fighting. Their power extended over much of Asia, and now their great army entered Greece. These women fought on horseback with javelins and bows. They carried shields shaped like the crescent moon. Led by their queen Hippolyte they had already conquered many armies of men, and, at their approach, the country people deserted their fields and farms, flocking into the city of Athens to escape the ferocity of this host of women. Theseus led his army out against them and for a long time the battle swayed this way and that. The arrows of the Amazons darkened the sky; their horses wheeled and charged again and again upon the Athenian infantry. It was not until, coming to close quarters, Theseus himself fought with the queen of the Amazons, dragged her from her horse and made her prisoner, that the ranks of the Amazons broke. Many of both sides lay dead upon the plain, but the Athenians were victorious. The Amazon army withdrew from Greece. Hippolyte, their queen, became the wife of Theseus and, before she died, gave birth to a son who was called Hippolytus, a strong and noble boy who devoted himself to hunting and to the worship of the goddess Diana.

The next invasion of the land of Athens ended without bloodshed and in a memorable friendship. Pirithous, king of the Lapiths who lived in the north near the country of the Centaurs, had heard of the fame of Theseus and decided to see for himself whether he was as brave as he was said to be. So, with a large army, he invaded the country and reached the plain of Marathon where Theseus, at the head of his own army, marched out to meet him. On one side lay the sea and on the other the mountains. The two great hosts were drawn up in order of battle, and both Theseus and Pirithous stood out conspicuous in their armor in front of their men. The two kings looked closely at one another and each was so struck with the beauty and nobility of the other that they immediately laid down their arms and became ever afterwards the most inseparable of friends. Pirithous offered to pay for any damage that his army had done in Attica. Theseus promised him help and alliance for ever in the future. So instead of fighting together the two friends entered Athens in peace and spent many days in feasting and rejoicing.

Not long afterwards Pirithous married a wife who was called Hippodamia. To the wedding feast he invited not only his friend Theseus but all the heroes of Greece. He invited also the Centaurs, half men, half horses, who lived on the borders of his territories. Also he invited the gods, but one of them he failed to invite. This was Mars, the god of war.

In anger at being passed over, Mars determined to make the wedding banquet a scene of blood and warfare. One of the Centaurs was already drunk with wine and Mars put into his heart the desire to offer violence to the bride. In a drunken fury he attempted to carry Hippodamia away with him; but Theseus immediately killed the insulter of his friend's wife. This was the signal for a general fight. The Centaurs sprang up, each on his four legs, and began to attack the Lapiths with arrows and with the short heavy clubs which they carried. The women fled shrieking from the palace and for long the battle raged. Theseus, Pirithous and Heracles were the chief champions on the one side. On the other was a mass of whirling clubs, clattering hooves and great hairy bodies that struggled and twisted in the battle. Finally the Centaurs were defeated. With wild cries they fled from the hall and Pirithous with his Lapiths pursued them as they galloped away over the plain to their haunts in the mountains.

Whether because this terrible battle had shocked her too deeply or for some other reason, Hippodamia died soon afterwards. Theseus also had lost his wife and now the two friends determined to find themselves other wives to marry. This was a natural thing to do, but the way in which they did it was both unnatural and wrong.

First they decided to carry off by force the young girl Helen, who much later was to be the cause of the great war at Troy. They seized her from her home in Sparta, and, since she was only ten years old, Theseus put her in the care of his mother Aethra until she should be old enough to marry him. But Helen's two great brothers, Castor and Pollux, soon heard what had happened and rode to Athens to rescue their sister. Theseus had never fought in an unjust war. He knew that what he had done was wrong, and he restored Helen safe and sound to her home.

But the next exploit of Theseus and Pirithous was even more wicked and even less successful. Pirithous actually dared to try to carry off Proserpine, the queen of the lower world and wife of Pluto. Theseus had promised to help his friend in everything and so he accompanied him down to the lower world. Successfully they passed the terrible watchdog Cerberus and advanced into the pale kingdoms of the dead. But both Pluto and Proserpine had been forewarned of their wicked plan which was destined to come to nothing. As they wandered through the murky darkness of the outskirts of Hell, Theseus sat down to rest on a rock. As he did so he felt his limbs change and grow stiff. He tried to rise, but could not. He was fixed to the rock on which he sat. Then as he turned to cry out to his friend Pirithous, he saw that Pirithous was crying out too. Round him were standing the terrible band of Furies, with snakes in their hair, torches and long whips in their hands. Before these monsters the hero's courage failed and by them he was led away to eternal punishment. As he vanished from Theseus's sight, a voice could be heard saying: "From this warning learn wisdom and not to despise the gods."

So for many months in half darkness Theseus sat, immovably fixed to the rock, mourning both for his friend and for himself. In the end he was rescued by Heracles who, coming to Hades to fetch the dog Cerberus, persuaded Proserpine to forgive him for the part he had taken in the rash venture of Pirithous. So Theseus was restored to the upper air, but Pirithous never again left the kingdom of the dead.

Theseus himself was not fated to end his life happily. During the time of his imprisonment in Pluto's kingdom, a usurper, Menestheus, had seized the throne of Athens and driven out the children of Theseus. Partly by bribes and partly by terror he had made himself secure, and, when Theseus returned, his ungrateful people refused to recognize their true king. Theseus was forced to retire into exile in the little island of Scyros, and there he was treacherously murdered by the king of the island, who, while pretending to show his guest the view from the top of a hill, pushed him over a steep precipice.

Many years later, when Athens was known as the great sea power which had conquered Persia, an Athenian admiral came to Scyros and found there in a huge coffin the bones of the great hero. In great state he brought the bones back to Athens, and there ever afterwards the people honored the shrine and temple where the bones were laid.

Why did Theseus choose the perilous land route rather than the safe sea route for his trip to Athens?

What do Medea, Deianeira, and Ariadne have in common? Do you think this is common among the wives of heroes? Why?

Theseus knew that his power should be used only for good—that, in fact, fighting for good was probably what gave him so much power. When did his downfall begin? How is Theseus' trip into the Underworld the opposite of Orpheus' trip into the Underworld?

The Round Table

From Camelot

ALAN JAY LERNER *and* FREDERICK LOEWE

Scene: ARTHUR'S *study.*

Time: Early evening.

At rise: GUENEVERE *is at a tapestry easel working with needle and thread.* ARTHUR *is standing next to her.*

ARTHUR (*heatedly*). You cannot deny the facts! Did I or did I not pledge to you five years ago that I would be the most splendid king who ever sat on any throne?

GUENEVERE. You did.

ARTHUR. And in five years, have I become the most splendid king who ever sat on any throne?

GUENEVERE. You have.

ARTHUR. Rubbish! I have not, and you know it well. I'm nothing of what I pledged to you I would be. I'm a failure, and that's that.

GUENEVERE. Arthur, it's not true. You're the greatest warrior in England.

ARTHUR. But for what purpose? Might isn't always right, Jenny.

GUENEVERE. Nonsense, dear, of course it is. To be right and lose couldn't possibly be right.

ARTHUR (*thinking*). Yes. Might and right, battle and plunder. That's what keeps plaguing me. Merlyn used to frown on battles, yet he always helped me win them. I'm sure it's a clue. If only I could follow it. I'm always walking down a winding dimly lit road, and in the distance I see the outline of a thought. Like the shadow of a hill. I fumble and stumble, and at last I get there; but when I do, the hill is gone. Not there at all. And I hear a small voice saying: "Go back, Arthur, it's too dark for you to be out thinking."

GUENEVERE. My poor love. Let me see you do it. Walk out loud.

ARTHUR. All right. (*He crosses to the end of the stage.*) Proposition: It's far better to be alive than dead.

GUENEVERE. Far better.

ARTHUR (*taking a step forward*). If that is so, then why do we have battles, where people can get killed?

GUENEVERE (*chews on it a moment*). I don't know. Do you?

ARTHUR. Yes. Because somebody attacks.

GUENEVERE (*sincerely*). Of course. That's very clever of you, Arthur. Why do they attack?

(ARTHUR *leaves "the road" and comes to her.*)

ARTHUR. Jenny, I must confess something I've never told you before for fear you would not believe me.

GUENEVERE. How silly, Arthur, I would never not believe you.

ARTHUR. You know Merlyn brought me up, taught me everything I know. But do you know how?

GUENEVERE. How?

ARTHUR. By changing me into animals.

GUENEVERE. I don't believe it.

ARTHUR. There, you see? But it's true. I was a fish, a bobolink, a beaver and even an ant. From each animal he wanted me to learn something. Before he made me a hawk, for instance, he told me that while I would be flying through the sky, if I would look down at the earth, I would discover something.

GUENEVERE. What did you discover?

ARTHUR. Nothing. Merlyn was livid. Yet tonight, on my way home, while I was thinking, I suddenly realized that when you're in the sky looking down at the earth, there are no boundaries. No borders. Yet that's what somebody always attacks about. And you win by pushing them back across something that doesn't exist.

GUENEVERE. It *is* odd, isn't it?

ARTHUR. Proposition: We have battles for no reason at all. Then why? Why?

GUENEVERE. Because knights love them. They adore charging in and whacking away. It's splendid fun. You've said so yourself often.

ARTHUR. It *is* splendid fun. (*Steps forward*) But that doesn't seem reason enough. (*He steps back.*)

GUENEVERE. I think it is. And from a woman's point of view, it's wonderfully exciting to see your knight in armor riding bravely off to battle. Especially when you know he'll be home safe in one piece for dinner.

ARTHUR. That's it! It's the armor! I missed that before. Of course! Only knights are rich enough to bedeck themselves in armor. They can declare war when it suits them, go clod-hopping about the country slicing up peasants and foot soldiers, because peasants and foot soldiers are not equipped with armor. All that can happen to a knight is an occasional dent. (*He takes a long run to the fireplace.*) Proposition: Wrong or right, they have the might, so wrong or right, they're always right—and that's wrong. Right?

GUENEVERE. Absolutely.

ARTHUR (*excitedly*). Is that the reason Merlyn helped me to win? To take all this might that's knocking about the world and do something with it. But what?

GUENEVERE. Yes, what?

(ARTHUR *sighs with resignation.*)

ARTHUR. It's gone. I've thought as hard as I can, and I can walk no further. (*He walks around and sits on the chaise longue.*) You see, Jenny? I'm still not a king. I win every battle and accomplish nothing. When the Greeks won, they made a civilization. I'm not creating any civilization. I'm not even sure I'm civilized . . .

GUENEVERE (*tenderly*). Dear Arthur. You mustn't belabor yourself like this. Let us have a quiet dinner, and after, if you like, you can stroll again.

ARTHUR. Bless you. (*He takes her hand, kisses her, rises and moves to exit. Then he stops and turns.*) Jenny, suppose we create a *new* order of chivalry?

GUENEVERE. Pardon?

ARTHUR. A new order, a new order, where might is only used for right, to improve instead of destroy. And we invite all knights, good or bad, to lay down their arms and come and join. Yes! (*Growing more and more excited*) We'll take one of the large rooms in the castle and put a table in it, and all the knights will gather at the table.

GUENEVERE. And do what?

ARTHUR. Talk! Discuss! Make laws! Plan improvements!

GUENEVERE. Really, Arthur, do you think knights would ever want to do such a peaceful thing?

ARTHUR. We'll make it a great honor, very fashionable, so that everyone will want to be in. And the knights of my order will ride all over the world, still dressed in armor and whacking away. That will give them an outlet for wanting to whack. But they'll whack only for good. Defend virgins, restore what's been done wrong in the past, help the oppressed. Might for right. That's it, Jenny! Not might is right. Might *for* right!

GUENEVERE. It sounds superb.

ARTHUR. Yes. And civilized. (*Calls*) Page! (*To* GUENEVERE) We'll build a whole new generation of chivalry. Young men, not old, burning with zeal and ideals. (*The* PAGE *enters.*) Tell the heralds to mount the towers. And to have their trumpets. And assemble the Court in the yard. Send word there is to be a proclamation.

PAGE. Yes, Your Majesty! (*He exits.*)

GUENEVERE. Arthur, it will have to be an awfully large table! And won't there be jealousy? All your knights will be claiming superiority and wanting to sit at the head.

ARTHUR. Then we shall make it a round table so there is no head.

GUENEVERE (*totally won*). My father has one that would be perfect. It seats a hundred and fifty. It was given to him once for a present, and he never uses it.

ARTHUR (*suddenly doubting*). Jenny, have I had a thought? Am I at the hill? Or is it only a mirage?

(*The* PAGE *enters.*)

PAGE. The heralds await, Your Majesty. Shall I give the signal, Your Majesty?

ARTHUR. No, wait. I may be wrong. The whole idea may be absurd. If only Merlyn were here! He would have known for certain. (*Disparagingly*) Knights at a table. . . .

GUENEVERE (*correcting him*). A round table.

ARTHUR (*corrected*). Round table. Might for right, a new order of chivalry, shining knights gallivanting around the countryside like angels in armor, sword-swinging apostles battling to snuff out evil! Why, its naïve . . . it's adolescent . . . it's juvenile . . . it's infantile . . . it's folly . . . it's . . . it's . . .

GUENEVERE. It's marvelous.

ARTHUR. Yes, it is. It's marvelous. Absolutely marvelous. (*To the* PAGE) Page, give the signal.

PAGE. Yes, Your Majesty. (*He exits.*)

ARTHUR (*sings*).

> We'll send the heralds riding through the country;
> Tell ev'ry living person far and near . . .

GUENEVERE (*interrupting him*).

> That there is simply not
> In all the world a spot
> Where rules a more resplendent king than here
> In Camelot.

(*The heralds appear in the towers and sound their horns.* ARTHUR *embraces* GUENEVERE *and goes to the window to make his procla-mation.*)

Dim Out

"I'm a failure, and that's that." What other heroes felt that way?

Sometimes the greatest struggle of a quest is to believe that it is worthwhile. Do you think Arthur's quest is a "hill" or a "mirage"? What other heroes faced the same dilemma?

Robin Hood
and the Greedy Butchers

1

THE ROAD TO NOTTINGHAM

Come to me, all you young gallants, O come
    From town and meadow and wood!
If you listen a while, I'll sing you a song
    Of an archer, bold Robin Hood.

Once, as he walked in the merry greenwood,
    It chanced bold Robin did see
A butcher astride a bonny fine mare,
    And riding to market was he.

"Good morrow, good fellow," said Robin Hood.
    "What carry you there in your pack?
And tell me your trade and where you dwell—
    I trust you'll safely get back."

The butcher he answered Robin Hood,
    "What matters it where I dwell?
For a butcher am I, and to Nottingham town
    I am going, my meat to sell."

"What is the price of your mare?" said Robin.
    "Tell me, I'm eager to learn.
And what is the price of your meat, for I wish
    As a butcher my living to earn?"

"The price of my meat?" the butcher replied.
    "I can reckon that up in a minute . . .
Four shillings, good sir, is none too dear—
    And a bonny fine mare to go with it."

"Four guineas I'll give you," said Robin Hood,
    "Four guineas in gold I'll pay."
They counted their money, exchanged their clothes,
    And each rode off on his way.

2
THE MARKET

So Robin Hood rode to Nottingham town
    On the butcher's bonny fine mare.
Though others might charge too dear for their meat,
    He vowed *his* price should be fair.

But the sheriff he was in league with these rogues,
    He too was a twister and cheat.
What cared he if the price was too high
    And the poor could buy no meat?

In their stalls the butchers opened their meat,
    On dish and platter displayed;
For many a year they'd swindled the poor,
    But Robin was new to the trade.

Yet not a bite, not a morsel they sold,
    While bountiful Robin did well:
He sold more meat for one penny piece
    Than the rest for three pennies could sell.

Those villainous butchers fell back, amazed;
    The sheriff he scratched his head.
"If this fellow continues in trade, we'll starve.
    We must teach him a lesson," they said.

The butchers stepped over to Robin, resolved
    That some pretty trick should be played.
"Good brother," said one, "will you join us for dinner?
    Do come — we are all in the trade."

"Such offers," said Robin, "I never refuse."
    And to dinner they hurried apace.

The sheriff sat down at the head of the table,
    And asked Robin Hood to say grace.

"And when you've said grace, you shall sit at my side
    And we'll drink to success and long life."
"I'll gladly say grace," said bold Robin Hood,
    "If I may sit next to your wife."

The sheriff agreed. "God bless us!" said Robin.
    "Good appetite! Drink your fill!
Though five pounds and more it cost me in gold,
    I vow that I'll settle the bill."

"This fellow is crazy," the butchers declared.
    Said the sheriff, "He's due for a fall.
He has sold all his land for silver and gold,
    And means to squander it all."

"May he squander it all in this house," said the butchers,
    "And part with it, quick as can be!"
"Be patient! I've thought of a trick," said the sheriff.
    "I beg you to leave it to me."

3

INTO THE GREENWOOD

Said the sheriff to Robin, "What have you to sell?
    Any cattle or horned beast?"
"Indeed, I have plenty, good master sheriff,
    Two or three hundred at least."

The sheriff saddled his dapple-gray,
    With three hundred pound in gold;
And away he went with bold Robin Hood,
    His horned beasts to behold

By hill and furrow and field they rode,
    To the forest of merry Sherwood.
"O, Heaven forbid," the sheriff exclaimed,
    "That we meet with Robin Hood!"

"Why do you tremble and shake?" said Robin.
    "You should trust, good sir, in me.
With my brave long-bow and arrows I'll show
    I can shoot as straight as he."

When to a leafy hollow they came,
    Bold Robin chanced to spy
A hundred head of good red deer
    Through the trees come tripping by.

"Good master sheriff, how like you my beasts?
    They're sleek—and see how they race!"
"I tell you, good fellow, I'd rather go home—
    I don't like the look on your face."

Then Robin Hood put his horn to his mouth,
    He blew blasts two and three—
And fifty bowmen with brave Little John
    Stood under the greenwood tree.

"What is your will?" then said Little John.
    "Good master, what must we do?"
"I have brought the sheriff of Nottingham town
    Today to have dinner with you."

"He is welcome indeed," said Little John.
    "I hope from his purse he will pay
Guineas and shillings to give to the poor,
    To gladden them many a day."

Robin Hood stripped the cloak from his back
    And, laying it down on the ground,
He emptied the purse—in silver and gold
    He counted three hundred pound.

Then lo! through the greenwood the sheriff he led,
    Sitting glum on his old dapple-gray.
"Remember me, sir, to your lady at home!"
    Laughed Robin, and galloped away.

Big Bad John

Every morning at the mine you could see him arrive,
He stood six-foot-six and weighed two-forty-five.
Kind of broad at the shoulder and narrow at the hip,
And everybody knew you didn't give no lip to BIG JOHN!

Refrain: Big John,
        Big John
        Big Bad John,
        Big John.

Nobody seemed to know where John called home,
He just drifted into town and stayed all alone.
He didn't say much, a-kinda quiet and shy,
And if you spoke at all, you just said, "Hi" to BIG JOHN!
Somebody said he came from New Orleans,
Where he got in a fight over a Cajun queen.
And a crashing blow from a huge right hand
Sent a Louisiana fellow to the promised land. BIG JOHN!
[*Refrain*]

Then came the day at the bottom of the mine
When a timber cracked and the men started crying.
Miners were praying and hearts beat fast,
And everybody thought that they'd breathed their last 'cept John.
Through the dust and the smoke of this man-made hell
Walked a giant of a man that the miners knew well.
Grabbed a sagging timber and gave out with a groan,
And, like a giant oak tree, just stood there alone. BIG JOHN!
[*Refrain*]

And with all of his strength, he gave a mighty shove;
Then a miner yelled out, "There's a light up above!"
And twenty men scrambled from a would-be grave,
And now there's only one left down there to save; BIG JOHN!
With jacks and timbers they started back down
Then came that rumble way down in the ground,
And smoke and gas belched out of that mine,
Everybody knew it was the end of the line for BIG JOHN!
[*Refrain*]

Now they never re-opened that worthless pit,
They just placed a marble stand in front of it;
These few words are written on that stand:
"At the bottom of this mine lies a big, big man: BIG JOHN!"
[*Refrain*]

JIMMY DEAN

What was John's motive? Do you think he had, like Morgan, "a desire for death"?

Why do you think people make heroes out of those who die for them?

JUST BEFORE THE DOOMED PLANET, KRYPTON, EXPLODED TO FRAGMENTS, A SCIENTIST PLACED HIS INFANT SON WITHIN AN EXPERIMENTAL ROCKET-SHIP, LAUNCHING IT TOWARD EARTH!

WHEN THE VESSEL REACHED OUR PLANET, THE CHILD WAS FOUND BY AN ELDERLY COUPLE, THE KENTS.

LOOK, MARY! —IT'S A CHILD!

THE POOR THING! —— ITS BEEN ABANDONED!

THE INFANT WAS TURNED OVER TO AN ORPHAN ASYLUM, WHERE IT ASTOUNDED THE ATTENDANTS WITH ITS FEATS OF STRENGTH.

WE —— WE COULDN'T GET THAT SWEET CHILD OUT OF OUR MIND.

WE'VE COME TO ADOPT HIM IF YOU'LL PERMIT US.

I BELIEVE IT CAN BE ARRANGED. (—WHEW! THANK GOODNESS THEY'RE TAKING HIM AWAY BEFORE HE WRECKS THE ASYLUM!:)

THE LOVE AND GUIDANCE OF HIS KINDLY FOSTER-PARENTS WAS TO BECOME AN IMPORTANT FACTOR IN THE SHAPING OF THE BOY'S FUTURE.

NOW LISTEN TO ME, CLARK! THIS GREAT STRENGTH OF YOURS —YOU'VE GOT TO HIDE IT FROM PEOPLE OR THEY'LL BE SCARED OF YOU!

BUT WHEN THE PROPER TIME COMES, YOU MUST USE IT TO ASSIST HUMANITY.

As the lad grew older, he learned to his delight that he could hurdle skyscrapers . . .

. . . leap an eighth of a mile . . .

. . . raise tremendous weights . . .

. . . run faster than a streamline train --

. . . and nothing less than a bursting shell could penetrate his skin!

What th' — ? This is the sixth hypodermic needle I've broken on your skin!

Try again, Doc!

The passing away of his foster-parents greatly grieved Clark Kent. But it strengthened a determination that had been growing in his mind.

Clark decided he must turn his titanic strength into channels that would benefit mankind · and so was created--

SUPERMAN

Champion of the oppressed, the physical marvel who had sworn to devote his existence to helping those in need!

The Peach Boy

A Japanese legend

Retold by HELEN *and* WILLIAM MCALPINE

By a river that flowed through a mountainous province of Japan, there lived a childless woodcutter and his wife. To all the children in the neighborhood they were known with warm affection as Grandmama and Grandpapa, because, in spite of their poverty, they always remembered to keep a part of their small meal for the hungry young people who came to greet them daily. It grieved them greatly that they were childless, and always as their young friends turned homeward and their gay voices showered the evening air with their "thanks" and "good-bys" and "good nights," they would slide the paper-screen doors of their small house together and pause, silent and dejected, as if they could not bear to enclose the emptiness within.

One fine summer morning Grandmama decided to wash their winter kimonos in the river. In customary fashion she drew out the threads that held the long seams together and took the kimonos apart piece by piece. Gathering them into a rice-straw basket, she went down to the river bank. The river tripped and lilted in the sunshine, swinging round bends, sidling by rocks, and shooting through the mosses of the shallows. Skimming birds played with the flies, the flies with the jumping fish, and the willow trees dipped their long branches to the cool water. The river curled and eddied through Grandmama's fingers and round her sunbaked arms as she chanted "Jabujabu, jabujabu," to the rhythm of her washing. The sun and the river cheered her old wintry body, flooding it with the warmth of summer, and soon her work was done.

She laid the kimono strips along the bank to dry and was about to start for home, when she noticed a round object riding and tossing on the breast of the river, as it rounded the bend just beyond. It was buoyant as a cork and even the most ebullient eddies could not douse it. As it came nearer, she saw first the soft curved ripeness and then the bloom-furred skin of a golden peach. Its glowing skin, tinged with blushes, outshone the golden day. In all her life she had never seen a peach so big and so beautiful.

Quickly tucking her kimono above her knees, she stepped into the river and waded out until the waters brushed her gown. The peach rode jauntily towards her. She reached out her arms, but a sudden eddy sent it just beyond her reach, and there it spiralled and danced as if teasing her eager longing. She turned and started wading back, when suddenly the eddy moved towards her bringing the peach bobbing to her side. Folding her hands round the wet velvety skin, she lifted it out of the water and returned to the bank. She arrived home panting and breathless with the weight of it, but brimming with happiness at the thought of her prize brought safely home.

The dusk came and with it the clack-clock of her husband's wooden shoes on the stony path outside. Barely had he time to put down his day's gathering of wood, when Grandmama rushed out and flooded him with the tale of her golden find. Grandpapa laughed at her excitement as he kicked off his wooden shoes and stepped on to the straw matting of their only room. Before him lay the peach, its smooth and glowing warmness filling the whole room. His eyes, still closed in a twinkling line of laughter, slowly opened in amazement. He touched the peach to assure himself that it was real and then sat down on the floor, his legs tucked under him, to gaze at this miracle of all peaches. It would be a glory to eat!

When they had finished their simple meal of rice and dried fish, Grandmama cleaned the big kitchen knife. Together they put their hands on the haft and gently sliced down the golden cleft of the peach. As it fell apart, there was a stirring in the heart of the fruit. They fell back in fear as a boy, gay as the first green of spring, stepped out before their astounded eyes. He smiled at their incredulous wonder, and with a swift confiding movement, turned to Grandmama and pulled the folds of her apron around him. He rested tranquilly against her knees while the old couple sat spellbound. Long they remained, silent and motionless, but with hope slowly rising in their hearts that Buddha had at last relented and sent a child to them in the evening of their days.

And so indeed it proved. For as the seasons of the planting and the gathering of the rice came and went, the boy gave nothing but pleasure and happiness in his new home, and Grandmama and Grandpapa never ceased to rejoice in their good fortune. They called him "Momotaro"—the son of a peach—and as the months rounded into years, Momotaro grew sturdy of body and firm of limb. His skin glowed tan and rosy-gold and he carried with him a stoutness of heart and a sweetness of disposition that might well be attributed to his strange foster-mother.

One day, soon after he had reached his fifteenth birthday, Momotaro asked leave to address his parents on a matter of great importance. Greatly wondering, they waited for him to speak. Momotaro bowed low to them in filial piety, then said:

"Honorable Grandpapa! Honorable Grandmama! Though I became your son in a most unusual way, I can never cease to be grateful to you for the good but disciplined manner in which you have brought me to manhood. Your kindness has been wider than the horizon of the sky and your love has flowed over me with the fulness of the river that brought me to you."

Never before had they heard him speak with such seriousness. No longer was it the voice of their gay child. Before them stood a Momotaro, for all his smallness and youth, grown into manhood. Overcome with the tenderness of Momotaro's words, and at the same time sensing that behind their seriousness lay some firm decision that would affect the joy of their home, Grandmama began to weep. Grandpapa, remembering the days of his own youth and the first time he had wished to prove his manhood, guessed that Momotaro was longing to go into the world to try his fortune, and before the boy could continue he said:

"My son, I can guess what you are going to say. And though we shall taste the bitterness of loneliness without you, yet I applaud the courage of your spirit that prompts you to this course. Please do not allow our sorrow or the tears of your foolish mother to deter you. Only, we beg you, always remember that we shall be waiting for you as long as our fading years permit, and our poor hut will for ever be your home."

"You read my thoughts well, honorable Grandpapa," replied Momotaro with the same serious bearing. "And when the time comes for me to leave, your understanding will make our parting easier."

"But when will you go?" wept Grandmama, unable to control her tears. "When will you go? Beyond the hills of our village and the river of our valley, the world is angry and evil. It is no place for you."

"It is beyond the hills of our village and the river of our valley that

I must go, and without a moment to lose," said Momotaro. "And for no other reason than to quell that anger and to put good where evil reigns."

He paused and then continued:

"It is a long story and I fear that I shall weary you with the telling of it. In the ocean that washes the shores of our country, there is an island of evil. It is inhabited by fearful horned ogres. They are taller than the tallest bamboo in the forest and their hearts know only darkness. The skins of some are red as the belching flames of Mount Fuji, some blue as the ocean's stormy depths, some green as the eyes of cats at night, and some are as black as the evil in their hearts. They come in swift boats to our shores to ravage and pillage the countryside, devouring the children and leaving grief, destruction, and death everywhere behind them. I am going to brave these monsters on their island and exterminate them. I will bring back to Japan all the treasures they have stolen and restore them to their rightful owners."

At this Grandmama's tears redoubled, but Grandpapa checked her and said sharply:

"Do not be so foolish, wife! This is no time for tears and certainly no time to display them. Our son is brave. His cause is just, and Buddha, who sent him to us, will protect him. Until today he has been a boy: now he is to prove himself a man. Therefore, cease these useless tears and help the boy to equip himself for the long journey and the battles that lie before him."

With these words, Grandpapa went out to the woods to cut Momotaro a stout staff. Grandmama, drying her tears, took from the cupboard a bag of millet and began grinding the seed in a heavy mortar. Then she made the ground millet into dumplings and cooked them over the charcoal fire. Very soon Grandpapa returned with a stout branch. He stripped off the bark, baring the gleaming white wood which he speedily polished into a shining staff.

When all was prepared and Momotaro was about to leave, Grandpapa took from a lacquer box a warrior's iron fan and, with many exhortations and blessings, handed it to Momotaro, who tucked it into his kimono sash. All knelt on the floor and bowed deeply many times. No words were spoken and no grief showed in their faces. The depth of their silent bowing expressed only too well the sorrow in their hearts. Finally Momotaro took his leave, and his grandparents watched the valiant little figure stride into the distance. For a moment he turned, and all bowed their last farewell before he disappeared over the brow of the hill. Now they could only wait and offer prayers at the family altar for his safe and speedy return.

Momotaro, once he had overcome the sadness of parting, strode forward full of exuberance. It was good to be out in the world and, come what might, he knew the justice of his cause. He walked the whole morning through and deep into the afternoon. The rice fields had long been left behind him as he climbed hill and mountain. Peak after peak had passed, and now a valley with a coppice in it lay before him. He stepped aside into the trees and for the first time since he left home, prepared to smooth the raw edge of his hunger. He had hardly untied his bag of millet dumplings when he heard a sudden scuffling behind him, and leaping to his feet he saw a large and lordly dog bound from an entanglement of bushes. The dog snarled fiercely and barked in a deep voice:

"Who gave you leave to travel through my country? I am the Lord Brindled Dog, and all who come here must obey and pay homage to me. If they don't, I bite off their heads!"

He snarled again and looked as fierce as a jungle full of tigers. Momotaro, instead of melting with fear, started laughing at his comical face.

"Lord Brindled Dog, I think you are more bark than bite! I am not afraid of you!"

With these words Momotaro waved his staff before the lordly creature, who suddenly, with his tail between his legs, retreated to a safe distance before saying in a most conciliatory voice:

"You must be the famous Momotaro—the Momotaro that even the winds speak of, and of whose coming the pike in the river tell tales. Do me the honor of informing me what brings you into my domain."

Momotaro smiled at the Lord Brindled Dog's sudden change of tone, but willingly told him of his plans to exterminate the ogres. Lord Brindled Dog's ears and tail reared stiff in excitement.

"Those are the monsters who killed my brindled heir and devastated my lands. I vowed vengeance and now my hour has come. Momotaro Sama, take me with you. I am big and strong. I can run faster than the fastest creature on land. With my crunching jaws and sword-edged teeth, I can snap their heads from their bodies in one bite."

"The proof of that pudding will be in the eating of it," chuckled Momotaro, and he agreed to have Lord Brindled Dog as his fighting companion.

They set out together, having first refreshed themselves by sharing one of the millet dumplings, and travelled quickly on the way. Lord Brindled Dog was ever speeding ahead, snuffling the ground and smelling out the best track for them to follow. Mile after mile sped under their feet, until, towards evening, they came to a small hollow among the foothills of a mountain. Here they decided to rest for the night. They settled down under the spreading branches of a tree, but hardly had their heads touched their pillows of leaves, when there was a rustling commotion overhead and a handsome monkey came swinging down with long-armed grace to their feet. He bowed to Momotaro and said with charming politeness:

"You are undoubtedly the Lord Momotaro of whom all the forests and mountains have heard. I have come to offer my services in the task of right and justice you have undertaken. I am the Lord Monkey of this Mountain and I beg you to accept me as your retainer."

Lord Brindled Dog, when he heard these words, jumped snarling forward and yelped:

"I am Lord Momotaro's retainer and he needs no other. What use would a monkey be in making battle against monster giants? Be off with you to the tree-tops where you belong."

But the Lord Monkey of the Mountain remained calm and looked steadily at Momotaro. Momotaro liked him at once and his mind was made up.

"You, Lord Brindled Dog, if you really wish to serve me faithfully, will remember that there is arduous and dangerous work ahead of us. You will need all your battle energy for that time. Do not waste it now. Come, Lord Monkey of the Mountain, here is a millet dumpling. Share it with Lord Brindled Dog. I am happy to have you as my second retainer."

As the first hazy light of morning filtered through the branches above them, Momotaro and his two retainers rose up, yawned, and set off on their way. The air was full of the perfume of wild flowers, and the trees and bushes were astir with the movement and song of the little bush-warblers. It seemed a day full of promise to the three warriors as they strode on their way. Lord Brindled Dog bounded ahead with Momotaro's staff; Lord Monkey swung gracefully above their heads from tree to tree; Momotaro himself strode out blithely, carrying his fan in his hand as befitted a lordly warrior. Foothills gave place to forests, forests to winding streams, and winding streams to moorland. It was country that delighted Lord Brindled Dog's heart. He ran and

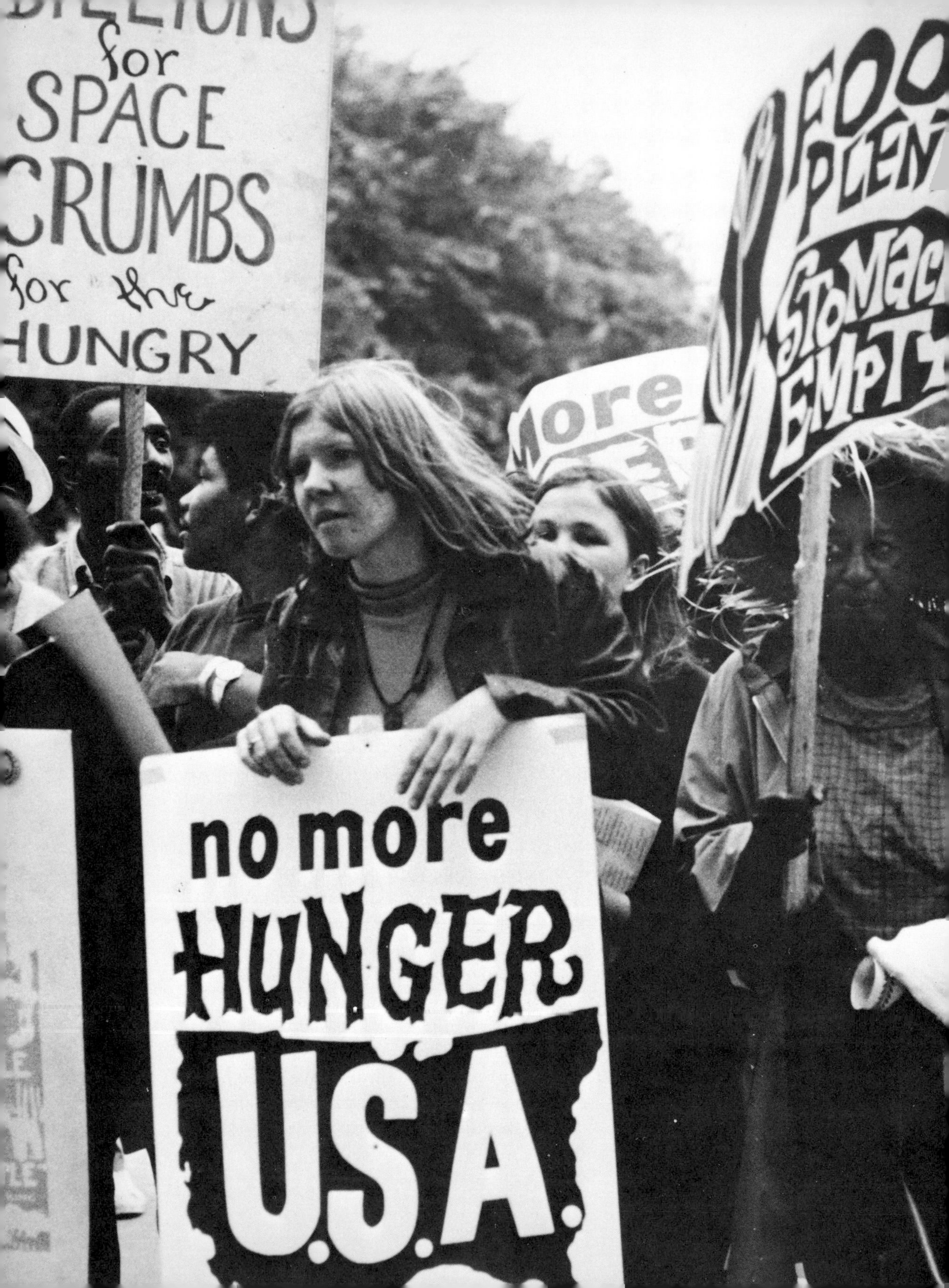

leaped, and snuffled and panted. Suddenly before his quivering nose a pheasant rose out of the gorse. Startled, the dog dropped Momotaro's staff and immediately sprang forward to bite off the pheasant's head. The pheasant, undaunted, whirled in the air and swooped to attack the dog. Momotaro watched and thought, "What a valiant creature! Just the follower I would have with me."

He picked up the fallen staff and brought it down with a thud on Lord Brindled Dog's rump, sternly ordering him to stop fighting. At the same time he spoke sharply to the pheasant and said:

"Who are you that dare molest my personal retainer? We are bound on a most important expedition and you are causing us much delay."

On hearing Momotaro's voice, the bird crouched low near his feet and said:

"You must be the great Lord Momotaro of whom all the moorfowl have heard. I am the humble Lord Pheasant of the Moor. I and my bird retainers know of your noble undertaking. We are wholeheartedly behind you and my only wish is to be allowed to serve under your leadership."

Momotaro was delighted with his new ally, and taking out another millet dumpling, he shared it among them all. Then all four continued across the moorland, the monkey riding on the dog's back, and the pheasant flying overhead and occasionally perching on Momotaro's shoulder.

The morning passed to noon and soon the scrub-covered moors were far behind. A wood of tall bamboo trees stretched endlessly through the afternoon and the four valiant heroes walked, ambled, hopped and swung under the cool shade of the leaves. Dusk was just falling gently over the forest when they emerged to see before them the blue expanse of the ocean. All four sat down, dusty, tired, and hungry, but overjoyed to be facing their first objective. They scanned the sea's glassy surface, but nothing rose to break its quiet immensity.

"We will sleep here tonight and tomorrow morning we will build a boat and start our search for the ogres' island," said Momotaro.

At the first light of dawn Lord Momotaro was up directing his three followers. Lord Brindled Dog felled the bamboo trees with savage bites of his fierce jaws; Lord Pheasant of the Moor brought long strands of creeper from distant fields to bind the trunks together; Lord Monkey of the Mountain and Momotaro worked quickly and deftly and soon their craft was shipshape and launched. Lord Brindled Dog took charge of the oar, which swivelled on a wooden pin at the stern of the boat.

His strong, powerful, curving strokes sent the boat speeding through the waveless blue. The land fell out of sight and the sun rose high in the sky. All day the little boat moved farther and farther out to sea, but from one end of the horizon to the other there was no sign of an island to be seen: nothing but the vast murmuring expanse of the ocean.

"Lord Pheasant of the Moor, now is the time for you to use your special gift of flight," said Momotaro. "Go before us and see what there is to be seen from your vantage point in the sky."

The pheasant rose swiftly in the air and flew towards the horizon, mounting steadily higher and higher until he vanished from sight. It seemed a long time to those waiting before the bright wings at last reappeared.

"Lord Momotar, I have seen the island's outline. It is still far away. But with good luck and swift rowing we should reach there before nightfall," cried the pheasant overhead. "Follow me and I will direct you."

Following the pheasant who flew on ahead, Lord Brindled Dog rowed with renewed strength and sent the boat skimming over the water. It was not long before a dot appeared on the skyline, which gradually grew into the outline of the island they sought. As they drew closer, its grim, forbidding look, its air of iron-clad isolation, cast a gloom upon the whole surroundings and made even the peach-stone heart of Momotaro chill for a moment. Looking at his followers, he saw that the dog's hair bristled along his spine and the monkey was chattering to himself in quiet undertones. Only the pheasant, now settled on his shoulder, looked unconcerned, his beady eyes as bright and alert as ever.

At the command of Momotaro, Lord Brindled Dog rowed quietly inshore. From there Momotaro could just see, through the falling dusk, the ogres' fortifications: a high iron-railed fence on the lower reaches, and behind, but farther up the rocky hill, a heavily spiked wall which encircled a massive fortress-like building. "That," concluded Momotaro, "holds our enemies."

He directed the boat to ground in the shelter of a large rock which jutted out beyond the iron-railed fence, and there took counsel with his followers. He explained to them his plan of attack, which had been formulating in his mind since he first saw the island's defences. They would attack under cover of darkness, but first they would rest a little to regain their strength. It was their best chance of success, if shrewdness, which they must depend on, was to beat the mighty ogres.

At the chosen hour, they started for the iron fence. Lord Brindled Dog quickly made an opening by biting through several of the uprights, and he and Momotaro stationed themselves one at each side of the massive wooden doors in the inner wall. Lord Monkey scaled the wall and waited at the top. Lord Pheasant went winging high over the fortress and alighted on the topmost turret. Suddenly, in the still darkness, the pheasant shrilled out his clear challenge, "Ken-ken, ken-ken, ken-ken," a cry which he knew all mortals took for the warning of an earthquake. The ogres, bleary-eyed with sleep, stumbled out into the darkness of the yard. The pheasant screeched again, while the monkey ran along the wall, tearing up the stones and hurling them at the heads of the ogres. Bewildered, the monsters flung open the great wooden doors, their howls filling the night. As they came through in blind confusion, Momotaro struck their legs with his dagger and, as they stumbled, Lord Brindled Dog tore their heads from their bodies with one snarling snap of his iron jaws. Inside, Lord Pheasant swooped in fury out of the dark sky and blinded them with his sharp beak; while Lord Monkey tore the hair from their heads with his strong fingers. The few that escaped rushed in panic to their boats, but were blinded by Lord Pheasant before they could reach them.

Only the ogre chief was left when morning came over the distant skyline. Surveying the ravages about him, he knew that defeat had come to him at last. He broke off his horns and taking the keys of his fortress treasure house, he laid them at the feet of Lord Momotaro in token of submission. Leaving Lord Brindled Dog to guard the ogre chief, Momotaro, with the pheasant and the monkey, went to ransack the storehouse for the treasures he had dreamed of returning to Japan. Many he saw that he thought had disappeared for ever: the precious stone with which the tides could be controlled; the garments which rendered their wearer invisible; the mallet which struck showers of gold at every blow; the precious coral which a famed empress brought from the depths of the ocean; and many priceless treasures of musk, emeralds, tortoiseshell, gold, silver and amber. All these they loaded into one of the ogres' boats and then set out for home, leaving the ogre chief solitary among his evil dead.

The flowing breeze bellied their sails: the tide ran fast in their course: and before long Lord Pheasant of the Moor announced from his heaven-high lookout that the coastline of their beloved Japan was in sight. Joyfully they landed and at once set about building a little cart, on which they loaded all the treasures from the ogres' storehouse. Soon they were eagerly striding homeward through the forests and moorlands.

As Momotaro descended the last hill with his faithful followers, there before him lay the village, with Grandpapa and Grandmama standing at the door of their little hut waiting to welcome him home. They bowed deeply and their eyes told the depth of the happiness in their hearts. The time had seemed endless while he had been away, but now it flew faster than the wings of morning as he told of all that had befallen him.

Momotaro's grandparents lived for many golden years to enjoy the good fortune their wonderful son had brought them, and Momotaro became a powerful but kindly and just lord as the years went by. Lord Brindled Dog, Lord Monkey of the Mountain, and Lord Pheasant of the Moor remained always his closest friends, paying him frequent visits from their own domains, where he in turn was always a most honored guest. And Momotaro spent the rest of his life in using the powers that the ogres' magic treasures had given him for the welfare of his people.

What is the Peach Boy's motive? How is it like Superman's?

Find these events in the lives of the Peach Boy and Superman: mysterious birth, growing up in obscurity, prophecy, quest, "supernatural" aid, triumph. Which other hero stories in this book contain the same events? Why do you think hero stories have the same basic "shape" no matter when they were written or to what culture they belong?

The Peach Boy leaves his mother and father. What other heroes did this? Why do you think this event is so significant in these stories? What do you think it represents in actual life? How is it an imaginative version of the same basic human event described in "A Ritual" in unit three?

What was special about the Peach Boy's relationship with nature and animals? What was extraordinary about Orpheus' relationship with nature? What was "more than human" about Asclepius' and Heracles' and Superman's relationships with nature? Why do you suppose this is true of heroes?

*Eric, a proud and mighty Viking
driven from his homeland, tells his
tale of strength and grief.*

Red Eric

WILLIAM CARLOS WILLIAMS

Rather the ice than their way: to take what is mine by single strength, theirs by the crookedness of their law. But they have marked me — even to myself. Because I am not like them, I am evil. I cannot get my hands on it: I, murderer, outlaw, outcast even from Iceland. Because their way is the just way and my way — the way of the kings and my father — crosses them: weaklings holding together to appear strong. But I am alone, though in Greenland.

The worst is that weak, still, somehow, they are strong: they in effect have the power, by hook or by crook. And because I am not like them — not that I am evil, but more in accord with our own blood than they, eager to lead — this very part of me, by their trickery must not appear, unless in their jacket. Eric was Greenland: I call it Greenland, that men will go there to colonize it.

I, then, must open a way for them into the ice that they follow me even here — their servant, in spite of myself. Yet they must follow.

It was so from the beginning. They drove me from Jaederen, my father and me. Who was this Christ, that he should come to bother me in my own country? His bishops that lie and falsify the records, make me out to be what I am not — for their own ends — because we killed a man.

Was he the first man that was ever killed, that they must sour over it? That he was important to their schemes, that he meant much to them — granted: one of their own color, we who altered him must be driven from Norway. Their courts and soft ways. Not that we killed him. One or the other of us had to die, under the natural circumstance.

He or we. But that if we had been killed, would he then have been driven from his country? They would have made him Archbishop.

To Iceland, then. Forget Norway. What there? My father dead. Land to the north cleared. A poor homestead. Manslaughter had driven me there. Then I married Thorhild, removed from the north and cleared land at Haukadal. Must I be meek because of that? If my slaves cause a landslide on Valthioff's farm and Valthioff's kinsman slays them, shall I not kill him? Is it proper for me to stand and to be made small before my slaves? I am not a man to shake and sweat like a thief when the time comes.

Rather say I killed two men instead of the one. They tried me among themselves and drove me out once more. To the north, then. Iceland wilderness.

There Thorgest comes to me and asks if I will lend him my outer dais-boards: ready to take me at a loss. Why else? For Eric the Red is a marked man, beyond the law, so it would seem: from that man one steals at will — being many in the act against his one. Thorgest keeps the decorated wood-pieces. I go to his house and remove my property. He gives chase and two of his sons are killed in the encounter.

This time they have done the thing. They search for us among the islands — me and my people.

This is the way of it, Thorhall, this has always been the way with me from the first. Eric loves his friends, loves bed, loves food, loves the hunt, loves his sons. He is a man that can throw a spear, take a girl, steer a ship, till the soil, plant, care for the cattle, skin a fox, sing, dance, run, wrestle, climb, swim like a seal. A man to plan an expedition and pay for it, kill an enemy, take his way through a fog, a snowstorm, read a reckoning by the stars, live in a stench, drink foul water, withstand the fierce cold, the black of winter and come to a new country with a hundred men and found them there. But they have branded me. They have separated murder into two parts and fastened the worse on me. It rides in the air around me. What is it to be killed? They have had their fling at me. Is it worse, so much worse, than to be hunted about the islands, chased from Norway to Iceland, from south to north, from Iceland to Greenland, because — I am I, and remain so.

Outlaws have no friends. Murderers are run down like rabbits among the stones. Yet my ship was built, fitted, manned, given safe conduct beyond the reefs. To Thorbiorn I owe much. And so to Greenland — after bitter days fighting the ice and rough seas. Pestilence struck us. The cattle sickened. Weeks passed. The summer nearly ended before we struck land. This is my portion. I do not call it not to my liking. Hardship lives in me. What I suffer is myself that outraces the water or the wind. But that it only should be mine, cuts deep. It is the half only. And it takes it out of my taste that the choice is theirs. I have the rough of it not because I will it, but because it is all that is left, a remnant from their coatcloth. This is the gall on the meat. Let the hail beat me. It is a kind of joy I feel in such things.

Greenland then. So be it. Start over again. It turns out always the one way. A wife, her two sons and a daughter. So my life was split up. The logic of it also. This is my proof. We lived at our homestead, well rid of the world. Traders visited us. Then Lief, Eric's son, sails to Norway, a thousand miles, in one carry. But on his return, Lief the Lucky, he is driven westward upon a new country, news of which he brings to Brattahild. At the same stroke he brings me back pride and joy-in-his-deed, my deed, Eric moving up, and poison: an edict from Olaf—from my son's mouth—solid as an axe to cut me, half healed, into pieces again.

Not that it was new. Only that here in Greenland I had begun to feel that I had left the curse behind. Here through the winters, far to the west, I had begun to look toward summer when I should be whole again. My people at work, my wife beside me, the boys free from my smear, growing in strength and knowledge of the sea. Here was an answer to them all: Thorstein and Lief Erickson, sons of Red Eric, murderer! Myself in the teeth of the world.

Eric convinces himself that he is using his might for right, yet he is shunned by his people. What other hero in this unit experienced the same rejection and isolation?

Do you think Eric is questing toward something or running from something? Why?

Eric seems to be a man of great strength and qualities of leadership. But he also seems to have failed in his quest. Do you think he has? Why?

What does Eric see as his final triumph?

"I am I, and remain so." What essential heroic quality does Eric possess?

The Final Problem

SIR ARTHUR CONAN DOYLE

It is with a heavy heart that I take up my pen to write these last few words in which I shall ever record the singular gifts by which my friend Mr. Sherlock Holmes was distinguished. In an incoherent and, as I deeply feel, an entirely inadequate fashion, I have endeavored to give some account of my strange experiences in his company from the chance which first brought us together at the period of the "Study in Scarlet," up to the time of his interference in the matter of the "Naval Treaty"—an interference which had the unquestionable effect of preventing a serious international complication. It was my intention to have stopped there, and to have said nothing of that event which has created a void in my life which the lapse of two years has done little to fill. My hand has been forced, however, by the recent letters in which Colonel James Moriarty defends the memory of his brother, and I have no choice but to lay the facts before the public exactly as they occurred. I alone know the absolute truth of the matter, and I am satisfied that the time has come when no good purpose is to be served by its suppression. As far as I know, there have been only three accounts in the public press: that in the *Journal de Genève* upon May 6th, 1891, the Reuter's dispatch in the English papers upon May 7th, and finally the recent letters to which I have alluded. Of these the first and second were extremely condensed, while the last is, as I shall now show, an absolute perversion of the facts. It lies with me to tell for the first time what really took place between Professor Moriarty and Mr. Sherlock Holmes.

It may be remembered that after my marriage, and my subsequent start in private practice, the very intimate relations which had existed between Holmes and myself became to some extent modified. He still came to me from time to time when he desired a companion in his investigations, but these occasions grew more and more seldom, until I find that in the year 1890 there were only three cases of which I retain any record. During the winter of that year and the early spring of 1891, I saw in the papers that he had been engaged by the French Government upon a matter of supreme importance, and I received two notes from Holmes, dated from Narbonne and from Nîmes, from which I gathered that his stay in France was likely to be a long one. It was with some surprise, therefore, that I saw him walk into my consulting-room upon the evening of the 24th of April. It struck me that he was looking even paler and thinner than usual.

"Yes, I have been using myself up rather too freely," he remarked, in answer to my look rather than to my words; "I have been a little pressed of late. Have you any objection to my closing your shutters?"

The only light in the room came from the lamp upon the table at which I had been reading. Holmes edged his way round the wall, and flinging the shutters together, he bolted them securely.

"You are afraid of something?" I asked.

"Well, I am."

"Of what?"

"Of air-guns."

"My dear Holmes, what do you mean?"

"I think that you know me well enough, Watson, to understand that I am by no means a nervous man. At the same time, it is stupidity rather than courage to refuse to recognize danger when it is close upon you. Might I trouble you for a match?" He drew in the smoke of his cigarette as if the soothing influence was grateful to him.

"I must apologize for calling so late," said he, "and I must further beg you to be so unconventional as to allow me to leave your house presently by scrambling over your back garden wall."

"But what does it all mean?" I asked.

He held out his hand, and I saw in the light of the lamp that two of his knuckles were burst and bleeding.

"It's not an airy nothing, you see," said he, smiling. "On the contrary, it is solid enough for a man to break his hand over. Is Mrs. Watson in?"

"She is away upon a visit."

"Indeed! You are alone?"

"Quite."

"Then it makes it the easier for me to propose that you should come away with me for a week on to the Continent."

"Where?"

"Oh, anywhere. It's all the same to me."

There was something very strange in all this. It was not Holmes's nature to take an aimless holiday, and something about his pale, worn face told me that his nerves were at their highest tension. He saw the question in my eyes, and, putting his finger tips together and his elbows upon his knees, he explained the situation.

"You have probably never heard of Professor Moriarty?" said he.

"Never."

"Aye, there's the genius and the wonder of the thing!" he cried. "The man pervades London, and no one has heard of him. That's what puts him on a pinnacle in the records of crime. I tell you, Watson, in all seriousness, that if I could beat that man, if I could free society of him, I should feel that my own career had reached its summit, and I should be prepared to turn to some more placid line in life. Between ourselves, the recent cases in which I have been of assistance to the Royal Family of Scandinavia, and to the French Republic, have left me in such a position that I could continue to live in the quiet fashion which is most congenial to me, and to concentrate my attention upon my chemical researches. But I could not rest, Watson, I could not sit quiet in my chair, if I thought that such a man as Professor Moriarty were walking the streets of London unchallenged."

"What has he done, then?"

"His career has been an extraordinary one. He is a man of good birth and excellent education, endowed by nature with a phenomenal mathematical faculty. At the age of twenty-one he wrote a treatise upon the Binomial Theorem, which has had a European vogue. On the strength of it, he won the Mathematical Chair at one of our smaller universities, and had, to all appearance, a most brilliant career before him. But the man had hereditary tendencies of the most diabolical kind. A criminal strain ran in his blood, which, instead of being modified, was increased and rendered infinitely more dangerous by his extraordinary mental powers. Dark rumors gathered around him in the university town, and eventually he was compelled to resign his Chair and to come down to London, where he set up as an army coach. So much is known to the world, but what I am telling you now is what I have myself discovered.

"As you are aware, Watson, there is no one who knows the higher criminal world of London so well as I do. For years past I have continually been conscious of some power behind the malefactor, some deep organizing power which for ever stands in the way of the law, and throws its shield over the wrongdoer. Again and again in cases of the

most varying sorts—forgery cases, robberies, murders—I have felt the presence of this force, and I have deduced its action in many of those undiscovered crimes in which I have not been personally consulted. For years I have endeavored to break through the veil which shrouded it, and at last the time came when I seized my thread and followed it, until it led me, after a thousand cunning windings, to ex-Professor Moriarty of mathematical celebrity.

"He is the Napoleon of crime, Watson. He is the organizer of half that is evil and of nearly all that is undetected in this great city. He is a genius, a philosopher, an abstract thinker. He has a brain of the first order. He sits motionless, like a spider in the center of its web, but that web has a thousand radiations, and he knows well every quiver of each of them. He does little himself. He only plans. But his agents are numerous and splendidly organized. Is there a crime to be done, a paper to be abstracted, we will say, a house to be rifled, a man to be removed—the word is passed to the Professor, the matter is organized and carried out. The agent may be caught. In that case money is found for his bail or his defence. But the central power which uses the agent is never caught—never so much as suspected. This was the organization which I deduced, Watson, and which I devoted my whole energy to exposing and breaking up.

"But the Professor was fenced round with safeguards so cunningly devised that, do what I should, it seemed impossible to get evidence which could convict in a court of law. You know my powers, my dear Watson, and yet at the end of three months I was forced to confess that I had at last met an antagonist who was my intellectual equal. My horror at his crimes was lost in my admiration at his skill. But at last he made a trip—only a little, little trip—but it was more than he could afford, when I was so close upon him. I had my chance, and, starting from that point, I have woven my net round him until now it is all ready to close. In three days, that is to say on Monday next, matters will be ripe, and the Professor, with all the principal members of his gang, will be in the hands of the police. Then will come the greatest criminal trial of the century, the clearing up of over forty mysteries, and the rope for all of them—but if we move at all prematurely, you understand, they may slip out of our hands even at the last moment.

"Now, if I could have done this without the knowledge of Professor Moriarty, all would have been well, But he was too wily for that. He saw every step which I took to draw my toils round him. Again and again he strove to break away, but I as often headed him off. I tell you, my friend, that if a detailed account of that silent contest could be written, it would take its place as the most brilliant bit of thrust-and-parry work in the history of detection. Never have I risen to such a height, and never have I been so hard pressed by an opponent. He cut deep, and yet I just undercut him. This morning the last steps were taken, and three days only were wanted to complete the business. I was sitting in my room thinking the matter over, when the door opened and Professor Moriarty stood before me.

"My nerves are fairly proof, Watson, but I must confess to a start when I saw the very man who had been so much in my thoughts standing there on my threshold. His appearance was quite familiar to me. He is extremely tall and thin, his forehead domes out in a white curve, and his two eyes are deeply sunken in his head. He is clean-shaven, pale, and ascetic-looking, retaining something of the professor in his features. His shoulders are rounded from much study, and his face protrudes forward, and is for ever slowly oscillating from side to side in a curiously reptilian fashion. He peered at me with great curiosity in his puckered eyes.

" 'You have less frontal development than I should have expected,' said he at last. 'It is a dangerous habit to finger loaded firearms in the pocket of one's dressing-gown.'

"The fact is that upon his entrance I had instantly recognized the extreme personal danger in which I lay. The only conceivable escape for him lay in silencing my tongue. In an instant I had slipped the revolver from the drawer into my pocket, and was covering him through the cloth. At his remark I drew the weapon out and laid it cocked upon the table. He still smiled and blinked but there was something about his eyes which made me feel very glad that I had it there.

" 'You evidently don't know me,' said he.

" 'On the contrary,' I answered. 'I think it is fairly evident that I do. Pray take a chair. I can spare you five minutes if you have anything to say.'

" 'All that I have to say has already crossed your mind,' said he.

" 'Then possibly my answer has crossed yours,' I replied.

" 'You stand fast?'

" 'Absolutely.'

"He clapped his hand into his pocket, and I raised the pistol from the table. But he merely drew out a memorandum-book in which he had scribbled some dates.

" 'You crossed my path on the 4th of January,' said he. 'On the 23rd you incommoded me; by the middle of February I was seriously inconvenienced by you; at the end of March I was absolutely hampered in my plans; and now, at the close of April, I find myself placed in such a position through your continual persecution that I am in positive danger of losing my liberty. The situation is becoming an impossible one.'

" 'Have you any suggestion to make?' I asked.

" 'You must drop it, Mr. Holmes,' said he, swaying his face about. 'You really must, you know.'

" 'After Monday,' said I.

" 'Tut, tut!' said he. 'I am quite sure that a man of your intelligence will see that there can be but one outcome to this affair. It is necessary that you should withdraw. You have worked things in such a fashion that we have only one resource left. It has been an intellectual treat to me to see the way in which you have grappled with this affair, and I say, unaffectedly, that it would be a grief to me to be forced to take any extreme measure. You smile, sir, but I assure you that it really would.'

" 'Danger is part of my trade,' I remarked.

" 'This is not danger,' said he. 'It is inevitable destruction. You stand in the way not merely of an individual, but of a mighty organization, the full extent of which you, with all your cleverness, have been unable to realize. You must stand clear, Mr. Holmes, or be trodden under foot.'

" 'I am afraid,' said I, rising, 'that in the pleasure of this conversation I am neglecting business of importance which awaits me elsewhere.'

"He rose also and looked at me in silence, shaking his head sadly.

" 'Well, well,' said he at last. 'It seems a pity, but I have done what I could. I know every move of your game. You can do nothing before Monday. It has been a duel between you and me, Mr. Holmes. You hope to place me in the dock. I tell you that I will never stand in the dock. You hope to beat me. I tell you that you will never beat me. If you are clever enough to bring destruction upon me, rest assured that I shall do as much to you.'

" 'You have paid me several compliments, Mr. Moriarty,' said I. 'Let me pay you one in return when I say that if I were assured of the former eventuality I would in the interests of the public, cheerfully accept the latter.'

" 'I can promise you the one but not the other,' he snarled, and so turned his rounded back upon me and went peering and blinking out of the room.

"That was my singular interview with Professor Moriarty. I confess that it left an unpleasant effect upon my mind. His soft, precise fashion of speech leaves a conviction of sincerity which a mere bully could not produce. Of course, you will say: 'Why not take police precautions against him?' The reason is that I am well convinced that it is from his agents the blow will fall. I have the best of proofs that it would be so."

"You have already been assaulted?"

"My dear Watson, Professor Moriarty is not a man who lets the grass grow under his feet. I went out about midday to transact some business in Oxford Street. As I passed the corner which leads from Bentinck Street on to the Welbeck Street crossing a two-horse van furiously driven whizzed round and was on me like a flash. I sprang for the footpath and saved myself by a fraction of a second. The van dashed round from Marylebone Lane and was gone in an instant. I kept to the pavement after that, Watson, but as I walked down Vere Street a brick came down from the roof of one of the houses and was shattered to fragments at my feet. I called the police and had the place examined. There were slates and bricks piled upon the roof preparatory to some repairs, and they would have me believe that the wind had toppled over one of these. Of course I knew better, but I could prove nothing. I took a cab after that and reached my brother's rooms in Pall Mall, where I spent the day. Now I have come round to you, and on my way I was attacked by a rough with a bludgeon. I knocked him down, and the police have him in custody; but I can tell you with the most absolute confidence that no possible connection will ever be traced between the gentleman upon whose front teeth I have barked my knuckles and the retiring mathematical coach, who is, I dare say, working out problems upon a blackboard ten miles away. You will not wonder, Watson, that my first act on entering your rooms was to close your shutters, and that I have been compelled to ask your permission to leave the house by some less conspicuous exit than the front door."

I had often admired my friend's courage, but never more than now, as he sat quietly checking off a series of incidents which must have combined to make up a day of horror.

"You will spend the night here?" I said.

"No, my friend; you might find me a dangerous guest. I have my plans laid, and all will be well. Matters have gone so far now that they can move without my help as far as the arrest goes, though my presence is necessary for a conviction. It is obvious, therefore, than I cannot do better than get away for the few days which remain before the police are at liberty to act. It would be a great pleasure to me, therefore, if you could come on to the Continent with me."

"The practice is quiet," said I, "and I have an accommodating neighbor. I should be glad to come."

"And to start tomorrow morning?"

"If necessary."

"Oh, yes, it is most necessary. Then these are your instructions, and I beg, my dear Watson, that you will obey them to the letter, for you are now playing a double-handed game with me against the cleverest rogue and the most powerful syndicate of criminals in Europe. Now listen! You will dispatch whatever luggage you intend to take by a trusty messenger unaddressed to Victoria tonight. In the morning you will send for a hansom, desiring your man to take neither the first nor the second which may present itself. Into this hansom you will jump, and you will drive to the Strand end of the Lowther Arcade, handing the address to the cabman upon a slip of paper, with a request that he will not throw it away. Have your fare ready, and the instant that your cab stops, dash through the Arcade, timing yourself to reach the other side at a quarter past nine. You will find a small brougham waiting close to the curb, driven by a fellow with a heavy black cloak tipped at the collar with red. Into this you will step, and you will reach Victoria in time for the Continental express."

"Where shall I meet you?"

"At the station. The second first-class carriage from the front will be reserved for us."

"The carriage is our rendezvous, then?"

"Yes."

It was in vain that I asked Holmes to remain for the evening. It was evident to me that he thought he might bring trouble to the roof he was under, and that that was the motive which impelled him to go. With a few hurried words as to our plans for the morrow he rose and came out with me into the garden, clambering over the wall which leads into Mortimer Street, and immediately whistling for a hansom, in which I heard him drive away.

In the morning I obeyed Holmes's injunctions to the letter. A hansom was procured with such precautions as would prevent its being one which was placed ready for us, and I drove immediately after breakfast to the Lowther Arcade, through which I hurried at the top of my speed. A brougham was waiting with a very massive driver wrapped in a dark cloak, who, the instant that I had stepped in, whipped up the horse and rattled off to Victoria Station. On my alighting there he turned the carriage, and dashed away without so much as a look in my direction.

So far all had gone admirably. My luggage was waiting for me, and I had no difficulty in finding the carriage which Holmes had indicated, the less so as it was the only one in the train which was marked "Engaged". My only source of anxiety now was the non-appearance of Holmes. The station clock marked only seven minutes from the time when we were due to start. In vain I searched among the groups of travellers and leave-takers for the lithe figure of my friend. There was no sign of him. I spent a few minutes in assisting a venerable Italian priest, who was endeavoring to make a porter understand, in his broken English, that his luggage was to be booked through to Paris. Then, having taken another look around, I returned to my carriage, where I found that the porter, in spite of the ticket, had given me my decrepit Italian friend as a travelling companion. It was useless for me to explain to him that his presence was an intrusion, for my Italian was even more limited than his English, so I shrugged my shoulders resignedly and continued to look out anxiously for my friend. A chill of fear had come over me, as I thought that his absence might mean that some blow had fallen during the night. Already the doors had all been shut and the whistle blown, when—

"My dear Watson," said a voice, "you have not even condescended to say good morning."

I turned in uncontrollable astonishment. The aged ecclesiastic had turned his face towards me. For an instant the wrinkles were smoothed away, the nose drew away from the chin, the lower lip ceased to protrude and the mouth to mumble, the dull eyes regained their fire, the drooping figure expanded. The next the whole frame collapsed, and Holmes had gone as quickly as he had come.

"Good heavens!" I cried. "How you startled me!"

"Every precaution is still necessary," he whispered. "I have reason to think that they are hot upon our trail. Ah, there is Moriarty himself."

The train had already begun to move as Holmes spoke. Glancing back I saw a tall man pushing his way furiously through the crowd and waving his hand as if he desired to have the train stopped. It was too late, however, for we were rapidly gathering momentum, and an instant later had shot clear of the station.

"With all our precautions, you see that we have cut it rather fine," said Holmes, laughing. He rose, and throwing off the black cassock and hat which had formed his disguise, he packed them away in a hand-bag.

"Have you seen the morning paper, Watson?"

"No."

"You haven't seen about Baker Street, then?"

"Baker Street?"

"They set fire to our rooms last night. No great harm was done."

"Good heavens, Holmes! This is intolerable."

"They must have lost my track completely after their bludgeon-man was arrested. Otherwise they could not have imagined that I had returned to my rooms. They had evidently taken the precaution of watching you, however, and that is what has brought Moriarty to Victoria. You could not have made any slip in coming?"

"I did exactly what you advised."

"Did you find your brougham?"

"Yes, it was waiting."

"Did you recognize your coachman?"

"No."

"It was my brother Mycroft. It is an advantage to get about in such a case without taking a mercenary into your confidence. But we must plan what we are to do about Moriarty now."

"As this is an express, and as the boat runs in connection with it, I should think we have shaken him off very effectively."

"My dear Watson, you evidently did not realize my meaning when I said that this man may be taken as being quite on the same intellectual plane as myself. You do not imagine that if I were the pursuer I should allow myself to be baffled by so slight an obstacle. Why, then, should you think so meanly of him?"

"What will he do?"

"What I should do."

"What would you do, then?"

"Engage a special."

"But it must be late."

"By no means. This train stops at Canterbury; and there is always at least a quarter of an hour's delay at the boat. He will catch us there."

"One would think that we were the criminals. Let us have him arrested on his arrival."

"It would be to ruin the work of three months. We should get the big fish, but the smaller would dart right and left out of the net. On Monday we should have them all. No, an arrest is inadmissible."

"What then?"

"We shall get out at Canterbury."

"And then?"

"Well, then we must make a cross-country journey to Newhaven, and so over to Dieppe. Moriarty will again do what I should do. He will get on to Paris, mark down our luggage, and wait for two days at the depot. In the meantime we shall treat ourselves to a couple of carpet bags, encourage the manufacturers of the countries through which we travel, and make our way at our leisure into Switzerland, via Luxemburg and Basle."

I am too old a traveller to allow myself to be seriously inconvenienced by the loss of my luggage, but I confess that I was annoyed at the idea of being forced to dodge and hide before a man whose record was black with unutterable infamies. It was evident, however, that Holmes understood the situation more clearly than I did. At Canterbury, therefore, we alighted, only to find that we should have to wait an hour before we could get a train to Newhaven.

I was still looking rather ruefully after the rapidly disappearing luggage van which contained my wardrobe, when Holmes pulled my sleeve and pointed up the line.

"Already, you see," said he.

Far away from among the Kentish woods there arose a thin spray of smoke. A minute later a carriage and engine could be seen flying along the open curve which leads to the station. We had hardly time to take our places behind a pile of luggage when it passed with a rattle and a roar, beating a blast of hot air into our faces.

"There he goes," said Holmes, as we watched the carriage swing and rock over the points. "There are limits, you see, to our friend's intelligence. It would have been a *coup de maître* had he deduced what I would deduce and acted accordingly."

"And what would he have done had he overtaken us?"

"There cannot be the least doubt that he would have made a murderous attack upon me. It is, however, a game at which two may play. The question now is whether we should take a premature lunch here, or run our chance of starving before we reach the buffet at Newhaven."

We made our way to Brussels that night and spent two days there, moving on upon the third day as far as Strasbourg. On the Monday morning Holmes had telegraphed to the London police, and in the evening we found a reply waiting for us at our hotel. Holmes tore it open, and then with a bitter curse hurled it into the grate.

"I might have known it," he groaned. "He has escaped!"

"Moriarty!"

"They have secured the whole gang with the exception of him. He has given them the slip. Of course, when I had left the country there was no one to cope with him. But I did think that I had put the game in their hands. I think that you had better return to England, Watson."

"Why?"

"Because you will find me a dangerous companion now. This man's occupation is gone. He is lost if he returns to London. If I read his character right he will devote his whole energies to revenging himself upon me. He said as much in our short interview, and I fancy that he meant it. I should certainly recommend you to return to your practice."

It was hardly an appeal to be successful with one who was an old campaigner as well as an old friend. We sat in the Strasbourg *salle à manger* arguing the question for half an hour, but the same night we had resumed our journey and were well on our way to Geneva.

For a charming week we wandered up the Valley of the Rhône, and then, branching off at Leuk, we made our way over the Gemmi Pass, still deep in snow, and so, by way of Interlaken, to Meiringen. It was a lovely trip, the dainty green of the spring below, the virgin white of the winter above; but it was clear to me that never for one instant did Holmes forget the shadow which lay across him. In the homely Alpine villages or in the lonely mountain passes, I could still tell, by his quick glancing eyes and his sharp scrutiny of every face that passed us, that he was well convinced that, walk where we would, we could not walk ourselves clear of the danger which was dogging our footsteps.

Once, I remember, as we passed over the Gemmi, and walked along the border of the melancholy Daubensee, a large rock which had been dislodged from the ridge upon our right clattered down and roared into the lake behind us. In an instant Holmes had raced up on to the ridge, and, standing upon a lofty pinnacle, craned his neck in every direction. It was in vain that our guide assured him that a fall of stones was a common chance in the springtime at that spot. He said nothing, but he smiled at me with the air of a man who sees the fulfilment of that which he had expected.

"*I don't know where the bad guys are. I'm a good guy.*"

And yet for all his watchfulness he was never depressed. On the contrary, I can never recollect having seen him in such exuberant spirits. Again and again he recurred to the fact that if he could be assured that society was freed from Professor Moriarty, he would cheerfully bring his own career to a conclusion.

"I think that I may go so far as to say, Watson, that I have not lived wholly in vain," he remarked. "If my record were closed tonight I could still survey it with equanimity. The air of London is the sweeter for my presence. In over a thousand cases I am not aware that I have ever used my powers upon the wrong side. Of late I have been tempted to look into the problems furnished by nature rather than those more superficial ones for which our artificial state of society is responsible. Your memoirs will draw to an end, Watson, upon the day that I crown my career by the capture or extinction of the most dangerous and capable criminal in Europe."

I shall be brief, and yet exact, in the little which remains for me to tell. It is not a subject on which I would willingly dwell, and yet I am conscious that a duty devolves upon me to omit no detail.

It was upon the 3rd of May that we reached the little village of Meiringen, where we put up at the Englischer Hof, then kept by Peter Steiler the elder. Our landlord was an intelligent man, and spoke excellent English, having served for three years as waiter at the Grosvenor Hotel in London. At his advice, upon the afternoon of the 4th we set off together with the intention of crossing the hills and spending the night at the hamlet of Rosenlaui. We had strict injunctions, on no account to pass the falls of Reichenbach, which are about halfway up the hill, without making a small detour to see them.

It is, indeed, a fearful place. The torrent, swollen by the melting snow, plunges into a tremendous abyss, from which the spray rolls up like the smoke from a burning house. The shaft into which the river hurls itself is an immense chasm, lined by glistening, coal-black rock, and narrowing into a creaming, boiling pit of incalculable depth, which brims over and shoots the stream onward over its jagged lip. The long sweep of green water roaring for ever down, and the thick flickering curtain of spray hissing for ever upwards, turn a man giddy with their constant whirl and clamor. We stood near the edge peering down at the gleam of the breaking water far below us against the black rocks, and listening to the half-human shout which came booming up with the spray out of the abyss.

The path has been cut half-way round the fall to afford a complete view, but it ends abruptly, and the traveller has to return as he came. We had turned to do so, when we saw a Swiss lad come running along it with a letter in his hand. It bore the mark of the hotel which we had just left, and was addressed to me by the landlord. It appeared that within a very few minutes of our leaving, an English lady had arrived who was in the last stage of consumption. She had wintered at Davos Platz, and was journeying now to join her friends at Lucern, when a sudden hemorrhage had overtaken her. It was thought that she could hardly live a few hours, but it would be a great consolation to her to see an English doctor, and, if I would only return, etc., etc. The good Steiler assured me in a postscript that he would himself look upon my compliance as a great favor, since the lady absolutely refused to see a Swiss physician, and he could not but feel that he was incurring a great responsibility.

The appeal was one which could not be ignored. It was impossible to refuse the request of a fellow-countrywoman dying in a strange land. Yet I had my scruples about leaving Holmes. It was finally agreed, however, that he would retain the young Swiss messenger with him as guide and companion while I returned to Meiringen. My friend would stay some little time at the fall, he said, and would then walk slowly over the hill to Rosenlaui, where I was to rejoin him in the evening. As I turned away I saw Holmes with his back against a rock and his arms folded, gazing down at the rush of waters. It was the last that I was ever destined to see of him in this world.

When I was near the bottom of the descent I looked back. It was impossible, from that position, to see the fall, but I could see the curving path which winds over the shoulder of the hill and leads to it. Along this a man was, I remember, walking very rapidly. I could see his black figure clearly outlined against the green behind him. I noted him, and the energy with which he walked, but he passed from my mind again as I hurried on upon my errand.

It may have been a little over an hour before I reached Meiringen. Old Steiler was standing at the porch of his hotel.

"Well," said I, as I came hurrying up, "I trust that she is no worse?"

A look of surprise passed over his face, and at the first quiver of his eyebrows my heart turned to lead in my breast.

"You did not write this?" I said, pulling the letter from my pocket. "There is no sick Englishwoman in the hotel?"

"Certainly not," he cried. "But it has the hotel mark upon it! Ha!

it must have been written by that tall Englishman who came in after you had gone. He said—"

But I waited for none of the landlord's explanations. In a tingle of fear I was already running down the village street, and making for the path which I had so lately descended. It had taken me an hour to come down. For all my efforts, two more had passed before I found myself at the fall of the Reichenbach once more. There was Holmes's alpenstock still leaning against the rock by which I had left him. But there was no sign of him, and it was in vain that I shouted. My only answer was my own voice reverberating in a rolling echo from the cliffs around me.

It was the sight of that alpenstock which turned me cold and sick. He had not gone to Rosenlaui, then. He had remained on that three-foot path, with sheer wall on one side and sheer drop on the other, until his enemy had overtaken him. The young Swiss had gone too. He had probably been in the pay of Moriarty, and had left the two men together. And then what had happened? Who was to tell us what had happened then?

I stood for a minute or two to collect myself, for I was dazed with the terror of the thing. Then I began to think of Holmes's own methods and to try to practise them in reading this tragedy. It was, alas, only too easy to do! During our conversation we had not gone to the end of the path, and the alpenstock marked the place where we had stood. The blackish soil is kept for ever soft by the incessant drift of the spray, and a bird would leave its tread upon it. Two lines of footmarks were clearly marked along the farther end of the path, both leading away from me. There were none returning. A few yards from the end the soil was all ploughed up into a patch of mud, and the brambles and ferns which fringed the chasm were torn and bedraggled. I lay upon my face and peered over, with the spray spouting up all around me. It had darkened since I had left, and now I could only see here and there the glistening of moisture upon the black walls, and far away down at the end of the shaft the gleam of the broken water. I shouted; but only the same half-human cry of the fall was borne back to my ears.

But it was destined that I should after all have a last word of greeting from my friend and comrade. I have said that his alpenstock had been left leaning against a rock which jutted on to the path. From the top of this boulder the gleam of something bright caught my eye, and, raising my hand, I found that it came from the silver cigarette-case which he used to carry. As I took it up a small square of paper, upon which it had lain, fluttered down on to the ground. Unfolding it I found that it consisted of three pages torn from his notebook and addressed to me. It was characteristic of the man that the direction was as precise, and the writing as firm and clear, as though it had been written in his study.

"My dear Watson," he said, "I write these few lines through the courtesy of Mr. Moriarty, who awaits my convenience for the final discussion of those questions which lie between us. He has been giving me a sketch of the methods by which he avoided the English police and kept himself informed of our movements. They certainly confirm the very high opinion which I had formed of his abilities. I am pleased to think that I shall be able to free society from any further effects of his presence, though I fear that it is at a cost which will give pain to my friends, and especially, my dear Watson, to you. I have already explained to you, however, that my career had in any case reached its crisis, and that no possible conclusion to it could be more congenial to me than this. Indeed, if I may make a full confession to you, I was quite convinced that the letter from Meiringen was a hoax, and I allowed you to depart on that errand under the persuasion that some development of this sort would follow. Tell Inspector Patterson that the papers which he needs to convict the gang are in pigeon-hole M, done up in a blue envelope and inscribed "Moriarty". I made every disposition of my property before leaving England, and handed it to my brother Mycroft. Pray give my greetings to Mrs. Watson, and believe me to be, my dear fellow,
Very sincerely yours,
SHERLOCK HOLMES."

A few words may suffice to tell the little that remains. An examination by experts leaves little doubt that a personal contest between the two men ended, as it could hardly fail to end in such a situation, in their reeling over, locked in each other's arms. Any attempt at recovering the bodies was absolutely hopeless, and there, deep down in that dreadful cauldron of swirling water and seething foam, will lie for all time the most dangerous criminal and the foremost champion of the law of their generation. The Swiss youth was never found again, and there can be no doubt that he was one of the numerous agents whom Moriarty kept in his employ. As to the gang, it will be within the memory of the public how completely the evidence which Holmes had accumulated exposed their organization, and how heavily the hand of the dead man weighed upon them. Of their terrible chief few details came out during the proceedings, and if I have now been compelled to make a clear statement of his career, it is due to those injudicious champions who have endeavored to clear his memory by attacks upon him whom I shall ever regard as the best and the wisest man whom I have ever known.

In this story, find: the quest, the monster, the faithful companion, the descent into the underworld, the glorification of the hero. What other heroes can you name who had faithful companions?

The detective and the cowboy are two very popular types of hero. Using some movies or television programs that you know, show how the "shape" or pattern of their quests is basically the same.

The more abstract the hero and villain become in a story, the more that story becomes like myth. Would you say this story is close to myth? Why?

"Might for right" can sometimes sound "put-on," making a hero seem artificially noble. But do you think "might for right" could be the hidden, almost unconscious, motive of a man who fights for his country or for his religion? How?

Many of the quest stories in this book, because they focus so clearly on a single hero, have perhaps suggested that the quest is a very personal affair. Actually, however, the hero's quest almost always has a larger social significance. This is most clearly seen in the romance quest, in which a clearly larger-than-life hero's journey and battle can be seen to have an effect on the whole civilization of which he is a part.

The quest of Theseus for his rightful kingdom has many points of contact with the quests of other heroes like Perseus, Heracles, the boy in "The Street," or the young hunter in "The Bear." But Theseus is also the legendary founder of Athenian civilization, and so he is even more a cultural hero than the others. The effects of his courageous deeds have social significance. He clears the road from Troizen to Athens of a whole series of terrible bandits, and leaves it safe for future travel. He saves the people in the plain of Marathon from the great bull. He rescues the Athenian hostages of Minos from the Minotaur, and his city from having to pay a dreadful yearly tribute. Subsequently he saves Athens from the invasion of the Amazons; makes peace with Pirithous and his army; and even defends his new ally from the attack of the Centaurs. With each of his victories, his own city and the surrounding country become freer, more secure places.

King Arthur's quest for the Round Table is similar. In the scene from *Camelot,* he wrestles with the dream of a "new order, where might is used only for right, to improve instead of destroy." The Peach Boy is a kind of Japanese King Arthur, rescuing the coastal villages from the horned ogres of the Island of Evil who had been "ravaging and pillaging the countryside." To Dr. Watson, the great detective Sherlock Holmes ("the best and wisest man" he has ever known) is the only fit man to execute justice on

Professor Moriarty, the "Napoleon of crime." Watson records for us Holmes' honest reflection at the end of his life: "I have not lived wholly in vain . . . in over one thousand cases I am not aware that I have ever used my powers on the wrong side." Robin Hood sells meat fairly to the townsfolk and uses his wits to cheat the cheaters by making the Sheriff's greed trap him into paying back what he had previously stolen from the poor. And even though his great strength saved only a few fellow miners, Big Bad John is celebrated in song as a "big, big man."

The romance hero is, of course, a highly idealized figure. In fact, he could be said to embody the best that human civilization has to offer—not just physical strength, but greatness of heart, imagination and vision. For these reasons, his quest has a great deal to do with the periodic renewal that human societies seem to require, in order to grow, or even to survive. These quests provide images of growth and change. They embody symbols that carry the human spirit forward in counteraction to the comfortable but limiting habits that hold it back. Each hero, to a greater or lesser degree, rescues a dying or bound social order from the rigidity of settled habits or the tyranny of evil laws. For these reasons, the significance of their quests may not always be understood by the society in which they live. So, leaders like Theseus and Red Eric may even be thrust out of their kingdoms, and it is left for later ages to tell of their exploits. Even to King Arthur himself, in a moment of cynicism, his dream of the Round Table seems naive," "adolescent," "folly." But to Guenevere, whose imagination is free and unclouded, such a quest, like man himself, seems only a "marvelous" thing.

1973

1959

1981

1939

274

Alan E. Cober '72

6

2008

1975

Oedipus

A Greek myth
Retold by REX WARNER

After Apollo and Diana had entirely destroyed the race of Amphion, Thebes was without a king, and the people summoned Laius, a descendant of Cadmus, to come to the throne which, indeed, was his by right.

Laius had been warned by an oracle that, if he had a son, this son was fated to kill his own father. When, therefore, his wife Jocasta bore a son, Laius, in fear of the oracle, decided to put the child to death. Soon after the baby was born, a spike was thrust through his feet and he was given to a goatherd, who was told to leave the child on the cold steep slopes of Mount Cithaeron, where he would be devoured by wild beasts. The goatherd reported to the king that he had carried out his orders and the king's mind was set at rest. In fact, however, the man had not had the heart to destroy the small child and had given it to one of the servants of Polybus, King of Corinth, whom he had met on the mountain. This servant took the child to Corinth and there he was brought up and adopted by Polybus and his wife Merope, who were childless. They gave him the name of Oedipus, or "swollen feet," because of the marks left on his feet by the spike with which they had been pierced.

So in Corinth Oedipus grew to manhood, believing himself to be the son of Polybus and Merope. He was distinguished in every way, and it was through jealousy of him that once at a feast a drunken young man mocked at him for not being the true son of his parents. Oedipus, in great anxiety, went to Merope and asked her for the truth. She attempted to set his mind at rest, but still he was not satisfied. He left Corinth alone and on foot, and went to ask the advice of Apollo's oracle at Delphi. What he heard terrified him. "Unhappy man," replied the oracle, "keep far away from your father! If you meet him, you will kill him. Then you will marry your mother, and have children who will be fated to crime and misfortune."

Now Oedipus believed that it was because of some knowledge of this dreadful fate that Polybus and Merope had given indefinite answers to his questions. He was determined not to do them any harm and vowed that never again would he set foot in what he believed to be his native city of Corinth.

So, still startled by the oracle's reply, he left Delphi, turning away from the sea and the way to Corinth, and traveling inland over the lower slopes of Mount Parnassus. On his left were the high mountains where eagles circled overhead; below him, on the right, was a long river valley where olive trees grew in such numbers that they themselves seemed a great flood of gray-green and silver flowing to the sea.

In the mountains there is a place where three roads meet, and here, as Oedipus was traveling on foot, he was overtaken by an old man in a chariot, with servants running at the side of the chariot. One of these servants struck Oedipus on the back with his staff, telling him rudely to make way for his betters. This was treatment that the young man, who had been brought up as a king's son, could not tolerate. He struck the servant down and killed him. He was then attacked by the old man in the chariot and by the other servants, and, defending his own life, he killed them all except for one who escaped and made his way back to Thebes with the news that King Laius had been killed. Since the man did not like to admit that he and the rest had been destroyed by one man singlehanded, he pretended that they had been attacked by a large band of robbers.

Oedipus, with no idea that he had killed his own father, went on his way in the direction of Thebes. He went past Helicon and came in sight of Mount Cithaeron, where, as an infant, he had been left to die. From the country people he learned not only that the King of Thebes had been killed, but that the whole land was terrorized by the Sphinx, a monster with lion's body and the head of a woman. The Sphinx guarded the approaches to the plain of Thebes. It had a riddle to which it demanded the answer from all whom it met. Already in the rocky plain were many piles of the bones of those who had failed to give the right answer, and now it had been proclaimed that if any man could answer the riddle and free the country of the Sphinx, he should have Queen Jocasta for his wife and himself become King of Thebes.

Oedipus resolved to make the attempt. Going out to a rock which towered above the plain, he found the Sphinx sitting on top of it, with great claws clutching the sandy ground. He demanded to know the riddle and the Sphinx said: "What is it that in the morning walks on four legs, in the midday walks on two, and in the evening on three?"

"It is Man," replied Oedipus. "In the morning of his childhood he crawls on hands and knees; in the midday of his youth he walks on his two legs; in the evening of his old age he needs a stick to support himself, and so goes on three legs."

The Sphinx, finding that at last her riddle was answered, threw herself down, as was fated, from the rock and died. Oedipus received his reward. He was made King of Thebes and took Jocasta, little knowing that she was his own mother, to be his wife. So the oracle was fulfilled, though none of those who had fulfilled it knew what the truth was.

Oedipus for many years ruled Thebes well and wisely. He was happy with Jocasta, who bore him four children—two twin sons Eteocles and Polynices, and two daughters Antigone and Ismene. It was not until these children had grown up that the truth was revealed and the happiness of Oedipus turned into the greatest misery.

Thebes, since the death of the Sphinx, had been prosperous and successful; but in the end a plague fell upon the land. The cattle died in the fields; blight fell upon the crops; then the people began to die, and the air was full of ravens and of vultures, ill-omened birds that came to feast upon the dead bodies of animals and of men. The people called in vain upon the gods to help. They looked also to their king, who had saved them before from the persecution of the Sphinx.

Oedipus sent Creon, the brother of Jocasta, to the oracle at Delphi to ask the god how Thebes might be free of the plague. The reply came back that the plague had been sent because of the murder of Laius and because not even yet had the murderer made atonement for the bloodshed.

Oedipus immediately and with his usual energy began to make inquiries into the murder which he had himself unknowingly committed so long ago. He examined those who had heard the story at the time, and he sent for the old prophet Tiresias, whose wisdom was greater than that of mortals. The gods had taken away his sight, but had given him knowledge of the future and the past.

When the old man was summoned before the king, he had no wish to speak. "Let me go home again," he said, "and do not ask me these questions. It would be better, far better, for you to remain in ignorance. Take my advice, which is meant kindly to you."

But Oedipus, anxious for his people, and determined to show himself once more their deliverer, pressed on with his inquiries. As the old prophet still refused to speak, he began to grow angry, and to insult him. "Either," he said, "you are an old cheat who knows nothing, or else you have been bribed by the murderer to conceal his name, or else perhaps you are the murderer yourself. Either speak, or suffer every punishment that I can think out for you."

Then Tiresias spoke: "You yourself, Oedipus, are the man who murdered Laius. You murdered him in the place where three roads meet on the way from Delphi. It is because of you that the plague has fallen on this city. And there is worse news still that waits for you."

Oedipus remembered the old man in the chariot whom he had killed so long ago. He was horrified at the thought that he might have killed his wife's husband and began to question her as to his appearance and the number of his servants. As she answered him, he became convinced that the prophet had spoken the truth.

But Jocasta attempted to persuade him that Tiresias should not be believed. "Even Apollo's oracle," she said, "sometimes tells lies. For example Laius was told that he would be killed by his own son, but the only son we ever had was killed and eaten by the wild beasts on Mount Cithaeron."

Oedipus was interested by this story and demanded proof of it. The goatherd, now a very old man, who had taken the baby to Mount Cithaeron, was summoned. Oedipus questioned him closely and now, thinking that he had nothing to fear, the goatherd admitted that he had not killed the child, as he had been told to do. Instead he had given the poor weak thing to a servant of the King of Corinth.

As he spoke, and as Oedipus, in increasing excitement, went on questioning him, Jocasta suddenly realized the truth. Oedipus had been brought up by the King of Corinth, he still had on his feet the marks of the iron that had pierced them; it was indeed he who had killed Laius, and he who, fulfilling the oracle, had married his own mother. She cried out once. "I am an unhappy woman," she said, and then, looking for the last time on Oedipus, she went into the house. Then she tied her girdle to a beam, made a running knot in it, and hanged herself.

Meanwhile Oedipus was sifting the evidence of the goatherd. His keen intelligence saw how all the story fitted together, but only gradually could his mind grasp the truth—that, though he had never known it or suspected it, the words of the oracle had for long been proved, in fact, that he had killed his father and become the husband of his mother. As he became fully conscious of his own position, he heard a cry from indoors. There he found Jocasta dead, hanging from the palace roof. In misery, despair and shame, he took the pins from the buckle of her girdle and with them pierced his eyes. Then, with the blood streaming down his face, and with all the world dark to him, he came back to his people, resolved finally to leave them and to go abroad in exile, so that he might atone for the guilt which he had never imagined as being his.

His daughters, Antigone and Ismene, went with him, and for long, guiding the steps of their blind father, they wandered in the hills and valleys of Cithaeron and the mountains of Attica. In the end they came to Colonus, a little town near Theseus's kingdom of Athens. It is a town where fine horses are bred and where all the summer the tawny nightingale sings among the berries of the ivy that cloaks the trees. Here at last Oedipus found peace. Theseus gave him sanctuary, partly for his own sake, partly because an oracle had revealed that the land where Oedipus died would be famous and prosperous. Yet if Oedipus died at all, he died in a way that was miraculous. Theseus alone saw, or might have seen the manner of his departing from life. For suddenly, in the sunshine and among the singing of the birds, the blind king began to feel the power of the gods upon him. He left his two daughters in the grove of Colonus and commanded Theseus to lead him forward over the rolling ground to the place where he had to be. Then, taking leave of Theseus also, he went on alone, with firm, though slow, steps, as though he still had the use of his eyes. From the clear sky came the roar of thunder and Theseus, in fear and reverence for the gods, hid his eyes. When he looked up again, Oedipus had gone, taken perhaps to heaven or lost in some invisible fold in the ground.

In leafy, well-watered Colonus, and in Athens itself he received for ever the honors due to a hero, and to one whom, in the end, the gods loved.

Compare the births and childhoods of Oedipus and Theseus. How are they alike?

Oedipus discovered much more about himself than the names of his mother and father. What did he come to realize about what it means to be a human being? Is this what caused him to blind himself? What do you think his blindness represents?

Oedipus performs a number of heroic deeds: leaving his home for a higher purpose, defending himself against insults and attack on the road, slaying a terrifying monster, saving a kingdom. Why, then, is his life filled with sorrow and death?

Do you think the gods loved Oedipus? Why? Do you think the love of the gods is a necessary requirement for being a hero? Why?

Heroes

Shall I ever believe again, having once believed
In fugitive heroes and the words they say?
How often from worship have I looked away
And wept I was a simpleton, deceived
By the captains of power and glory. I was a child bereaved
Of childhood. Even my closest, even they
Who loved me, had lessened into faulty clay:
And I was the one hero, I who grieved. . . .

A simpleton, indeed, choosing despair:
Either great heroes and myself a child,
Or else myself the only faultless one!
I beg you, anybody, have a care
Not to be like me—though at last I smiled . . .
We are all such little heroes in the sun.

WITTER BYNNER

What has this poet discovered about himself? How is it like what Oedipus realized?

If this poet has stopped believing in heroes, what does he believe in now?

Sonnet 26

We travel on a familiar road every day
To return to the place we live,
But in this forest, there are hidden
Many narrow paths, secluded and strange.

When we walk on one of these strange paths we panic,
Afraid of getting farther and farther, getting lost;
Yet, without knowing, through a clearing in the woods
Suddenly we see the place where we live,

Displayed on the horizon, like a new island.
So many things around us demand that we
Make new discoveries.

Think not that everything is already familiar.
When you lie dying and touch your own hair and skin,
You will wonder: Whose body is this?

FENG CHIH
Translated by KAI-YU HSU

Red Eric was able to say "I am I." Do you think this poet can say that? Why?

What is the perilous journey the poet is talking about?

How was Heracles' journey, like this poet's, a return to his original "home"?

What is the one journey everyone makes?

The Man Whose Luck Was Asleep

A Persian legend
Retold by ELEANOR BROCKETT

Once upon a time there were two brother who had each inherited an equal share of their father's property, but while the land of the younger brother flourished and prospered although he took no trouble with it at all, that of the elder remained totally unproductive however hard he worked. The elder brother therefore came to the conclusion that the younger brother's land must be more rich and fertile than his and suggested that they should exchange. The younger brother happily agreed, but this made no difference. The younger brother continued to have good crops and reap plentiful harvests while the elder brother's land was producing nothing at all.

The elder brother, now more puzzled than ever, pondered on what he should do and one day he decided that he would go to his brother's corn heap at night, take some of his corn and spread it upon his own. He duly arrived at the spot after darkness had fallen, tethered his donkey, and was just about to open the sack he had brought with him when a strange man suddenly appeared in front of him and asked him what he was doing there.

"I think I should ask you that," said the elder brother. "Who are you?"

"I," said the stranger, "am your brother's Luck and it is part of my duty to watch over his corn and see that no one steals it."

"Oh, you are my brother's Luck, are you?" said the elder brother. "Well, I should very much like to know where my Luck is."

The stranger told the elder brother that his Luck was to be found on the top of a far-distant mountain and gave him directions how to get there. "If you want your affairs to prosper," he added, "you must find your Luck and wake him up."

The elder brother, now convinced that his fortune was about to change, gathered together all he would need for his long journey, placed his land in his younger brother's care, and set off.

He had travelled some distance when he was terrified to see a fierce lion in his path, moving threateningly towards him as if to devour him. The elder brother went on his knees and begged the lion to spare him and allow him to continue on his way in safety.

"I will let you go," said the lion, "provided you tell me exactly where you are off to and what you are going to do."

The elder brother told the lion all about his troubles and that he was making this journey to find his Luck and wake him up.

"Oh," said the Lion. "Well, when you have found your Luck and wakened him, please oblige me by asking him why it is that however much I eat I never feel satisfied, and inquire of him if there is any cure for this condition."

The elder brother agreed to do this, and continued on his way until he came to a village where he met an old farmer who offered him shelter for the night. In the course of the evening the elder brother told the farmer all about himself and how he was going to find his Luck and wake him up.

"When you have found your Luck and wakened him," said the farmer, "please do me the kindness of asking him why it is that a certain piece of ground I have, however much I tend it, will not yield."

Next morning, the elder brother started off on his journey once more and went on and on until he reached the gates of a city. As was the custom in this place, the stranger was at once led into the presence of the King, who inquired what business had brought him there. Once more the elder brother told his story, and the King too asked a favor of him.

"When you have found your Luck and wakened him," said the King, "please ask him on my behalf why it is that however much I care for my country and my people, my realm does not prosper as it should."

Having agreed to the King's request, the elder brother left the city and continued on his journey which was now nearing its end. Soon the mountain was in sight and before long the elder brother was toiling up its slopes. On the summit he found a large, well-set-up man lying asleep and snoring loudly. The elder brother bent down and roused him: "Come on," he called. "Wake up! Do you sleep all your time away?"

The man rubbed his eyes, yawned loudly and stretched. "Ah," he said, "now I am awake I shall not go to sleep again. Do not worry."

When the man was thoroughly awake the elder brother put to him the questions he had promised the lion, the farmer and the King he would ask, and when he had got the answers he started on his way down again.

First he came to the city gates and was once more led before the King.

"Well," said the King, "did you manage to find your Luck and waken him and put my question to him?"

"Yes, I did," said the elder brother, mightily pleased with himself.

"And what was the answer?" inquired the King.

"We shall need to be alone before I can tell you that," said the elder brother. "I must tell you in private."

The King accordingly gave orders that everyone should leave the audience chamber and when the King and the elder brother were alone, the latter said:

"My Luck said that you, your Majesty, are really a woman and that a country never prospers under a woman's rule."

The King became greatly agitated and implored the elder brother never to let anyone else know the secret. "But," he added, "now that you have discovered it, you shall become king in my stead and marry me."

"Oh, I cannot possibly do that," exclaimed the elder brother. "I must get back to my land. Now that my Luck is awake I can expect an end to my troubles and my next harvest will doubtless be a good one."

The King thereupon inquired as to the extent of his land and offered him estates many times its value, but the elder brother would hear none of it and continued on his way.

And once again he approached the village where he had spent the night with the farmer. His former host greeted him and gave him a great welcome, inquiring eagerly whether he had managed to find his Luck and waken him.

"Yes, I did," replied the elder brother.

"And what is his answer to my question?" asked the farmer.

"He says that the reason that certain piece of ground does not yield is that there is treasure buried beneath it. If you will dig and recover the treasure, the ground will become fertile again."

Thereupon the old farmer led the elder brother to the piece of ground in question and fetched a spade for each of them. Together they dug and dug until they came upon one, then two, then three— in all seven fabulous jars full of gold.

"My friend," said the farmer, "I am old and have not much longer to live. Stay with me, marry my daughter and this land and this treasure will be yours."

"Oh, I could not possibly do that," replied the elder brother. "I must get back to my land. Now that my Luck is awake I can expect an end to my troubles and my next harvest will doubtless be a good one."

The old farmer did his best to persuade him, but his mind was made up and once more he set off on his homeward way.

And then he met again the lion who asked him how he had fared. The elder brother told the lion of all his adventures so far, finishing with an account of how the King who was a woman had wanted him to marry her and become ruler of the kingdom and how the farmer with the buried treasure had wanted him to stay and marry his daughter.

"And what was your Luck's answer to my question?" asked the lion.

"My Luck," said the elder brother importantly, "said there certainly is a cure for your trouble."

"And what is it?" said the lion. "I cannot wait."

"My Luck said," continued the elder brother, "that whenever you meet a man who is a complete fool you should at once tear him to pieces and gobble him up."

There was a little pause while the lion pondered on these words. Then he said: "Well, I never in all my life met a more complete fool than you!"

And that was the end of the elder brother.

The man in this story searches so blindly for what he thinks is important, that he misses what is obvious. What does he miss? What does this tell you about the difficulty of the quest for identity?

A Bao A Qu

A Malay Legend
Retold by JORGE LUIS BORGES

If you want to look out over the loveliest landscape in the world, you must climb to the top of the Tower of Victory in Chitor. There, standing on a circular terrace, one has a sweep of the whole horizon. A winding stairway gives access to this terrace, but only those who do not believe in the legend dare climb up. The tale runs:

On the stairway of the Tower of Victory there has lived since the beginning of time a being sensitive to the many shades of the human soul and known as the A Bao A Qu. It lies dormant, for the most part on the first step, until at the approach of a person some secret life is touched off in it, and deep within the creature an inner light begins to glow. At the same time, its body and almost translucent skin begin to stir. But only when someone starts up the spiraling stairs is the A Bao A Qu brought to consciousness, and then it sticks close to the visitor's heels, keeping to the outside of the turning steps, where they are most worn by the generations of pilgrims. At each level the creature's color becomes more intense, its shape approaches perfection, and the bluish light it gives off is more brilliant. But it achieves its ultimate form only at the topmost step, when the climber is a person who has attained Nirvana and whose acts cast no shadows. Otherwise, the A Bao A Qu hangs back before reaching the top, as if paralyzed, its body incomplete, its blue growing paler, and its glow hesitant. The creature suffers when it cannot come to completion, and its moan is a barely audible sound, something like the rustling of silk. Its span of life is brief, since as soon as the traveler climbs down, the A Bao A Qu wheels and tumbles to the first steps, where, worn out and almost shapeless, it waits for the next visitor. People say that its tentacles are visible only when it reaches the middle of the staircase. It is also said that it can see with its whole body and that to the touch it is like the skin of a peach.

In the course of centuries, the A Bao A Qu has reached the terrace only once.

Translated by NORMAN THOMAS DI GIOVANNI

The Frog Prince

Retold by JOSEPH JACOBS

Once upon a time, and a very good time it was, though it wasn't in my time, nor in your time, nor any one else's time, there was a girl whose mother had died, and her father married again. And her stepmother hated her because she was more beautiful than herself, and she was very cruel to her. She used to make her do all the servant's work, and never let her have any peace. At last, one day, the stepmother thought to get rid of her altogether; so she handed her a sieve and said to her: "Go, fill it at the Well of the World's End and bring it home to me full, or woe betide you." For she thought she would never be able to find the Well of the World's End, and, if she did, how could she bring home a sieve full of water?

Well, the girl started off, and asked every one she met to tell her where was the Well of the World's End. But nobody knew, and she didn't know what to do, when a queer little old woman, all bent double told her where it was, and how she could get to it. So she did what the old woman told her, and at last arrived at the Well of the World's End. But when she dipped the sieve in the cold, cold water, it all ran out again. She tried and she tried again, but every time it was the same; and at last she sat down and cried as if her heart would break.

Suddenly she heard a croaking voice, and she looked up and saw a great frog with goggle eyes looking at her and speaking to her.

"What's the matter, dearie?" it said.

"Oh, dear, oh dear," she said, "my stepmother has sent me all this long way to fill this sieve with water from the Well of the World's End, and I can't fill it no how at all."

"Well," said the frog, "if you promise me to do whatever I bid you for a whole night long, I'll tell you how to fill it."

So the girl agreed, and the frog said:

> "Stop it with moss and daub it with clay,
> And then it will carry the water away;"

and then it gave a hop, skip, and jump, and went flop into the Well of the World's End.

So the girl looked about for some moss, and lined the bottom of the sieve with it, and over that she put some clay, and then she dipped it once again into the Well of the World's End; and this time, the water didn't run out, and she turned to go away.

Just then the frog popped up its head out of the Well of the World's End, and said: "Remember your promise."

"All right," said the girl; for thought she, "what harm can a frog do me?"

So she went back to her stepmother, and brought the sieve full of water from the Well of the World's End. The stepmother was angry as angry, but she said nothing at all.

That very evening they heard something tap-tapping at the door low down, and a voice cried out:

> "Open the door, my hinny, my heart,
> Open the door, my darling;
> Mind you the words that you and I spoke,
> Down in the meadow, at the World's End Well."

"Whatever can that be?" cried out the stepmother, and the girl had to tell her all about it, and what she had promised the frog.

"Girls must keep their promises," said the stepmother. "Go and open the door this instant." For she was glad the girl would have to obey a nasty frog.

So the girl went and opened the door, and there was the frog from the Well of the World's End. And it hopped, and it hopped, and it jumped, till it reached the girl, and then it said:

> "Lift me to your knee, my hinny, my heart;
> Lift me to your knee, my own darling;
> Remember the words you and I spoke,
> Down in the meadow by the World's End Well."

But the girl didn't like to, till her stepmother said: "Lift it up this instant, you hussy! Girls must keep their promises!"

So at last she lifted the frog up on to her lap, and it lay there for a time, till at last it said:

"Give me some supper, my hinny, my heart,
Give me some supper, my darling;
Remember the words you and I spake,
In the meadow, by the Well of the World's End."

Well, she didn't mind doing that, so she got it a bowl of milk and bread, and fed it well. And when the frog had finished, it said:

"Go with me to bed, my hinny, my heart,
Go with me to bed, my own darling;
Mind you the words you spake to me,
Down by the cold well, so weary."

But that the girl wouldn't do, till her stepmother said: "Do what you promised, girl; girls must keep their promises. Do what you're bid, or out you go, you and your froggie."

So the girl took the frog with her to bed, and kept it as far away from her as she could. Well, just as the day was beginning to break what should the frog say but:

"Chop off my head, my hinny, my heart,
Chop off my head, my own darling;
Remember the promise you made to me,
Down by the cold well so weary."

At first the girl wouldn't, for she thought of what the frog had done for her at the Well of the World's End. But when the frog said the words over again she went and took an axe and chopped off its head and lo! and behold, there stood before her a handsome young prince, who told her that he had been enchanted by a wicked magician, and he could never be unspelled till some girl would do his bidding for a whole night, and chop off his head at the end of it.

The stepmother was surprised indeed when she found the young prince instead of the nasty frog, and she wasn't best pleased, you may be sure, when the prince told her that he was going to marry her step-daughter because she had unspelled him. But married they were, and went away to live in the castle of the king, his father, and all the step-mother had to console her was that it was all through her that her step-daughter was married to a prince.

Little Boxes

Little boxes on the hillside,
Little boxes made of ticky tacky,
Little boxes on the hillside,
Little boxes all the same.

There's a green one, and a pink one,
And a blue one, and yellow one,
And they're all made out of ticky tacky,
And they all look just the same.

And the people in the houses,
All went to the University,
Where they were put in boxes,
And they came out all the same.
And there's doctors, and there's lawyers,
And business executives,
And they're all made out of ticky tacky,
And they all look just the same.

And they all play on the golf course,
And drink their martinis dry,
And they all have pretty children,
And the children go to school,
And the children go to summer camp,
And then to the university,
Where they are put in boxes,
And they come out all the same.

And the boys go into business,
And marry and raise a family;
In boxes made of ticky tacky
And they all look just the same.
There's a green one, and a pink one,
And a blue one, and a yellow one,
And they're all made out of ticky tacky,
And they all look just the same.

MALVINA REYNOLDS

Who are the heroes in this song? What is their quest? How is it like the quests of others in this book? How is it different?

Do you think these people can say "I am I"? Why or why not?

The ancient heroes often had gods or oracles tell them exactly what their quests were. How do you think people of our own time discover their quests? Do you think it is easier or more difficult to say "I am I" in our age? Why?

Saturday's Child

Some are teethed on a silver spoon,
  With the stars strung for a rattle;
I cut my teeth as the black raccoon—
  For implements of battle.

Some are swaddled in silk and down,
  And heralded by a star;
They swathed my limbs in a sackcloth gown
  On a night that was black as tar.

For some, godfather and goddame
  The opulent fairies be;
Dame Poverty gave me my name,
  And Pain godfathered me.

For I was born on Saturday—
  "Bad time for planting a seed,"
Was all my father had to say,
  And, "One mouth more to feed."

Death cut the strings that gave me life,
  And handed me to Sorrow,
The only kind of middle wife
  My folks could beg or borrow.

COUNTEE CULLEN

How is this poet's birth quite different from the marvelous births of the mythic heroes we have seen?

Given the circumstances of his birth, what will this boy's quest become? What monsters will he have to slay?

Knoxville: Summer 1915

From A Death in the Family
JAMES AGEE

We are talking now of summer evenings in Knoxville, Tennessee in the time that I lived there so successfully disguised to myself as a child. It was a little bit mixed sort of block, fairly solidly lower middle class, with one or two juts apiece on either side of that. The houses corresponded: middle-sized gracefully fretted wood houses built in the late nineties and early nineteen hundreds, with small front and side and more spacious back yards, and trees in the yards, and porches. These were softwooded trees, poplars, tulip trees, cottonwoods. There were fences around one or two of the houses, but mainly the yards ran into each other with only now and then a low hedge that wasn't doing very well. There were few good friends among the grown people, and they were not poor enough for the other sort of intimate acquaintance, but everyone nodded and spoke, and even might talk short times, trivially, and at the two extremes of the general or the particular, and ordinarily nextdoor neighbors talked quite a bit when they happened to run into each other, and never paid calls. The men were mostly small businessmen, one or two very modestly executives, one or two worked with their hands, most of them clerical, and most of them between thirty and forty-five.

But it is of these evenings, I speak.

Supper was at six and was over by half past. There was still daylight, shining softly and with a tarnish, like the lining of a shell; and the carbon lamps lifted at the corners were on in the light, and the locusts were started, and the fire flies were out, and a few frogs were flopping in the dewy grass, by the time the fathers and the children came out. The children ran out first hell bent and yelling those names by which they were known; then the fathers sank out leisurely in crossed suspenders, their collars removed and their necks looking tall and shy. The mothers stayed back in the kitchen washing and drying, putting things away, recrossing their traceless footsteps like the lifetime journeys of bees, measuring out the dry cocoa for breakfast. When they came out they had taken off their aprons and their skirts were dampened and they sat in rockers on their porches quietly.

It is not of the games children played in the evening that I want to speak now, it is of a contemporaneous atmosphere that has little to do with them: that of the fathers of families, each in his space of lawn, his shirt fishlike pale in the unnatural light and his face nearly anonymous, hosing their lawns. The hoses were attached at spigots that stood out of the brick foundations of the houses. The nozzles were variously set but usually so there was a long sweet stream of spray, the nozzle wet in the hand, the water trickling the right forearm and the peeled-back cuff, and the water whishing out a long loose and low-curved cone, and so gentle a sound. First an insane noise of violence in the nozzle, then the still irregular sound of adjustment, then the smoothing into steadiness and a pitch as accurately tuned to the size and style of stream as any violin. So many qualities of sound out of one hose: so many choral differences out of those several hoses that were in earshot. Out of any one hose, the almost dead silence of the release, and the short still arch of the separate big drops, silent as a held breath, and the only noise the flattering noise on leaves and the slapped grass at the fall of each big drop. That, and the intense hiss with the intense stream; that, and that same intensity not growing less but growing more quiet and delicate with the turn of the nozzle, up to that extreme tender whisper when the water was just a wide bell of film. Chiefly, though, the hoses were set much alike, in a compromise between distance and tenderness of spray (and quite surely a sense of art behind this compromise, and a quiet deep joy, too real to recognize itself), and the sounds therefore were pitched much alike; pointed by the snorting start of a new hose; decorated by some man playful with the nozzle; left empty, like God by the sparrow's fall, when any single one of them desists: and all, though near alike, of various pitch; and in this unison. These sweet pale streamings in the light lift out their pallors and their voices all together, mothers hushing their children, the hushing unnaturally prolonged, the men gentle and silent and each snail-like withdrawn into the quietude of what he singly is doing, the urination of huge children stood loosely military against an invisible wall, and gentle happy and peaceful, tasting the mean goodness of their living like the last of their suppers in their mouths; while the locusts carry on this noise of hoses on their much higher and sharper key. The noise of the locust is dry, and it seems not to be rasped or vibrated but urged from him as if through a small orifice by breath that can never give out. Also there is never one locust but an illusion of at least a thousand. The noise of each locust is pitched in some classic locust range out of which none of them varies more than two full tones: and yet you seem to hear each locust discrete from all the rest, and there is a long, slow, pulse in their noise, like the scarcely defined arch of a long and high set bridge. They are all around in every tree, so that the noise seems to come from nowhere and everywhere at once, from the whole shell heaven, shivering in your flesh and teasing your eardrums, the boldest of all the sounds of night. And yet it is habitual to summer nights, and is of the great order of noises, like the noises of the sea and of the blood her precocious grandchild, which you realize you are hearing only when you catch yourself listening. Meantime from low in the dark, just outside the swaying horizons of the hoses, conveying always grass in the damp of dew and its strong green-black smear of smell, the regular yet spaced noises of the crickets, each a sweet cold silver noise threenoted, like the slipping each time of three matched links of a small chain.

But the men by now, one by one, have silenced their hoses and drained and coiled them. Now only two, and now only one, is left, and you see only ghostlike shirt with the sleeve garters, and sober mystery of his mild face like the lifted face of large cattle enquiring of your presence in a pitchdark pool of meadow; and now he too is gone; and it has become that time of evening when people sit on their porches, rocking gently and talking gently and watching the street and the standing up into their sphere of possession of trees, of birds hung havens, hangars. People go by; things go by. A horse, drawing a buggy, breaking his hollow iron music on the asphalt; a loud auto; a quiet auto; people in pairs, not in a hurry, scuffling, switching their weight of aestival body, talking casually, the taste hovering over them of vanilla, strawberry, pasteboard and starched milk, the image upon them of lovers and horsemen, squared with clowns in hueless amber. A street car raising its iron moan; stopping, belling and starting; stertorous; rousing and raising again its iron increasing moan and swimming its gold windows and straw seats on past and past and past, the bleak spark crackling and cursing above it like a small malignant spirit set to dog its tracks; the iron whine rises on rising speed; still risen, faints; halts; the faint stinging bell; rises again, still fainter; fainting, lifting, lifts, faints forgone: forgotten. Now is the night one blue dew.

Now is the night one blue dew, my father has drained, he has coiled the hose.

Low on the length of lawns, a frailing of fire who breathes.

Content, silver, like peeps of light, each cricket makes his comment over and over in the drowned grass.

A cold toad thumpily flounders.

Within the edges of damp shadows of side yards are hovering children nearly sick with joy of fear, who watch the unguarding of a telephone pole.

Around white carbon corner lamps bugs of all sizes are lifted elliptic, solar systems. Big hardshells bruise themselves, assailant: he is fallen on his back, legs squiggling.

Parents on porches: rock and rock: From damp strings morning glories: hang their ancient faces.

The dry and exalted noise of the locusts from all the air at once enchants my eardrums.

On the rough wet grass of the back yard my father and mother have spread quilts. We all lie there, my mother, my father, my uncle, my aunt, and I too am lying there. First we were sitting up, then one of us lay down, and then we all lay down, on our stomachs, or on our sides, or on our backs, and they have kept on talking. They are not talking much, and the talk is quiet, of nothing in particular, or nothing at all in particular, of nothing at all. The stars are wide and alive, they seem each like a smile of great sweetness, and they seem very near. All my people are larger bodies than mine, quiet, with voices gentle and meaningless like the voices of sleeping birds. One is an artist, he is living at home. One is a musician, she is living at home. One is my mother who is good to me. One is my father who is good to me. By some chance, here they are, all on this earth; and who shall ever tell the sorrow of being on this earth, lying, on quilts, on the grass, in a summer evening, among the sounds of the night. May God bless my people, my uncle, my aunt, my mother, my good father, oh, remember them kindly in their time of trouble; and in the hour of their taking away.

After a little I am taken in and put to bed. Sleep, soft smiling, draws me unto her: and those receive me, who quietly treat me, as one familiar and well beloved in that home: but will not, oh, will not, not now, not ever; but will not ever tell me who I am.

The author of "Sonnet 26" talked about the discovery of the familiar. What is this boy discovering in the ordinary world around him?

Not all quests lead out and away. Some lead into the heart. But what does the boy realize he must do in order to find out who he really is?

Now that you have read the stories of many different heroes, go back to the poem that opens this book. Name all the different kinds of quests that the poem describes. Choose any sentence or phrase from the poem and tell how it describes a specific hero in this book.

In what ways could you see all these heroes as being "one hero"? What is the pattern that all hero stories seem to follow? How could all the quests in literature really be "one quest"? What do you think that one quest is? How do you share in it?

The quests in this unit focus on the personal, on the notion that all quests—whether to gain the rightful kingdom or to break out of human limitations or to destroy evil—are man's attempts to find out "who I am."

For the narrator of "Knoxville," this quest has not yet been fulfilled. In other selections, like "Oedipus," or "Little Boxes," or "Heroes," the final discovery of "who I am" produces bitter, tragic, or ironic visions. Oedipus discovers that he is himself the murderer he seeks. The singer of "Little Boxes" realizes that in an immense and impersonal society, one's "self" may not be very different from the "self" of anyone else. And in "Heroes" the speaker finds that the definition of "hero" is very different from what he thought it was. The Man Whose Luck Was Asleep misses himself completely because he thinks he is really looking for something else. Sometimes, as in "The Frog Prince," the love and trust of someone else is necessary to achieve true identity. But whatever the discovery may be, all these stories affirm the experience of the beast in "A Bao A Qu"—"the creature suffers when it cannot come to completion." The creature is the spirit of man.

In a sense, all the quests in this book are quests for identity. They all have one fundamental shape: each hero wanders far from his home in strange lands, whether "real" or in the imagination, often alone, or accompanied by a sympathetic guide. During his wandering, he must prove that he has sufficient strength and wit to survive and to take his adult place in society upon his return. This constantly recurring process suggests that the hero's quest has something to do with the periodic renewal that human societies and individuals seem to require, in order to grow, and even to survive. In fact, the personal and the social come together in the quest.

All primitive societies have tribal rituals called

301

"rites of passage" (one example is in unit three). At certain moments in the life of the individual, such as birth, initiation into manhood, marriage, and even death, these societies prescribe certain symbolic actions, or rituals, which must be performed by the individual whose status is changing. The purpose of these rituals is to conduct the person across the critical threshold of transformation. Such a passage will produce a radical change in the patterns of both his outward and inward life. The details of these rituals differ considerably from tribe to tribe, but their basic stages are remarkably consistent: separation from the tribe; isolation; instruction by the tribal wise ones; an ordeal; return to the tribe; new clothes, a new name; and finally joining in a dance with all the tribe to celebrate rebirth. In other words, the ritual repeats the pattern of the quest.

It is by standing back and looking at such rituals that we can best see the connections among personal growth, the renewal of human civilization, and the patterns of the imagination that show up in stories of quest. Hero stories provide symbols that carry the human spirit forward, in opposition to the comfortable and limiting habits that hold it back. These stories rehearse for us all the pattern of trial, death, and rebirth that all members of every society must undergo to become mature, to take a proper place in society, and to help civilization renew itself. For it is in the world of the imagination that we learn what it is to be truly human—and learn how to bring the rightful golden garden back again.

Index of Authors and Titles

A 1
B 2
C 3
D 4
E 5
F 6
G 7
H 8
I 9
J 0